Graphics Guide
to the Commodore 64

Graphics Guide
to the Commodore 64™

Charles Platt

Berkeley · Paris · Düsseldorf

Cover art by Patrice Larue
Design by Ingrid Owen

Commodore and Commodore 64 are trademarks of Commodore Business Machines, Inc.
The Connection is a trademark of Tymac Controls Corp.
FoxSoft and SpriteByter are trademarks of FoxSoft.
Spritemaster is a trademark of Access Software, Inc.

SYBEX is not affiliated with any manufacturer.

Every effort has been made to supply complete and accurate information. However, SYBEX assumes
no responsibility for its use, nor for any infringements of patents or other rights of third parties which
would result.

Library of Congress Card Number: 83-51570
ISBN 0-89588-138-1
Printed in the United States of America
10 9 8 7 6 5 4 3 2 1

ACKNOWLEDGEMENTS

In 1983, having been commissioned to write some new educational video games, I spent two difficult weeks unravelling the quirks and complexities of an early model of the Commodore 64. I resolved to try to pass on my hard-won knowledge to others, so that they wouldn't have to go through the same trial-and-error learning process that I had experienced.

To do this properly, I needed the assistance of a good publisher; by which I mean one that would do more than merely buy the manuscript, print it, and distribute it, as is so often the case these days. A good publisher takes the time to edit, check, expand, and otherwise enhance an author's work.

Sybex is such a publisher, and I would like to thank the people there who helped to make this a better book. Specifically: Jonathan Kamin, my editor; Ingrid Owen, art and design; Valerie Brewster, typesetting; Valerie Robbins and Laura Meany, word processing; Ian Hughes and Dawn Amsberry, proofreading; and Guy Orcutt, photography. I have never before encountered such enthusiasm, attention to detail, and promptness.

All the program listings in this book are directly derived from my own working versions on disk, and should consequently be free from any typographical errors. If any errors are present, either in the programs or the text, the responsiblility is mine.

—Charles Platt

TABLE OF CONTENTS

11 *Sprites: The Final Confusing Facts Explained*

12 *Beyond BASIC*

Appendices

INTRODUCTION

Why This Book Is Necessary

Commodore supplies two instruction texts for the Commodore 64. One of them, the *User's Guide*, is an introduction for beginners, included free with every computer. The other, the *Programmer's Reference Guide*, is sold as an optional extra. It assumes that the reader has some programming experience and describes every last little detail of the computer, in nearly 500 pages.

Why, then, is my *Graphics Guide* necessary?

For several reasons. First, the computer industry is so competitive that manufacturers are under great pressure to get their product on the market as quickly as possible. This gives them very little time to produce high quality, accurate instruction manuals. This is certainly true of the *User's Guide* supplied with the Commodore 64, which has many omissions and even errors. I had to figure out how to operate many aspects of the computer on my own.

Second, even though the *Programmer's Reference Guide* is very complete, it is not very easy to understand. The Commodore 64 contains some graphics features which are advanced and versatile, but they are not easy to program or to explain, and the *Programmer's Reference Guide* is virtually incomprehensible for any reader who lacks programming experience.

There's an obvious need for a book which explains all the complicated graphics features of the Commodore 64, without omissions, in a way that a beginner can understand. And that is exactly what this book tries to do.

The chapters take you step by step through writing a simple game program, making use of each graphics feature in turn. If you have never programmed a computer before, you will also need a reference book, such as Douglas Hergert's *Commodore 64/VIC 20 BASIC Handbook,* also published by SYBEX, for explanations of the most frequently used BASIC techniques: FOR/NEXT loops, DATA statements, and string variables, and the like. But you will not need any previous programming experience.

Once you understand the way the Commodore 64 works, you'll find this *Guide* a useful reference book. Its appendices summarize all the facts, including memory maps which I think are easier to use than the ones supplied by Commodore; a sprite-building guide which involves much less arithmetic than the Commodore system; a complete scale drawing of all the character sets (not available even in Commodore's own *Programmer's Reference Guide*); and some hints on how to handle the 1541 disk drive, which can be troublesome at times.

This *Guide* deals only with graphics. It is not a tutorial in general BASIC programming, and it doesn't deal with other specific subjects, such as sound. A thorough explanation of sound on the Commodore 64 would require two or three chapters, and there was not enough space for this additional material. Also, in my experience, it is seldom practical to control both graphics and sound in a BASIC video game, because the BASIC statements are executed quite slowly.

However, in the course of developing a sample game, I will describe some fundamental principles of memory management and some relatively advanced programming techniques. By the time you finish Chapter Eleven, you should have all the information you need to write ambitious video games of your own.

The pleasure in programming doesn't come from learning techniques out of a book. The real pleasure, I think, is in going off on your own and figuring out new ways of doing things for yourself. I hope my book will take you to the point where you can start doing exactly that.

ONE
Mysteries
of Memory

Screen Background Color

Turn on the Commodore 64, and the first thing you see is pale blue lettering against a bright blue background. Or, if you have a black-and-white monitor, you see murky gray lettering against a pinstriped gray background. Either way, typing text and trying to read what you've written is apt to cause instant eyestrain. So the first thing any Commodore 64 user needs to know about graphics is how to change screen and text color to something a bit more sensible—such as black and white, for instance.

If you've read your Commodore instruction manual, you already know how to take four simple steps to get black text on a white background.

1. Hold down the key marked CTRL (the Control key) and press the numeral 1, to turn the text black.
2. Type:

   POKE 53280,1

   and press RETURN, to turn the screen border white.
3. Type:

   POKE 53281,1

   and press RETURN, to turn the screen background white.
4. Hold down a SHIFT key and press the CLR/HOME key (which means clear/home). This clears the screen and homes the cursor (the blinking square) to the top-left corner.

Now adjust your video monitor or TV. Do you find black letters on a white background too dazzling? Personally, I prefer a gray background. To get it, you simply type:

POKE 53281,12

and press RETURN.

Do you want the border of the screen also to be gray? Then type:

POKE 53280,12

and press RETURN.

I'm going to pause here and explain exactly what these statements are doing, for those of you who don't know already. This silly-sounding word, POKE, isn't explained in every beginner's guide to BASIC, because the way it works is a bit technical. However, it controls just about every graphics feature on the Commodore 64, so we have to make use of it right from the start.

First, notice that POKE 53281,1 turned the screen white, while POKE 53281,12 turned the screen gray. The only difference between these two statements is the number that follows the comma.

Figure 1.1 is a list of all the colors that the Commodore 64 can display on its screen. (For future reference, this list also appears in Appendix A.)

To display the screen background color of your choice, first look up its number, then type:

POKE 53281

and then type a comma, followed by the color number. Then press RETURN. To change the color of the screen border, you do the same thing, except you POKE 53280 instead of POKE 53281.

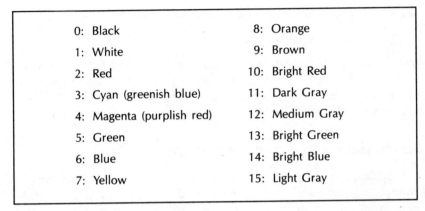

0: Black	8: Orange
1: White	9: Brown
2: Red	10: Bright Red
3: Cyan (greenish blue)	11: Dark Gray
4: Magenta (purplish red)	12: Medium Gray
5: Green	13: Bright Green
6: Blue	14: Bright Blue
7: Yellow	15: Light Gray

Figure 1.1: Color codes for POKE statements.

The POKE Statement

You may be wondering, why do those long numbers 53280 and 53281 control border and background color, and what does this POKE word really do?

To ask why 53281 and 53280 control the screen color is like asking why you happen to have a particular Social Security number. Some clerk in Washington gave you that number. It was an arbitrary decision. Well, some programmer at Commodore made the same sort of arbitrary decision about which number should control screen background color.

As for how POKE works. . . . In this book, I won't bother to explain most BASIC statements, because you can look them up in any general reference guide. But I will explain this one.

First you must consider the nature of computer memory. You know, of course, that it's made of tiny little silicon chips. But I don't want you to think of it that way. Instead, use your imagination, and think of it as a row of little boxes, like mailboxes on a very long, straight street. Each box is numbered. This number is its *address*—just like the number painted on the outside of a mailbox. The Commodore 64 contains addresses numbered from 0 through 65535—quite a long "street" of memory.

When a mailman delivers mail, he might put 12 items of mail in the mailbox at address number 53281, and 12 items of mail in the address numbered 53280. You see the similarity? Each address in the computer can be loaded with a number (such as 12) just as a mailbox can be loaded with mail. In the Commodore 64, most of the addresses can hold any number from 0 up to 255. To tell the computer to load an address with a number, you use the word POKE. Thus:

POKE 53281,12

tells the computer to find memory address 53280 and put the number 12 in it. A moment later (so quickly, the whole thing seems to happen immediately) the computer checks to see what number is in 53281, and uses that number as an instruction to update screen background color.

Immediate and Programmed Instructions

I said that the computer updates screen color so quickly, it seems to happen "immediately." In fact, the computer is obeying you in what's known as *immediate mode*. This means, as soon as you hit the RETURN key, the computer carries out the instruction you just typed. Then it says it is READY for more instructions.

What if you want to give a whole, long series of instructions? You number them, and put them on separate lines. Then you type:

RUN

and press RETURN, and the computer obeys the instructions in numerical order. Make sure you're clear about this:

- When you type an instruction *without* a line number, the computer responds immediately, in immediate mode.
- When you precede an instruction *with* a line number, the computer waits until you tell it to RUN that instruction and all the others that follow it. A list of numbered instructions is a *program*.

Instead of coloring screen background and coloring the border as two separate commands in immediate mode, you could write them as:

10 POKE 53280,12
20 POKE 53281,12

Then type:

RUN

and press RETURN. Then both screen and border colors would change.

I've used line numbers 10 and 20 (instead of 1 and 2) to leave a gap in case extra lines need to be inserted later. The computer doesn't care how big the gap is between each line number and the next. It just starts at the lowest line number and works up to the highest (which is 63999 on this computer).

The advantage of writing your series of instructions as a program is that you can save it on tape or disk, then reload it later, and RUN it again. You cannot save and re-run statements typed in immediate mode.

Putting Images on the Screen

So far, I've dealt with screen color, POKE statements, and the difference between a program and immediate mode. Perhaps you've noticed that I haven't explained how pressing CTRL and numeral 1 turns video text black, or how pressing SHIFT and CLR/HOME clears the screen. We'll deal with these details later. Right now, I want to go further with this POKE word, and show how it can put little images on the screen "in front of" screen background color, and move them around.

Did someone say, "What about PRINT"? Well, it's true that the easiest way to display messages on the screen is to PRINT them there. You type:

PRINT "A"

and the computer displays a letter A—or just about anything else you type between the quote marks.

But this isn't much use to us in video games, where we want to move an image freely around the screen. To do this on the Commodore 64, we *have* to use POKE statements. So I'm going to deal with POKE first, and leave PRINT till Chapter Four.

What letters, numbers, and symbols can we display in front of background color, with POKE statements? Well, there are two whole sets, called character sets. You can only display one set at a time, and you can switch between them by holding down either of the SHIFT keys while you press the C= key at the bottom-left corner of the keyboard.

In this book we will use only Character Set One, which is what the computer displays when you first turn it on. Figure 1.2 is an enlarged look at the alphabet that Commodore provides for us.

Check Appendix C for a complete display of all the characters in Character Set One and Character Set Two.

Every character is code-numbered, just as the screen colors are code-numbered. The code of a character is called its ASCII code. These code numbers run from 0 through 255. ASCII stands for American Standard Code for Information Interchange, and people pronounce it "ask-key." Actually Commodore's version of ASCII is a non-standard variant called PET-ASCII, but I'll call it ASCII anyway. In the Commodore system, A is code-numbered 1, and the rest of the alphabet is numbered through to Z, which has code number 26.

Now look at the video memory map in Figure 1.3. This shows the way the computer thinks of the video screen: divided into lots of little

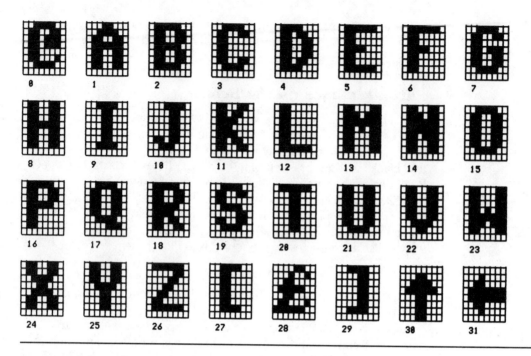

Figure 1.2: The Commodore Alphabet.

rectangles. These rectangles are called *pixels* (short for "picture cells") and you can think of them as memory addresses ("mailboxes") stacked up so that they fill the screen. The top-left pixel has address 1024. The bottom-left pixel has address 2023. Remember, an address is like the number on the outside of a mailbox. Don't confuse it with a number that you POKE into the address, which is like the number of pieces of mail you deliver to that address.

When you POKE a character's ASCII code into one of the video addresses, the character appears in that pixel. So POKE 1024,1 places letter A in the top-left corner.

Coloring Your Characters

Unfortunately, there's a snag—the first of many, where this computer is concerned. Not all models of the Commodore 64 were built the same way. On some of the early ones, when you POKE the number of a character into a video address, you don't see that character on the screen, because the computer automatically gives the character the same color as the screen background. A white character doesn't show up very well on a white background!

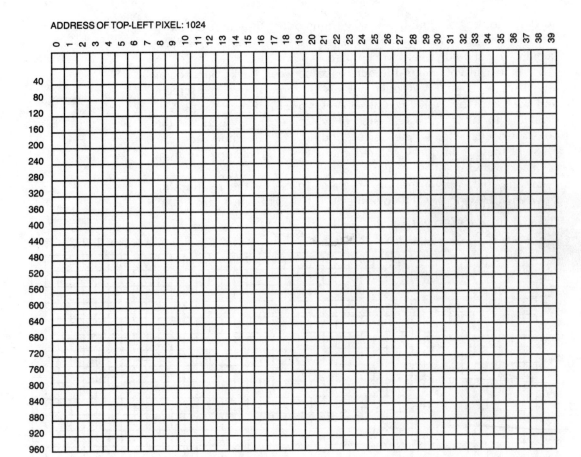

ADDRESS OF TOP-LEFT PIXEL: 1024

Figure 1.3: The Commodore 64's video memory map.

Luckily, however, when we POKE a character into video memory, we can also tell the computer what color we want that character to be. We do this by POKEing another stretch of memory called color memory.

Color memory is arrayed in a map, just like video memory. Each color memory address controls the color of the character displayed in the corresponding video memory address.

Check Figures 1.4 and 1.5. The top-left color-memory pixel is color address number 55296. It controls the color of the character in video address 1024. Since 1024 + 54272 = 55296, there's a general rule here: add 54272 to any video address to find the color memory address that controls it.

Numbers, and more numbers. There's no escape from them when

you want to program graphics on the Commodore 64. But if you keep a pocket calculator at hand, and refer to the video memory map frequently, you shouldn't get too confused.

Keep clear in your mind the difference between background color and character color. Background color is the same all over the screen, and you set it by POKEing one address: 53281. Color memory is divided into 1000 addresses, each of which separately controls the color of a character in the corresponding video memory address. Think of these individually colored characters as appearing "in front of" background color (see Figure 1.6).

Try this short demonstration program, to clarify the relationship between video memory and color memory. Use SHIFT plus CLR/HOME

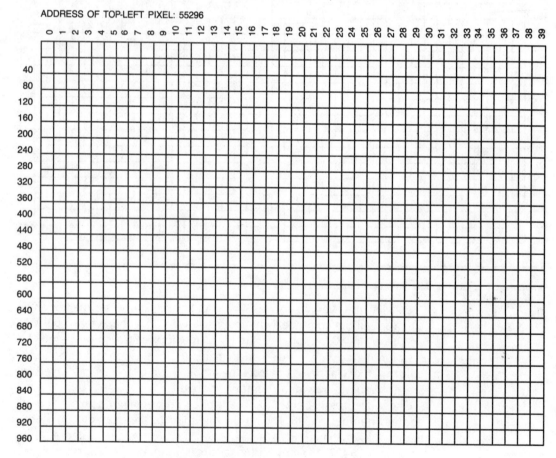

Figure 1.4: The Commodore 64's color memory map.

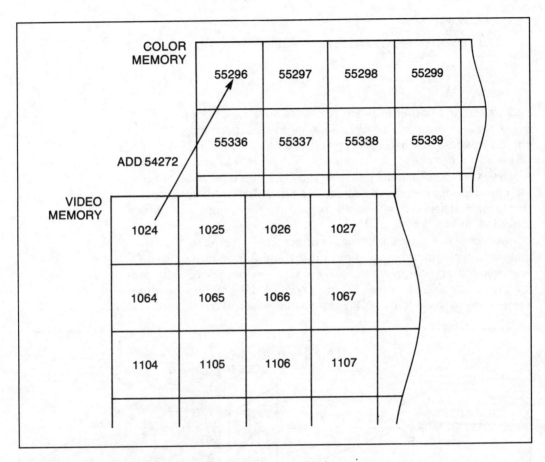

Figure 1.5: The correspondence between video memory and color memory.

to clear the screen before you start typing, and remember to press RETURN at the end of each line.

You don't have to insert spaces between statements in Commodore BASIC, but if you do the program listings are easier to read. Note that on the Commodore keyboard, you should not press the SHIFT key when typing * or + or − signs. You may get something that looks like a + sign, but it won't act like one.

In the programs in this book, I'll use VA to stand for the Video Address where video memory begins. Likewise, CA is the Color Address where color memory begins. Defining these constants makes it easier to see what a program is doing, and it will be useful when our programs become more complicated.

In this little program, line 10 defines VA and CA, line 20 selects a value for C, the character color (0 being black), line 30 sets screen

```
10 VA=1024:CA=55296
20 C=0
30 POKE 53280,1:POKE 53281,1
40 FOR A=0 TO 255
50 POKE CA+A,C
60 POKE VA+A,A
70 NEXT A
```

background and border to white, and lines 40–70 are a loop to POKE every character into successive video addresses, beginning with the character whose ASCII code is 0, and ending with ASCII 255.

Line 50 POKEs color memory before line 60 POKEs video memory. Always POKE color memory first. If you do it the other way around, the character appears on the screen for just an instant before its correct color is assigned to it, and this results in a flickering image, which looks bad in video games.

Make sure your program listing is correct. You remember, of course, that when typing numbers you must use 1 and 0, not letters L and O. Also, *you must get all the numbers right*. Commodore BASIC lacks useful words like DRAW and PLOT that control the graphics on other computers. We have to use POKE statements, which allow no room for

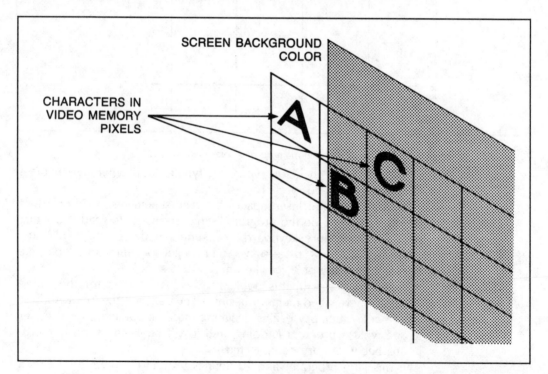

Figure 1.6: Think of each character in video memory as being "in front of" screen background color.

error. If you POKE an address outside the range of video memory by mistake, you'll accidentally give some sort of instruction to the operating system, or you'll disrupt your program listing itself. This will "confuse" the computer, at which point it may stop responding to you. You'll have to turn it off and then on again, which will wipe out your program. So type carefully!

Editing Your Program

If you notice you've made a typing error, you can fix it by moving the cursor to it and retyping. How do you move the cursor? Simple. The left-hand key marked CRSR moves the cursor down. The right-hand CRSR key moves the cursor right. Now press one of the SHIFT keys while you hold down the CRSR key, and the cursor will reverse direction. Fairly simple, isn't it? But if you try to move the cursor after you type a quote mark ("), the CRSR keys don't work. To bring them back to normal, press RETURN.

When you've located the cursor at your error, you can type new text to replace old text. Or, you can edit that line by pressing the key marked INST/DEL, which means Insert/Delete. By itself, this key deletes. If you hold it down and press a SHIFT key at the same time, INST/DEL inserts extra space into a line, so that you can insert anything you forgot to type before.

Remember—always remember!—that the computer keeps its own record of your program, separate from what you see on the screen. If you correct an error on the screen, the computer pays no attention at all, and *does not update its record of the program*, until you press RETURN. Then, it updates its record of that one line, where the cursor is. So press RETURN after every separate change you make on the screen. Otherwise, what you see will not be what you get.

When everything looks right, clear the screen, type:

LIST

and press RETURN. This lets you check that any changes you made have been properly recorded by the computer.

Now save the program on disk or tape. Always save a program before you run it, just in case. If you're using tape, type:

SAVE"FILE NAME"

and press RETURN. Instead of FILE NAME you can use any name you like, so long as it contains no more than sixteen letters and spaces.

If you use a disk drive, take a look at Appendix S, which offers some tips on how to handle Commodore's 1541 disk drive. Then, to save your program, type:

SAVE"FILE NAME",8

and press RETURN. The comma and number 8 at the end of the statement tell the computer you want to use the disk drive (device #8) instead of the cassette recorder.

Now clear the screen again, and press the left-hand CRSR key to move the cursor half-way down, to make room for the characters which the program is going to POKE into video addresses along the top of the screen. Type:

RUN

and press RETURN. You should see a complete set of black characters, just as they appear in Appendix C.

Now LIST the program and move the cursor to line 20. Change it to read C = 3 instead of C = 0. Press RETURN to record this change, clear the screen, move the cursor down, and run the program again. This time, all the characters should be color number three, which is cyan, a greenish blue.

Now type a new program line:

45 C = INT(RND(1)∗16):IF C = 1 THEN 45

Press RETURN to record this new line. Clear the screen and list your program again. The new line should appear between line 40 and line 50.

Line 45 sets the color code number, C, to a new random value each time the program goes through one cycle. The statement RND(1) tells the computer to calculate a pseudo-random number. Its value will range from 0 to slightly less than 1. This means that RND(1)∗16 will give a result ranging from 0 to 15.99999999. By putting INT ("integer") in front of the expression, we tell the computer to leave off the decimal fractions, so we end up with a pseudo-random whole number ranging from 0 through 15, which can be used to choose a color from 0 through 15.

Because we want all the characters on the screen to be visible, none of them should be the same color as the background, i.e., white. So if C is equal to 1 (the color code for white), line 45 repeats itself, till it finds a new random value for C, other than 1.

Run the program. The character set now appears multicolored. Note that the program runs more slowly now—it has to pause and find a new random color for each character it POKEs onto the screen. This slowing down can be a problem in games written in BASIC. Making game programs run fast enough in BASIC is something we'll tackle in detail later in the book.

Making Things Move

Clear the screen and type another new line:

65 GET A$:IF A$ = "" THEN 65

There must be no space between the "" marks. GET A$ tells the computer to scan its keyboard, see which key is being pressed, and assign it to the string named A$. If no key has been pressed, A$ is equal to "", i.e., nothing at all, in which case line 65 repeats again and again, until a key *is* pressed, at which point the program continues.

Run the program. It places one character on the screen, then waits for you to touch any key. Hold down the space bar. After half a second, the space bar *repeats*—it sends a stream of spaces. So the program proceeds. The space bar, CRSR keys, and INST/DEL are the only keys that repeat (but you can change this by POKEing address 650—see the memory listing in Appendix J).

Let go of the space bar and the program stops, stuck on line 65 again, waiting for another keyboard entry. The program is responding to your keyboard commands. We'll use this principle when we design a game program.

Interrupt the program by pressing the RUN/STOP key. The computer says BREAK IN 65, meaning it stopped during line 65. Now it's READY again for your further instructions.

Here's what we want to do now. To get rid of line 45, clear the screen, type

45

and press RETURN.

When you type a new line that has the same line number as an old line, and you press RETURN, the computer remembers the new line instead of the old line. You may still see the old line on the screen, but next time you list the program, to check how the computer remembers it, the old line won't be there.

If you type a line number by itself you replace the old line with no-line, i.e., nothing at all.

List the program to make sure line 45 has gone. Now edit line 60, and type a new line 67, so you have:

60 POKE VA + A,1
67 POKE VA + A,32

Run the program again. Hold down the space bar, and you should see a little blue A running along the screen. Line 60 POKEs video memory with 1 (the code for an A). Line 65 stops the program till you press a key, as before. Then line 67 POKEs video memory with 32, a blank space, which wipes out the blue A and lets background color (white) show through again. The process repeats over and over, in successive video addresses, and it happens fast enough so that the symbol seems to move. This is how we animate images in simple video games—as you'll see, when we write our first game in the next chapter.

Summary

If you've managed to remember everything in this chapter, you now know:

- How to set screen background and border color by POKEing a color code (0 through 15) into 53281 and 53280, respectively.
- How a POKE statement works, putting a number into a memory address like mail into a mailbox.
- How to type instructions in Immediate Mode (without line numbers) or as a program (with line numbers).
- How to display characters on the screen by POKEing their ASCII codes into video addresses, and POKEing corresponding addresses in color memory.
- How to clear the screen, move the cursor, and edit program lines (remember, press RETURN after editing each line, to update the computer's record of the program, which isn't necessarily the same as what you see on the screen).
- How to delete, insert, and replace whole program lines.
- How to save a program.
- How to GET a character from the keyboard.
- How to move an image from one pixel to the next across the screen.

TWO
Super-Simple
Shoot-'Em-Up

  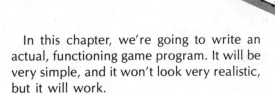

In this chapter, we're going to write an actual, functioning game program. It will be very simple, and it won't look very realistic, but it will work.

Video Game Basics

Most video games are really rather simple. There's a token on the screen, which you control. It's either attacking other images, or running away from them. In our game we'll go for the first of these two options, because it's easier to program.

Our game will be called *Air Attack*. You will be in charge of an anti-aircraft gun, shooting at a plane which moves around randomly in the middle of the screen.

This sounds good, but it won't look very good, because at this point I want to keep everything simple. So we won't have a very convincing airplane. To be moved easily, it must be represented by just one character, like the letter A that we moved across the screen at the end of the last chapter.

Look at the characters available, in Appendix C. Does any of them look like an airplane? Not in the slightest! So we'll have to pretend one of them is an airplane. (In Chapter Five, we'll build images that *do* look detailed and realistic; but not yet.) I'm going to use the big X symbol (on the front of the V key), which has an ASCII code of 86, as our airplane.

Now, what about an anti-aircraft gun? None of the characters looks like a gun, either. So I'll use the up-arrow, ASCII code 30.

And what about a bullet? The solid blob, code 81, will do. Figure 2.1 gives a rough idea of how our game will look.

Now we have to figure out how to fire the gun, how to move the bullet, how to move the plane, and how to check whether the bullet has hit the plane. Firing the gun is easy; we'll use a key on the keyboard as the "trigger," and have the computer check frequently to see if that key has been pressed. The space bar is the easiest key to find and touch, so we'll use that.

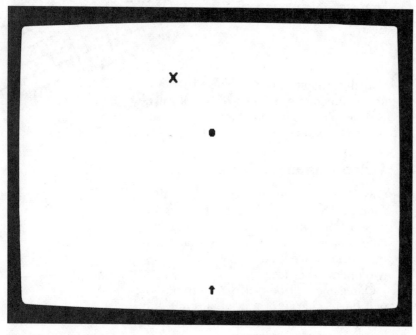

Figure 2.1: The basic ingredients of our super-simple beginning video game.

What about moving the bullet? To keep things simple, we'll have it move straight up the screen. In the last chapter, we saw that adding 1 to the video address of a screen image made it move one space to the right. To make the image move one space upward, we subtract 40 from its address. Figure 2.2 shows why.

And the "airplane"? We'll move it randomly, using a RND(1) statement. To make the game interesting, the plane should shift in as many different, unexpected ways as possible. We'll allow it eight directions. Imagine that North is at the top of the screen. Then we can call the other directions North-East, East, South-East, South, South-West, West, and North-West. The airplane moves from one position to another when we blank out its image and add one of these numbers to its old address, to find its new address:

$$-40, \ -39, \ 1, \ 41, \ 40, \ 39, \ -1, \ \text{or} \ -41.$$

Figure 2.2 helps to explain this. These numbers are called the *increments* that we add to the airplane's address.

Lastly, to discover whether the bullet has hit the airplane, we compare their two addresses in video memory. If the program tries to move the bullet to occupy the same address as the plane, we have a hit.

Putting Principles into Practice

Now I'll explain how these ideas are translated into an actual program. I'm including the complete listing in Figure 2.3, so you can check your version against it when you've finished typing and are looking for errors. In a moment, I'll explain each section of the program individually.

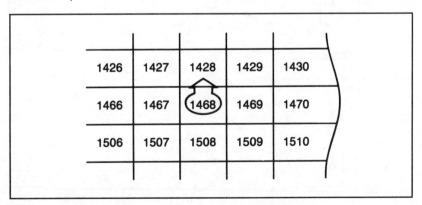

Figure 2.2: Video memory is laid out so that you subtract 40 from any address to move to the one above it.

```
10 GOSUB 1000
97 REM
98 REM--------- Move Airplane ---------
99 REM
100 D=INT(RND(1)*9)-4
110 IF ABS(D)>1 THEN D=D+(37*SGN(D))
120 IF AA+D>VA+879 OR AA+D<VA THEN D=-D
170 POKE AA,32:AA=AA+D
180 POKE AA+54272,2:POKE AA,86
197 REM
198 REM-------- Check Keyboard --------
199 REM
200 GET A$
297 REM
298 REM---------- Move Bullet ---------
299 REM
300 IF A$=CHR$(32) AND AB=0 THEN 380
310 IF AB=0 THEN 100
320 POKE AB,32:AB=AB-40
330 IF AB<VA THEN AB=0:GOTO 100
340 POKE AB+54272,0:POKE AB,81
350 IF AB=AA THEN 800
360 GOTO 100
365 REM---------- Fire Gun --------
380 AB=AG-40
390 POKE AB+54272,0:POKE AB,81:GOTO 100
797 REM
798 REM------ Bullet Hits Target ------
799 REM
800 POKE AA,160
900 POKE 53280,1:POKE 53281,1
970 END
997 REM
998 REM----- Establish Constants ------
999 REM
1000 VA=1024
1047 REM
1048 REM----- Establish Variables -----
1049 REM
1070 AA=0:AB=0:AG=0:D=0
1097 REM
1098 REM------ Establish Strings ------
1099 REM
1140 A$=""
2697 REM
2698 REM-------- Set Up Screen --------
2699 REM
2700 POKE 53280,3:POKE 53281,3
2710 PRINT CHR$(147);
2800 AA=VA+380
2810 POKE AA+54272,2:POKE AA,86
2820 AG=VA+980
2830 POKE AG+54272,5:POKE AG,30
2890 RETURN
```

Figure 2.3: Complete listing for Air Attack.

You may notice that none of the lines in this program is more than 39 characters long. This is because the screen of the Commodore 64 is only 40 characters wide (and we need the 40th space at the end of each line for the cursor when we edit the program).

You can type longer program lines, but as you continue adding characters, they "wrap around" onto the line below. This makes the program hard to read, because the program statements become mixed up with the line numbers. So almost all the programs in this book use short lines for the sake of clarity, even when this entails a bit of extra typing and a little repetition.

There are big gaps between some of the line numbers, because we'll be modifying the program by adding extra lines, in future chapters. For this reason, *do not change any of the line numbers!*

Clear the screen, type:

NEW

and press RETURN, to get rid of the program you typed in the last chapter. Then begin by typing the following lines:

```
997 REM
998 REM----- Establish Constants ------
999 REM
1000 VA=1024
1047 REM
1048 REM----- Establish Variables -----
1049 REM
1070 AA=0:AB=0:AG=0:D=0
1097 REM
1098 REM------ Establish Strings ------
1099 REM
1140 A$=""
2697 REM
2698 REM-------- Set Up Screen --------
2699 REM
2700 POKE 53280,3:POKE 53281,3
2710 PRINT CHR$(147);
2800 AA=VA+380
2810 POKE AA+54272,2:POKE AA,86
2820 AG=VA+980
2830 POKE AG+54272,5:POKE AG,30
2890 RETURN
```

The lines that begin with REM are REMarks. The computer ignores them. Their only purpose is to insert some space in the layout of the program, and explain to you what each piece of it is for. You can leave out these REM lines altogether, if you want to. But if you do you may find your program listing hard to understand when you look at it again a few weeks later.

This section of the program establishes the constants and variables, before the game begins. Here's what they all mean:

> VA is the top-left Video Address, just as it was in the last chapter.
>
> AA will be the Address of the Airplane in video memory.
>
> AB will be the Address of the Bullet.
>
> AG will be the Address of the Gun.
>
> D will be the Direction the airplane moves—the "increment" added to its old address, when we want to find its new address.

It's not really necessary to establish the variables on line 1070. BASIC allows us to invent a new variable and introduce it at any point in a program. But as this game gets bigger in the next few chapters, we'll use more and more variables, and keeping them all listed in one place makes the program easier to follow. Apart from anything else, it's a way of checking that the same letter or letters haven't accidentally been used to mean two different things in different parts of the program.

Line 2700 establishes the screen color, just as we did in the last chapter. I'm assuming you'll play the game in color, so I've chosen cyan as the background, to look like a blue sky. If you're using a monochrome monitor, this won't look good. Use a different background: 1 for white, or 15 for pale gray.

Line 2710 homes the cursor, just as if you pressed SHIFT and CLR/HOME in immediate mode. I'll explain this command in Chapter Four. Make sure you type the semicolon at the end of the line.

Line 2800 chooses a beginning address for the airplane, in the middle of the screen. Line 2810 POKEs color memory—remember, you add 54272 to the video address to find the corresponding color address. I'm coloring the airplane red (color number 2). But if you play this game in black-and-white, your airplane should be black, so you should substitute a 0 for the 2 on this line, and also on line 180.

Having set color memory, line 2810 POKEs the actual airplane symbol (ASCII 86) into video memory.

Lines 2820 and 2830 do the same thing for the gun, which I've colored green (color number 5). Use 0 instead, if you are playing this in black and white.

Using GOSUB for Lower Line Numbers

This whole section from line 1000 through 2890 is a *subroutine.* Check back to the full listing of the program, and you'll see that line 10, the first line, says:

GOSUB 1000

which means that as soon as the computer begins executing the program, it's told to go find the subsection that begins on line 1000. The computer obeys all the instructions in this subsection until it comes to the word RETURN on line 2890, which ends the subroutine and sends the computer back to the line immediately following the initial GOSUB command.

Having obeyed the set-up instructions in the subroutine, the computer then plays the actual game, which begins on line 100.

But why put the set-up of the program in a subroutine down at the bottom? For two reasons. First, it's easier to understand a program that's divided into separate blocks which take care of clearly defined functions. Second, it's important to make a game program run as fast as possible, and one way to do this is to put the routine parts at the bottom and the more active parts at the top.

Like most BASIC programs, this one contains the statement GOTO. For instance, line 390 ends with GOTO 100, which tells the computer to look for line 100, go to it, and obey whatever instruction it finds there. (The difference between GOSUB and GOTO is that GOTO is a permanent jump, whereas GOSUB is temporary, and the subroutine always ends with the word RETURN.)

Every time the program tells the computer to GOTO a line number, the computer has to convert that line number into its own system of numbering before it can obey. It takes less time to figure out GOTO 100 than GOTO 10000. So we keep line numbers low where time is of the essence, and use higher-numbered lines for less crucial operations.

Moving the Airplane

As soon as the computer has finished obeying the set-up subroutine, it starts playing the actual game by finding a direction for the airplane to move. Type these lines:

```
10 GOSUB 1000
97 REM
98 REM-------- Move Airplane ---------
99 REM
100 D=INT(RND(1)*9)-4
110 IF ABS(D)>1 THEN D=D+(37*SGN(D))
120 IF AA+D>VA+879 OR AA+D<VA THEN D=-D
170 POKE AA,32:AA=AA+D
180 POKE AA+54272,2:POKE AA,86
```

Line 100 chooses a random direction for the airplane. The RND formula here gives the following range of values for direction D:

$$-4, -3, -2, -1, 0, 1, 2, 3, 4.$$

If you check back to our "airplane increment" list you'll see that these aren't the values we really need. −1, 0, and 1 are usable; the others need to be adapted.

Line 110 takes care of this. The expression:

$$\text{IF ABS(D)} > 1$$

means, take the value of D, ignore its minus sign (if there is one), and see whether it's greater than 1. If so, line 110 continues:

$$D = D + (37 * SGN(D))$$

which means: First take the SGN of D. SGN(D) is −1 if D is negative, +1 if D is positive. Multiply this by 37; so we get either −37 or +37. Add this to D itself, which will be −4, −3, −2, 2, 3, or 4, since the first part of line 110 has screened out the −1, 0, and 1 values. The result will be −41, −40, −39, 39, 40, or 41, which are precisely the increments we want for the airplane.

This sounds complicated. Yes, it could be simpler. We could have a whole lot of IF statements:

$$\text{IF } D = 4 \text{ THEN } D = 41$$
$$\text{IF } D = 3 \text{ THEN } D = 40$$

and so on. But the computer would take time to interpret all these statements, and time is what we don't have in a BASIC game program. So the trick is to find one formula, or *algorithm*, which generates all the figures we need, as quickly as possible.

Having chosen a new random direction for the airplane, we have to check whether this direction might move it off the top or bottom of the screen. This is very important. If the airplane runs out of control, the program may POKE addresses outside of video memory. So line 120 says, IF incrementing AA with D will take the airplane too high or low, THEN reverse the direction, by making new D equal to minus-old-D.

Line 170 POKEs the old location of the airplane with a blank space and adds the new D to the old value of AA to get the new value of AA. Then line 180 POKEs color memory with the airplane color (2 = red), and POKEs new AA with 86, the airplane image.

Having moved the airplane, it's time to see what the player wants to do, so we check the keyboard. Type these lines:

```
197 REM
198 REM-------- Check Keyboard --------
199 REM
200 GET A$
```

We don't want the program to stop and wait till the player presses a key. So this program tells the computer to GET its keyboard just once, find which key has been pressed (if any), then move right on to the next important part of the game.

Firing the Gun and Moving the Bullet

Here are the lines of the program that deal with this:

```
297 REM
298 REM---------- Move Bullet ---------
299 REM
300 IF A$=CHR$(32) AND AB=0 THEN 380
310 IF AB=0 THEN 100
320 POKE AB,32:AB=AB-40
330 IF AB<VA THEN AB=0:GOTO 100
340 POKE AB+54272,0:POKE AB,81
350 IF AB=AA THEN 800
360 GOTO 100
365 REM---------- Fire Gun
380 AB=AG-40
390 POKE AB+54272,0:POKE AB,81:GOTO 100
```

The program can only keep track of one bullet at a time, which means that, so long as a bullet is moving on the screen, the player is not allowed to fire another one. I'm using AB, the Address of the Bullet, to show whether a bullet is currently being animated across the screen or not. If *not*, AB = 0.

Line 300 says, IF the space bar has been pressed (i.e. if A$ = CHR$(32), a space), AND IF AB = 0 (no bullet currently on the screen), THEN go to the "fire gun" routine on line 380, which starts AB at the video pixel just above the gun, and POKEs the bullet image there.

Why doesn't line 300 say (more simply):

IF A$ = " "

in other words, a space between two quote marks? Because when you type a space after typing a quote mark, on the Commodore 64, the computer gives you a blank that has ASCII code 96; whereas, when you press the space bar later, that produces a code of ASCII 32. Yes, there are *two kinds of space* on the Commodore 64. Oddly enough, this will come in handy later.

If the player hasn't pressed the space bar, program execution continues on line 310. This says, IF AB = 0 (i.e., no bullet on the screen), THEN skip the whole bullet-moving thing, because there is no bullet to move. Go back to line 100 and move the airplane some more.

But if there *is* a bullet on the screen, line 320 prepares to move it by blanking its image and decrementing its address by 40. (A *decrement* is an increment that is negative, rather than positive. It diminishes, instead of increasing.)

Then line 330 checks to see whether this has moved the bullet beyond video memory, in which case AB is assigned the value 0 (bullet no longer on screen).

But if the bullet still is within video memory, its new image is POKEd in on line 340.

Most important, line 350 now checks to see whether AB, the new address of the bullet, is the same as AA, the airplane's address. If not, the program recycles back to line 100.

The Climax of the Game

If the bullet and the airplane *do* now have the same address, the target has been hit. This is the end of the game (this primitive version of it).

```
797 REM
798 REM------ Bullet Hits Target ------
799 REM
800 POKE AA,160
900 POKE 53280,1:POKE 53281,1
970 END
```

Line 800 POKEs the bullet/airplane pixel with a black square, to indicate a hit. Line 900 restores the screen background to white. The END statement on line 970 is needed to stop the computer from running on down into the subroutine on line 1000.

Room for Improvement

If you seem to have made no errors in typing this program, save it first, and then RUN it.

What do you see, when you run it? You see a little red X dancing around. Press the space bar, and a black blob moves up like a bubble rising through molasses. Why, it's . . . pathetic! Is this all you get in return for all your typing?

Well, the fact is, the first version of any program is often a failure, especially if it's written in a rather primitive version of BASIC. In the next chapter, we'll refine this program out of all recognition.

First we must list all the improvements that need to be made:

- The game should run faster. The bullet should move like a bullet, not like a bubble.
- The bullet image shouldn't flicker, as it does now.
- Most important, the airplane shouldn't dance around like a demented mosquito. It shouldn't change direction so often. And when it reaches the left or right edge of the screen, it should double back, rather than go off the edge and reappear at the opposite edge.
- The player should have a better chance of winning. Perhaps the bullet should move faster than the plane.

- The gun should be movable, from side to side, like the gun in Space Invaders. Otherwise, you have to sit waiting for the airplane to wander into range.
- Ideally, the player shouldn't have to wait for one bullet to leave the screen before he can fire another.

Well, that's quite a list. Some of the changes are easy. Others are hard; but we'll make all of them in the next chapter.

Summary

In this chapter, I've tried to explain:

- Basic principles of shoot-'em-up video games.
- How to add increments to a video address, to move an image in various different directions.
- How to develop the program listing (no lines longer than 39 characters).
- How to use a subroutine, and keep line numbers low where fast action is needed.
- How to develop an algorithm (a simple formula) to generate numbers you need.
- How to stop an image from wandering off the top or bottom of the screen.
- How to test for a collision between two images (when they try to share the same video address).
- How to make a list of all the things that don't work properly, so you can fix them in the next version of the program.

THREE
Improving Speed and Realism

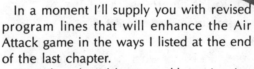

In a moment I'll supply you with revised program lines that will enhance the Air Attack game in the ways I listed at the end of the last chapter.

First, though, I'd better tackle an inevitable question: is this the final version of the program? After you laboriously type this new listing, will it be finished?

Well . . . no program is ever really *finished*. There's always one more little thing that it would be nice to add. It's a process of gradual evolution and refinement.

In fact, there will be three more versions of Air Attack before we're through with it. But I hope you'll take the time to make the revisions that I list in each chapter, because this is the best way to learn game-programming techniques.

And I've made things as easy as possible for you by designing each new version of the program so that it "grows out of" the preceding one. Here's all you have to do.

If you saved last chapter's listing of Air Attack on tape or disk, type:

NEW

and press RETURN, then load last chapter's version of Air Attack and list it.

Some of the old lines from that listing can be retained, without any changes. All the headings in the program, and the sections it is divided into, remain the same.

Some new lines must be added, and some can be made by editing old lines on the screen.

To add new lines:

1. Clear the screen.
2. Type the new lines with their correct line numbers.
3. Clear the screen again.
4. List the program. Use the CTRL key to slow the listing. Press RUN/STOP to stop it at any point.
5. You'll find that the computer has inserted your new lines automatically among the old ones, in numerical order.

To edit old lines:

1. List the appropriate section of the program.
2. Move the cursor to the line to be edited.
3. Delete obsolete statements and insert new ones, using the INST/DEL key.
4. Remember to press RETURN when you have finished editing each line.
5. Clear the screen.
6. List the program and check that each line you edited has been remembered in its new form.

To avoid confusion, in the listings in this chapter I will show an asterisk (*) beside lines that are totally new, and an E beside lines which you can make by editing old program lines.

Speeding Up BASIC

Speed is the first enhancement that I want to deal with. BASIC doesn't run very fast to start with, and as we add more features to make the game do more, images begin literally crawling across the screen.

There are standard ways of coping with this problem. First, you can leave out the REM lines where speed is important, so that the computer doesn't waste time scanning through REMs to find the next active line of the program. Second, you can omit spaces between BASIC statements. Both these changes make program listings harder to read, so I won't adopt them here, but you can do so when you type in *your* program.

Next, CC can use much lower line numbers. Instead of numbering lines 10, 20, 30, you can renumber them 1, 2, 3, and modify line numbers referred to in GOTO and GOSUB statements to match. This is most easily done in pencil on a paper print-out, which you then use as a guide for screen editing.

However, you should not do this till we finish the final version of the program. Don't change any line numbers in Air Attack just yet. Just remember this technique as something to do later on.

The most important change we can make right now is to use constants in the arithmetical operations. Each time the computer is given an instruction such as POKE VA + 54272, it has to convert 54272 into its own numbering system before it can obey. We can speed things up by establishing a constant at the beginning of the program, and use it instead of 54272. Let's call this constant CC, to mean Color Constant. Remember, it's the difference between the video starting address and the color-memory starting address. We can tell the computer, then, that:

$$CC = CA - VA$$

which instructs the computer to make a record of the value of CC in its own numbering system. When it encounters CC later in the program, it will know its value without having to do a number conversion.

Here are some lines to type. Remember, E means you can make this line by editing the old line of this number that already exists. But the lines marked * must be typed from scratch; they are completely new.

Don't actually type an E or a * in *your* program. These are just the symbols I'm using to show you what you have to do.

```
E 1000 VA=1024:CA=55296:CC=CA-VA
* 1005 AP=86:GU=30:BU=81:IB=40
* 1006 T=10:FT=15:BS=32:NS=96
* 1010 VU=VA+80:VD=VA+879
* 1020 D(0)=41:D(1)=39:D(2)=-41:D(3)=-39
* 1021 D(4)=-1:D(5)=1:D(6)=1:D(7)=-1
* 1040 POKE 650,128
```

Here's what these new constants stand for:

VA is the Video Address; start of video memory, as before.

CA is the Color Address; start of color memory, as before.

CC = CA − VA, which is the new color constant.

AP is the AirPlane symbol.

GU is the GUn symbol.

BU is the BUllet.

IB is the Increment of the Bullet; the amount by which it moves.

T will be used in moving the airplane.

FT won't be used till a later game version, but we might as well include it now.

BS is the Blank Space symbol, ASCII code 32.

NS will be used to define the edges of the screen.

VU is the Video Up limit of movement.

VD is the Video Down limit of movement.

There are some other numbers in the program that I won't bother to represent as constants. They are either low numbers which don't take long for the computer to convert, or numbers that occur at parts of the program where speed isn't important. For instance, I won't bother to use a constant instead of 53281, in POKE 53281,3 when background color is selected.

New line 1040 makes any key on the keyboard repeat after it has been held down for half a second. This will be useful when the player moves the gun in this new version of the program. Instead of tapping a key repeatedly, the player can simply hold the key down.

New lines 1020 and 1021 are needed to move the airplane in a new way. Type them just as they are listed here, and I'll explain what they mean in the next section.

Subscripted Variables

First, we can leave out some of the directions that the airplane used to move. We won't have it moving straight up or down, since those sudden vertical shifts aren't the way real airplanes behave. And we won't have it hover motionless. Really, we shouldn't allow any sudden reversals of direction, either; but if we make it as true to life as that, the image will be too easy to hit, and the game will be too simple. So we'll compromise by allowing some sudden reversals, but less often. And we'll adjust the randomness so that the plane flies level more, and dives and climbs less.

How on earth do we build all this into the program? We can use a whole series of IF statements, which will take too long to execute. Or, we can find a shortcut—an algorithm.

My shortcut uses a new kind of variable, D, to describe the direction our airplane flies. D will now be followed by a *subscript*, which is a number in brackets. Lines 1020 and 1021 define $D(0)$, $D(1)$ . . . all the way through $D(7)$.

D(1) does not mean that D is equal to 1. The number in the brackets is like the label on the track suit of someone running in a race. It has nothing to do with his real identity. It simply allows us to refer to him easily as "runner number 1."

The subscripts in our program will be used the same way: to pick out, for convenience, eight different directions, numbered arbitrarily 0 through 7. The actual *values* assigned to these directions are defined on lines 1020 and 1021, and illustrated in Figure 3.1. For instance, D(1) = 39. Check back to our list of direction increments, and you'll see that adding 39 to the airplane's address moves it downward and to the left. So D(1) = 39 really means that "direction #1 is downward and to the left." This is much the same as announcing at the beginning of a race, "runner #1 is Jack Smith." Just as runner #1 is Jack Smith all through the race, D(1) will have the value 39 all through our program. (Our "subscripted variables" are really constants—which is why they're listed in the 'Establish Constants' section of the program. But for some reason, no one ever talks about "subscripted constants.")

Using subscripts offers advantages. First, it cuts out a lot of the calculation we had to do before, to find a new random direction. All we need to do now is say:

$$N = INT(RND(1) * 8)$$

where N is the number of the direction we're randomly selecting. Having chosen a value for N, we put it in the brackets after D, and then use D(N) as our increment for the airplane's position.

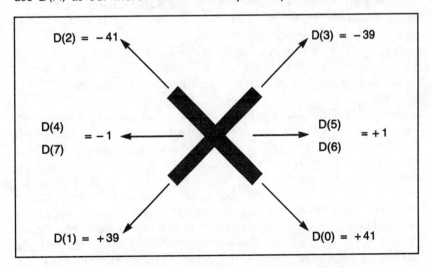

Figure 3.1: The values assigned to each subscripted variable, and the direction they represent on the screen.

If we want our airplane to spend more time flying level than climbing or diving, all we have to do is give more of the direction numbers the level-flight values, + 1 or − 1. Then, if we keep picking directions at random, we'll tend to pick level flight more often, because more of the D( )s have that value.

In addition, by setting up the subscripted variables cleverly, we can simplify figuring the plane's changes of direction when it reaches the edge of the screen. If the airplane tries to fly off the top or bottom of the screen, we can give it a new direction very simply. We say N (the number of the new direction) = 3 − N (three minus the number of the old direction). That's all!

Here are two lines to accomplish this:

```
E 120 IF AA+D(N)<VU THEN L=0:N=3-N
* 130 IF AA+D(N)>VD THEN L=0:N=3-N
```

Remember, we decided to leave out the vertical directions of flight, so the plane can only fly off the top or bottom of the screen if it's moving diagonally. The four diagonal directions are D(0), D(1), D(2), and D(3). (Listed on line 1020.)

To look realistic, the plane should dip down if it flies too high, or pull up if it flies too low, without changing its rightward or leftward progress, as indicated in Figure 3.2. For instance, if it's climbing, moving rightward, its video address is incrementing by − 39 each time, and we want it to start incrementing by + 41 instead. Well, D(3) = − 39 (as you can see from the list), and D(0) = 41. So we want N, the number of the direction, to change from 3 to 0. Well, the statement N = 3 − N has exactly this effect, saying that new N = three-minus-old-N.

Check all the other ways the plane can fly off the top or bottom of the screen, and you'll find that N = 3 − N works every time, to set the airplane back on course. You'll find this statement on new lines 120 and 130.

Now, what about the edges of the screen? This is a tougher problem, because of the way the pixels are numbered. The computer doesn't see the screen as having left and right "edges;" it just sees a long string of video addresses from 1024 to 2023. How do we specify every fortieth address as lying at the right-hand edge of the screen?

We don't. We cheat. Remember I mentioned in Chapter Two that there are two kinds of blank space, with ASCII codes 32 and 96? Check Appendix C, and you'll see. Well, we can use this to our advantage now.

Type the following lines. Remember, E means you can get this line by Editing an existing line. * means this is a new line you must type from scratch.

In addition, there are a few lines with a hyphen (-) beside them.

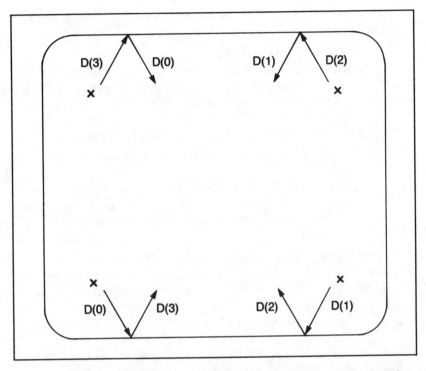

Figure 3.2: When the airplane tries to fly off the bottom edge of the screen, this is how it should respond. In each case, the number of the new direction is equal to the number of the old direction subtracted from 3. That is: N = 3 – N.

These are old lines that do not need to be changed at all. I include them simply because you'll see them on the screen in your old listing, and I don't want you to think they shouldn't be there. You must retain them exactly as they are.

You should also still have the REM lines giving the names of the sections of the program. I have not bothered to list them all over again.

```
*  1050 A=0:B=0:C=0
*  1060 K=0:L=0:N=0:SC=0:IG=0
-  1070 AA=0:AB=0:AG=0
R  1140 A$="":U$=CHR$(145):C$=CHR$(147)
-  2700 POKE 53280,3:POKE 53281,3
E  2710 PRINT C$;
*  2720 FOR A=VA TO VA+960 STEP 40
*  2730 POKE A,NS:POKE A+39,NS
*  2740 NEXT A
-  2800 AA=VA+380
E  2810 POKE AA+CC,2:POKE AA,AP
-  2820 AG=VA+980
E  2830 POKE AG+CC,5:POKE AG,30
-  2890 RETURN
```

Lines 1050 through 1070 establish variables. We have some new variables now.

> A, B, C are arbitrary letters which will be used as loop variables in a later version of the game.
>
> K and L will be used in this version to count cycles of the program when moving the airplane; I'll explain them in a moment.
>
> N is the Number of the direction the plane moves in.
>
> SC will be used when we keep SCore in a later version of the game.
>
> IG is the Increment that the Gun moves, left and right, in this new version. Since IG is negative when the gun moves left, and positive when it moves right, IG is a variable, not a constant.

As for the strings: for convenience, to save typing CHR$ followed by a number over and over again, I've given string names to CHR$(145) and CHR$(147). The latter is the screen-clear command; the former is a cursor-up command that I'll explain in Chapter Four.

Line 2700 selects background color, just as before. Line 2710 uses C$ instead of CHR$(147). Remember to include the semicolon.

Now we get to the part that uses spaces with value ASCII 96.

PEEK vs. POKE

Lines 2720 through 2740 POKE spaces of ASCII 96 (remember, NS = 96) down the right and left edges of the picture. These spaces won't look any different from the rest of the screen, which is full of ASCII 32 spaces that were put there by the automatic screen-clearing at the beginning of the program. But we can detect the difference between a 32 blank space and a 96 blank space by using a PEEK statement.

PEEK is the opposite of POKE. POKE loads an address with a number; PEEK finds out what number has been loaded. If we say, X = PEEK(1024), X will be assigned the value that the computer finds in address 1024. A PEEK is like looking in a mailbox to find out how many envelopes are in there—and then closing the box without disturbing the mail at all.

All we do, then, to test whether the airplane has reached the edge of the screen, is PEEK the video address it's about to move to. If that PEEK is 32, we're all right. If it's 96, the airplane has reached the edge and must double back.

How do we double back? It's not quite as elegant as the maneuver when the plane reaches the top or bottom of the screen. But it's still just one general-purpose line:

$$N = N + 4:IF \ N > 7 \ THEN \ N = N - 8$$

You'll find this statement on lines 140 and 150, listed below.

Suppose N is 5—the airplane flying in direction number 5. D(5) = 1, an increment which results in rightward, horizontal flight. When the airplane reaches the right-hand edge of the screen and needs to change direction, new N equals old N plus 4, so we add 5 to 4, making 9, but that's greater than 7, so we take away 8, leaving 1. So the new direction is direction number 1, and from the chart we see D(1) = 39, which is downward and leftward. The plane doesn't precisely reverse direction, but does move away from the right-hand edge, which will do for our purposes. Figure 3.3 shows all the possibilities.

Well, I warned you this part was complicated. Refining a program so that everything works in a realistic way is often much harder than thinking up the program in the first place.

There are two other things we want from the airplane: it has to move more slowly than the bullets being fired at it, and it has to change direction less often. Both these problems are solved the same way, with the two new variables K and L.

Here's the whole new airplane-moving routine (the preceding lines, 10 through 99 aren't listed because they remain the same). Remember, E means you can edit an old line. * means this is a new line.

```
E 100 K=K+1:IF K<3 THEN 200
E 110 K=0:L=L+1
* 140 IF PEEK(AA+D(N))=NS THEN L=0:N=N+4
* 150 IF N>7 THEN N=N-8
* 160 IF L>T THEN L=0:N=INT(RND(1)*8)
E 170 POKE AA,BS:AA=AA+D(N)
E 180 POKE AA+CC,2:POKE AA,AP
```

Line 100 adds 1 to the value of K, each time the program runs through a single cycle. IF K < 3 THEN we skip the airplane moving routine. When K = 3, we move the airplane but re-set K to 0. This means the plane only moves on every third cycle of the program, whereas a bullet on the screen will be incremented on every cycle. So the bullet will move three steps for every one step the airplane moves.

Similarly, line 110 uses L to count from 0 up to 10, and line 160 only chooses a new random direction for the airplane when L is greater than T (T is the new constant whose value is 10). In other words, the airplane moves ten steps before we use the RND statement on line 160 to find a new direction.

Lastly, lines 170 and 180 are edited to use the new constants we've established, instead of the old numerical values for the ASCII codes of the airplane, direction, and blank-space.

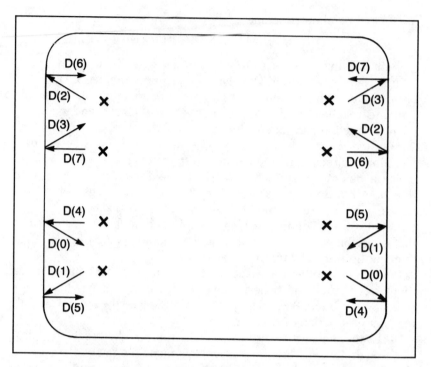

Figure 3.3: This is how the airplane should behave when it tries to fly off the left or right edge of the screen. In each case, the number of the new direction is equal to the number of the old direction, plus 4; except that, if the result exceeds 7, then 8 should be subtracted. In other words: N = N + 4 : IF N > 7 THEN N = N − 8.

Now, we can deal with the gun. Here are the new lines that will move it from side to side when the player presses keys on the keyboard:

```
E 198 REM----------- Move Gun -----------
- 199 REM
- 200 GET A$
* 210 IG=0
* 220 IF A$="1" THEN IG=-1
* 230 IF A$="2" THEN IG=1
* 240 IF IG=0 OR PEEK(AG+IG)=NS THEN 300
* 250 POKE AG,BS:AG=AG+IG
* 260 POKE AG+CC,5:POKE AG,GU
```

I'm using the 1 key on the keyboard to move the gun left, and 2 to move it right. To stop the gun from moving off the left or right edges of the screen, we have to PEEK for the 96 ASCII code, just as we now do for the airplane.

Line 210 establishes IG, the Increment of the Gun, as zero. But IF A$ (the keyboard entry) is "1", THEN IG = −1, i.e., leftward.

Line 230 says IF A$ is "2" THEN IG = 1, i.e., rightward.

Line 240 says if the player doesn't want to move the gun, or is trying to move off the edge of the screen, we'll leave the gun where it is, and skip to line 300, animating the bullet (if any).

Lines 250 and 260 blank out and re-POKE the gun's ASCII code in its new video address, just as we blank out and re-POKE the bullet and the airplane.

Now, the new bullet-moving routine. We want a player to be able to fire the gun without waiting for the previous bullet to leave the screen. How can this be done? One way would be by adding extra bullet-moving sections of the program, to control the position of extra bullets. But this would slow the program down too much. There's a simpler solution.

Let's assume that if the player wants to fire a new bullet, it must be because he realizes the previous bullet is going to miss, so he doesn't care about it any more. In this case, why not have the program blank out the old bullet as soon as the player tries to fire a new one, and start a new bullet down at the gun position right away? We'll still only have one bullet on the screen at a time, but the player will be able to start it again whenever he likes.

When I saw this solution to the problem, I wondered how it would look. Wouldn't it seem strange, for a previous bullet to vanish each time the player fired a new one? The only way to find out was to try it. And it works just fine.

Here is the new routine:

```
E 300 IF A$=CHR$(BS) THEN 370
- 310 IF AB=0 THEN 100
E 320 IF AB<VU THENPOKEAB,BS:AB=0:GOTO100
E 330 POKE AB,BS:AB=AB-IB
E 340 POKE AB+CC,0:POKE AB,BU
- 350 IF AB=AA THEN 800
- 360 GOTO 100
- 365 REM---------- Fire Gun
* 370 IF AB>0 THEN POKE AB,BS
E 380 AB=AG-IB
E 390 POKE AB+CC,0:POKE AB,BU:GOTO 100
```

On line 300, the constant BS (Blank Space) is used instead of the number 32, and the condition that AB = 0 is abolished—the player can now fire the gun any time. The GOTO is to a new line (line 370) which is needed to blank out the old image of the bullet, if it hasn't already left the screen.

The other modifications to the bullet-moving routine are needed to stop the image of the bullet from flickering. Remember, in the previous version of the game, the program blanked out the bullet's image, then checked to see if it had hit the airplane, and then POKEd the bullet into its new address, so long as a hit had not occurred. Well, checking for a hit takes just enough time for there to be a noticeable moment when the bullet's image is missing on the screen, in the previous game version. Hence the appearance of flicker.

The new version first moves the bullet and then checks for a collision.

The old 'Bullet Hits Target' section of the program is the same as before.

You should now have finished typing all the necessary revisions, and when you LIST the program you should find the computer has faithfully inserted all your new lines among the old—provided you typed the line numbers correctly.

Quickly go through the listings in this chapter and check to see that each line marked with an asterisk has been added to your listing. Check, also, that lines marked E have been edited correctly. If you forgot to press RETURN after doing an edit, that new line won't have been remembered and the old line will still be there.

When you're convinced you've made no errors, save the new version of the program on disk or tape, *in a different file from the old version*. Keep the old version, just in case.

Now run the program.

Assuming your listing works properly, you'll find the "playability" of the game has improved a lot. The X symbol moves more like an airplane, and you can use some strategy in trying to hit it.

But it's easy to think up a lot more improvements. How about instructions at the beginning, so anyone can play the game? How about a flash, or something, when the bullet hits the plane? How about setting a time limit, and seeing how many hits a player can make before time runs out? How about having the game automatically restart after every hit, and show the score and the remaining time right on the screen?

Why not? These improvements are easy, because they don't affect the logic of the program. All we need to know is how to add a few PRINT statements. And that's exactly what the next chapter is about.

Summary

To make the enhancements in this chapter, we've had to understand:

- How to increase running speed by replacing decimal numbers with constants, using lower line numbers, and omitting REM statements and spaces.
- How to use a subscripted variable to stand for "direction #1," "direction #2," and so on, to make programming easier.
- How to keep an image from moving off the top, bottom, and side edges of the screen.

- How to use PEEK, the opposite of POKE.
- How to set up an "invisible barrier" of ASCII 96 spaces on the screen.
- How to make some parts of a program run more slowly than others, by using a variable to count program cycles, activating some program sections only after a set number of cycles.
- How to move an image left and right in response to keyboard commands.

FOUR
Peculiarities of PRINT

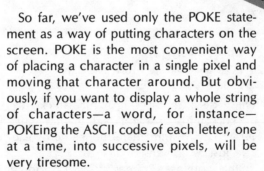

So far, we've used only the POKE statement as a way of putting characters on the screen. POKE is the most convenient way of placing a character in a single pixel and moving that character around. But obviously, if you want to display a whole string of characters—a word, for instance—POKEing the ASCII code of each letter, one at a time, into successive pixels, will be very tiresome.

There is, of course, a shortcut: the BASIC word, PRINT. If you clear the screen, type:

PRINT "HELLO"

and press RETURN, the computer inserts the ASCII code of each letter of HELLO into video memory automatically, and does it so fast, it looks as if the whole word appears all at once. Also, the computer will automatically set color memory for each letter at the same time. The PRINT statement, then, is the best and quickest way to display text.

Programmed Cursor Control

The text will commence on the screen at the position of the cursor. Now, in immediate mode (when a program is *not* running) you can move the cursor fairly easily by using the two CRSR keys. But how do you move it while a program *is* running? In other words, how can you write a program that will control where PRINTed text will appear on the screen?

There are two ways, neither of them very convenient. If you've used other computers, you may have come across a statement such as PRINT AT, which lets you specify the line where text will be PRINTed. But Commodore hasn't given us a PRINT AT command or anything like it. So what we have to do is home the cursor (i.e. move it to the top-left corner) and then move it down the necessary number of lines, then across the necessary number of columns, to the pixel where we want the first letter of our PRINTed word to appear.*

Unless a program uses the INPUT statement, the cursor will be invisible while the program is running. However, the computer always knows the cursor position, regardless of whether you can see it or not.

So how do you write a program to home and move the cursor? First, make sure you have saved your last program. Then type:

NEW

and press RETURN, and type the following:

```
10  PRINT CHR$(147)
20  FOR N = 1 TO 12:PRINT:NEXT N
30  PRINT TAB(17)"HELLO"
```

We used that statement, PRINT CHR$(147), in Air Attack. It clears the screen and homes the cursor, just as if you held down a SHIFT key and pressed the CLR/HOME key in immediate mode. I'll explain this special CHR$ statement in just a moment.

Line 20 seems to say, PRINT nothing, 12 times. But the computer follows any PRINT statement with an automatic line feed and a carriage return, even when nothing is being PRINTed. The line feed moves the cursor to the next line down, and the carriage return returns the cursor to the left edge of the screen.

Lastly, line 30 TABs the cursor across seventeen columns before it

---

*There is a simpler way of moving the cursor, but there are times when it won't work as you expect. It involves POKEing a screen line number (from 0–24) into address 214. See Appendix J, page 190, for a full discussion.

prints the word HELLO. Refer to the tab and line number map in Appendix G to see exactly what's going on.

There were twelve PRINT statements, moving the cursor down twelve lines. So you might think the word HELLO appears on line 12. Wrong! It's on line 13. Can you see why? Because that mysterious statement, PRINT CHR$(147), is a PRINT statement, in addition to its special screen-clearing function. So it, too, is automatically followed by a carriage return and line feed, making thirteen line feeds in all. You have to keep track of things like this, to be sure of where the cursor is.

Special CHR$ Codes

All right, now I'll explain this PRINT CHR$ business. On most computers, it's very simple. If you tell the computer to PRINT CHR$(N), it will display the character whose ASCII code is N. In other words, it has the same effect as POKEing video memory with that code.

Why do you need this feature? Well, perhaps you want to PRINT a special graphics character, among other ordinary characters. It's easier to say:

PRINT "AAA"CHR$(127)"BBB"

than it would be to figure out the video memory address where you need to POKE a graphics character between "AAA" and "BBB".

Actually, this is one of the things the Commodore 64 makes easy. It allows us to type graphics characters on the keyboard, and insert them between quote marks, as strings to be PRINTed. All you have to do is hold down a SHIFT key or the special C= key while you type. The symbols you get are shown on the front edges of the keys.

This causes no trouble unless you try to print the program listing on a printer other than one made by Commodore. No normal printer will display those funny graphics characters when they appear in a program listing. So in this book we will use the CHR$ expression when PRINTing any graphics character that doesn't appear on a normal computer keyboard, just to make listing easier.*

There is one other use for the PRINT CHR$ statement: if you want to PRINT a quote mark on the screen, you have to tell the computer to PRINT CHR$(34). The computer will not understand PRINT """".

---

*There is one way to list programs that include the graphics characters. Several manufacturers produce "smart interfaces" to connect non-Commodore printers with your Commodore 64. You can choose between PET-ASCII and regular ASCII on some; others will let you print the graphics characters, provided your printer has dot-addressable graphics; some will even translate the graphics characters inside quote marks in your PRINT statements into CHR$ codes or special three-letter codes that let you know which key you pressed. However, these interfaces tend to be expensive. Among them are Cardco's Card "?", Tymac's The Connection, Midwest Micro's Smart ASCII, and Micro World Electronix' MW-302. Inquire at your local dealer if you are interested.

Now, we saw in the last chapter that POKE 1024,1 places a letter A in the top left pixel of the screen. Does this mean that if we tell the Commodore 64 to PRINT CHR$(1) it will display a letter A?

It ought to mean exactly that, but it doesn't, because Commodore uses *two different systems* for numbering characters, depending on whether you're using the POKE statement or the PRINT CHR$ statement. The PRINT CHR$ codes are listed in Appendix D. You'll see that PRINT CHR$(65), not PRINT CHR$(1), produces a letter A.

To make things even more difficult, some CHR$ numbers are *special* numbers. Instead of displaying a character, they produce a special effect. Type:

PRINT CHR$(28)

and press RETURN. What happens? No character appears on the screen. Instead, all subsequent text turns red.

The special CHR$ codes are summarized in Appendix B. The screen-clearing, cursor-homing code, CHR$(147), is one of them.

Generally speaking, you can use the special CHR$ codes in a program to do all the graphics-control operations you can perform on the keyboard in immediate mode. For instance, in Chapter One, we turned the text black by holding down CTRL and pressing the 1 key. That's fine, until a program is running, and you want the text to be colored black. You don't want the program to stop and prompt the user to press CTRL and 1. You want the program itself to turn the text black. The way to do this is by a special PRINT CHR$ command—PRINT CHR$(144)—which can be written into the program. (You can, of course, hold down the Control key and press 1 inside quote marks of a PRINT statement, but you might not recognize the meaning of the character that appears when you look at your listed program.)

To control cursor movement, there are four special codes. PRINT CHR$(157) moves the cursor one step to the left, for instance. If you want to use these codes in a program, it saves a lot of time and space to give them string-variable names at the start of the program. I generally do it like this:

D$ = CHR$(17)		D for Down
R$ = CHR$(29)		R for Right
U$ = CHR$(145)		U for Up
L$ = CHR$(157)		L for Left

Then, if you want to move the cursor four spaces right and two lines down, you can say:

PRINT RRRRDD;

Don't forget to include that semicolon (;) mark at the end. The semicolon *suppresses* the carriage return and line feed that normally follow any PRINT statement. If you leave out the semicolon, the computer obeys the special CHR$ commands and moves the cursor as you wish, and then does the automatic carriage return and line feed. As a result, the cursor ends up somewhere quite different from where you wanted it.

At this point, you may have decided that moving the cursor as we did with PRINT and TAB statements is easier than moving it with cursor-control CHR$ commands. Maybe so, but bear in mind PRINT can only move the cursor down, and TAB moves it out toward the right edge of the screen. To move the cursor to the left, or up, you have to use CHR$ commands.

Do you still have our little three-line PRINT/TAB demo program? If so, add a semicolon after the word "HELLO" on line 30. Then type this extra line:

40 PRINT CHR$(145)CHR$(157)"GOODBYE"

Run the program, and the word GOODBYE should appear with its G directly above the O of HELLO—as you will see in Figure 4.1. The semicolon after the PRINT statement on line 30 suppresses the carriage

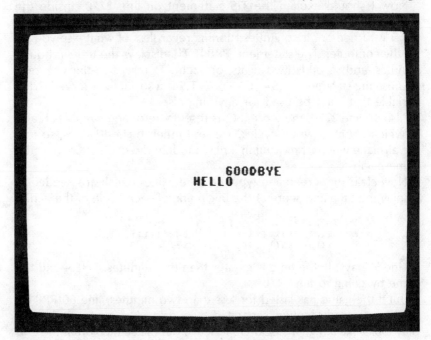

Figure 4.1: Using cursor-control commands to add extra text.

return and linefeed, the cursor is then moved one line up and one space left, and the new word is PRINTed.

Have you grasped all this? I don't blame you if you need to read it more than once, because it's a bit complicated.

Adding PRINT to Your Program

If you've grasped the basic principles involved, you're ready to add some new lines to the Air Attack game. First load the new version of the game that we completed in the last chapter, and list the program to make sure you have the new version and not an earlier version. Then clear the screen and type these new lines:

```
* 2750 PRINT SPC(5)"TIME"SPC(10)"HITS"
* 2760 PRINT U$;
* 2770 TI$="000000":SC=0:L=10:K=3
```

These lines will insert themselves in the Set Up Screen routine. Line 2750 puts a heading at the top of the screen, ready to display time and score. A line feed is allowed after this PRINT statement, and then PRINT U$; on line 2760 moves the cursor up again (remember to include the semicolon).

Now I should explain the TI$ statement on line 2770. Inside the Commodore 64 is a clock that begins from zero each time the computer is turned on. It continues running regardless of what else you do on the computer. The statement: PRINT TI$ displays the time in hours, minutes, and seconds (two digits for each). To reset the clock to zero you use the statement: TI$= "000000". TI$ is a specially reserved string variable that can't be used for anything else.

Also on line 2770, the score, SC, is reset to zero, and variables K and L, which count program cycles, are set to their highest values, so that the airplane will start moving in a new random direction as soon as the game begins.

Now clear the screen and type these new lines which are needed to display the time and score at the beginning of each cycle of the game:

```
* 50 IF TI$>"000200" THEN 900
* 60 PRINT MID$(TI$,4,1)":"RIGHT$(TI$,2);
* 70 PRINT TAB(FT)SC:PRINT U$;
```

Line 50 says, IF the time is greater than two minutes, THEN end the game by going to line 900.

But if the game has lasted for less than two minutes, line 60 PRINTs the minutes and seconds, separated by a colon (":" mark) so the display looks like a digital clock. Don't leave out the semicolon at the end of this line.

Line 70 TABs across to column 15 (FT is a constant whose value is 15) and inserts the score, SC, in the TIME and HITS heading that has already been placed on the screen. Then PRINT U$; moves the cursor back up to the start of this PRINT line.

The previous version of the game began each cycle on line 100. Now, however, we want each cycle to begin with new line 50, as above. This means we need to change some lines later in the program so that they say GOTO 50 instead of GOTO 100.

These are the lines you need to edit:

```
E 310 IF AB=0 THEN 50
E 320 IF AB<VU THENPOKEAB,BS:AB=0:GOTO 50
E 360 GOTO 50
E 390 POKE AB+CC,0:POKE AB,BU:GOTO 50
```

To display these lines, type:

LIST 310–390

and press RETURN, then move the cursor to the line number at the end of each line, change it from 100 to 50, and press RETURN to record each change.

You'll also see on your screen other lines between the ones I've shown here. These other lines don't have to be changed at all. Leave them exactly as they are. If you accidentally make changes in them, you can type NEW and then reload your program from disk or tape. You can then make the changes anew.

Now here's a new routine for when the bullet hits the airplane. In the past, a black square appeared on the screen and the game ended. With these changes, the image will flash, the score will increase by 1 point, and the game will continue.

```
E 800 FOR A=1 TO 5
* 810 B=160:GOSUB 860
* 820 B=BS:GOSUB 860
* 830 NEXT A
* 840 AB=0:SC=SC+1
* 845 POKE AA,BS:POKE AG,BS
* 850 GOSUB 2800:GOTO 50
* 855 REM---------- Delay Loop
* 860 POKE AA,B
* 880 FOR C=1 TO 100:NEXT C
* 890 RETURN
```

Line 800 starts a loop which will run through five cycles (the image will flash five times). Line 810 specifies a black square, then uses subroutine 860 to POKE that square into video memory and count from 1 to 100 so that the square has time to be seen on the screen. Line 820 substitutes a blank space for the black square, and the process is repeated.

Line 840 removes the bullet from the screen with the statement AB = 0 and adds 1 point to the score, SC.

Line 845 blanks out the position of airplane and gun. Then line 850 tells the computer to GOSUB 2800, which resets the gun and airplane to their beginning positions. And the game continues.

Now we need to improve the sequence of events when time runs out and the game ends. Line 900 remains the same as before. New lines 910 through 960 show the player's score and ask if he or she wants to play again. If the answer is "Y" for Yes, subroutine 2700 resets the score and screen and restarts the game from scratch.

Clear the screen and type these new lines:

```
* 897 REM
* 898 REM--------- Time Runs Out --------
* 899 REM
* 910 PRINT C$
* 920 PRINT"YOUR SCORE:";SC
* 930 PRINT:PRINT
* 940 PRINT"PLAY AGAIN?"
* 950 GET A$:IF A$="" THEN 950
* 960 IF A$="Y" THEN GOSUB 2700:GOTO 50
```

Old line 970 remains the same, so I haven't bothered to show it.

This is almost the end of the improvements to be made in this chapter. As promised, they have been simpler than the improvements in the last chapter, because none of them affects the logic of the game. We're simply adding "frills" that make the game easier to play and more professional in appearance.

Adding User Friendliness

The most important "frill" is still to come: instructions for playing the game. Many people don't bother to include instructions, but I believe computers should be as easy to use as possible, and a program should be understandable to anyone, not just the person who wrote it.

All of the following lines are new lines. Clear the screen first, and then type:

```
1997 REM
1998 REM-------- Instructions ---------
1999 REM
2000 POKE 53280,1:POKE 53281,1
2010 PRINT C$;CHR$(144)
2020 PRINT"THE OBJECT OF THIS GAME"
2030 PRINT"IS TO SHOOT DOWN AN ENEMY"
2040 PRINT"AIRPLANE.":PRINT:PRINT
2050 PRINT"USE KEYS 1 AND 2 TO MOVE"
2060 PRINT"YOUR GUN LEFT AND RIGHT."
2070 PRINT"PRESS THE SPACEBAR"
2080 PRINT"TO FIRE.":PRINT:PRINT
```

```
2090 PRINT"YOU HAVE TWO MINUTES"
2100 PRINT"TO SCORE AS MANY HITS"
2110 PRINT"AS YOU CAN.":PRINT:PRINT
2120 PRINT"PRESS ANY KEY TO BEGIN."
2130 GET A$:IF A$="" THEN 2130
2160 GOSUB 2700
2170 RETURN
```

Save the new version of your program in a new file. Call it something like GAME VERSION 3 so you can keep it separate from the previous versions.

We have now developed the game as far as possible, using single graphics characters that move from one pixel to the next.

I could make the game *look* a little more interesting by adding some scenery—a skyline at the bottom of the picture, for instance, and maybe some clouds behind the airplane. In the Chapter Five I'll describe a program that makes it easy to create this kind of background.

But scenery doesn't do anything to improve the crude and simple appearance of the symbols on the screen, and the jerky way they move. To upgrade that aspect of the game, we will need what are called Sprite graphics—the most powerful feature of the Commodore 64, which I'll explain a little later, in Chapter Six.

Summary

This chapter has tackled the topic of PRINT statements, and has explained:

- How PRINT works as a routine for inserting characters in video memory automatically, and setting their color at the same time.
- How to use PRINT and TAB to control cursor position.
- How line feeds and carriage returns work, and how to suppress them.
- How special PRINT CHR$ commands control cursor position and clear the screen.
- How CHR$ codes differ from ASCII codes.
- How to reset the Commodore clock to zero, and display the time with PRINT TI$.
- How to add the following features to a video game:
    - a display of the score;
    - a timed playing cycle, with a display clock;
    - a restart after an impact;
    - a replay option.

FIVE
Sketching on the Screen

  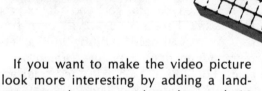

If you want to make the video picture look more interesting by adding a landscape or other scenery, how do you do it?

First, make some photocopies of the video memory map in Appendix E and sketch a picture on it, using the shapes of Commodore graphics characters. Then, you have to find a way of POKEing the code and the color of each character into video memory.

The most obvious method of doing this is to use a series of DATA statements. Your program would have a some lines in it like this:

```
10  X = VA
20  READ C:POKE X + CC,C
30  READ A:POKE X,A
40  X = X + 1:IF X < 1000 THEN 20
.....
(Rest of program here)
.....
5000  DATA 2,160, ... etc
```

Line 10 establishes X as the first address in video memory.

Line 20 READs the first number in the DATA statement, a Color code which is assigned to variable C and POKEd into the first address in color memory.

Line 30 reads the next number in the DATA statement, an ASCII code which is assigned to variable A and POKEd into the first address in video memory.

The result of this is a solid pixel (ASCII code 160) in the top-left corner of the screen, colored red (color code 2).

Line 40 then adds 1 to the value of X. If X has not yet reached the address of the end of video memory, the cycle of lines 20 through 40 repeats over again. Provided you add enough DATA statements, you can fill the whole screen this way.

But this means a lot of tiresome typing for you, and a lot of program space taken up with DATA. Isn't there a better way?

Well, of course there is. What you need is a program that lets you use cursor-control commands to draw a picture straight onto the screen. Then the program should PEEK each video and color address for you and save those numbers onto disk or tape. This way, you will never have to type any numbers yourself. The program will take care of them for you.

Later, you can write into your game program a little routine to re-load the numbers from disk or tape and POKE them back into color and video memory, to re-create the picture.

This chapter describes such a picture-drawing program. I call it a Graphics Generator, and I used it to draw the picture of the house in color plate 3 and the landscape for Air Attack in color plate 6. If you don't want the work of typing the long listing, you can obtain the program from me on tape or disk, ready to run (see Appendix Y).

The Graphics Generator Program

Be sure you have saved your most recent version of Air Attack. Then type:

NEW

and press RETURN. Then type the following lines:

```
997 REM
998 REM------------START-UP------------
999 REM
1000 POKE 53281,1:POKE 53280,1
1010 PRINT CHR$(147)CHR$(144)
1020 PRINT"GRAPHICS GENERATOR":PRINT
1030 PRINT"COMMAND CODES:":PRINT
1040 PRINT"U = UP"
1050 PRINT"D = DOWN"
1060 PRINT"L = LEFT"
1070 PRINT"R = RIGHT"
1080 PRINT"I = INSERT"
1090 PRINT"E = ERASE"
1110 PRINT"C = NEW COLOR"
1120 PRINT"A = NEW ASCII CODE"
1130 PRINT"S = SAVE"
1140 PRINT"H = HELP":PRINT
1200 P=0:Q=0:D=0:M=0:N=0
1300 VA=1024:CC=54272:X=1524:Y=VA+959
1310 A=160:C=0:CU=86:S=32:SF=64:NN=999
1350 DIM A(40),B(40)
1400 A$="":B$="":F$=""
1500 POKE 650,128
1600 INPUT"SCREEN BACKGROUND COLOR";M
1610 POKE 53281,M:PRINT
1620 INPUT"SCREEN BORDER COLOR";M
1630 POKE 53280,M:PRINT
1650 PRINT"WANT TO LOAD & EDIT?":PRINT
1660 GOSUB 2000:IF A$="Y" THEN 1800
1700 PRINT"WHICH FILE WILL YOU"
1710 INPUT"SAVE THE PICTURE IN";F$
1720 PRINT CHR$(147)
1730 RETURN
```

Line 1000 turns the screen white. Line 1010 clears the screen and specifies black text. Lines 1020 through 1140 are instructions. When the program is running, there will be a little X marker, which will be our cursor. To move this marker around you'll press U for Up, D for Down, etc. To draw with it, other single-letter codes will be used, as defined in the following list.

Lines 1200 through 1350 establish variables and constants:

P and Q will temporarily store the color and ASCII code of the pixel on the screen being marked by the cursor.

D is the Direction the cursor moves.

M and N are used as loop variables.

VA is the first Video Address.

CC is the Color Constant.

X is the video address of the cursor.

Y is an address where video messages will be displayed.

A is the ASCII code of the graphics symbol being used to draw the picture.

C is the Color of that symbol.

CU is the CUrsor's ASCII code (a constant).

S stands for blank Space.

SF and NN are constants that will be used in some simple arithmetic.

A( ) and B( ) will be used to memorize, temporarily, contents of video and color memory addresses which are used to display messages on the screen.

Lines 1600 through 1630 allow you to choose screen and border colors. Then line 1650 offers the option of loading an old picture, to edit it. I'll explain the load routine a little later.

Sequential Files

If you don't want to load an old picture, the program asks for the name of the file that the new picture will be saved in, when it's finished. This file name is like a program name. The only difference is that this file won't hold instructions that make up a program. Instead, it will hold a sequence of data—numbers that, in this case, will create a video picture.

This kind of file is called a *sequential file,* and it works much the same way on disk or on tape. Giving each file a different name allows you to choose which one you want to load.

After assigning the file name to F$, the program begins executing at the top of the listing, as it did in Air Attack.

Type these lines:

```
10 REM--------GRAPHICS GENERATOR-------
20 REM
30 GOSUB 1000
40 P=PEEK(X):Q=PEEK(X+CC)
50 POKE X+CC,0:POKE X,CU
60 GET A$:IF A$="" THEN 60
70 IF A$="U" THEN D=-40:GOTO 180
80 IF A$="D" THEN D=40:GOTO 180
90 IF A$="L" THEN D=-1:GOTO 180
100 IF A$="R" THEN D=1:GOTO 180
110 IF A$="I" THEN P=A:Q=C:D=1:GOTO 180
120 IF A$="E" THEN P=S:Q=1:D=1:GOTO 180
130 IF A$="A" THEN 300
140 IF A$="C" THEN 500
150 IF A$="S" THEN 800
160 IF A$="H" THEN 600
170 GOTO 60
180 POKE X+CC,Q
190 POKE X,P
200 IF X+D>VA+NN THEN X=X-1000
210 IF X+D<VA THEN X=X+1000
220 X=X+D:GOTO 40
```

Line 30 refers to the subroutine you've just typed, which sets up the variables and constants.

Line 40 assigns to P and Q the ASCII code and color code of the pixel where the cursor will appear. Since the cursor will displace the graphics and color of that point on the screen, we need P and Q to remember these values, so they can be replaced when the cursor moves to a different position.

Line 50 POKEs the cursor into video memory and colors it black.

Line 60 GETs a keyboard instruction. If no key has been pressed, line 60 repeats till a key is pressed.

Lines 70 through 160 check for all the possible keyboard instructions that make sense to this program. Look back at lines 1040 through 1140 to see what each key letter means. Lines 70 through 100 change cursor direction, if U, D, L, or R have been pressed.

Line 110 says, "If I has been pressed, we want to Insert a new graphics code and color on the screen when the cursor moves on. So we assign to P the ASCII code A of the graphics character, and assign to Q its color, C."

Line 120 goes through a similar operation, except that it specifies a blank space.

Lines 130 through 160 branch to other sections of the program that we'll deal with in a moment.

Line 180 POKEs cursor position with color Q, which was either the color that was there before the cursor, or is the new color that is being used to draw on the screen.

Line 190 POKEs cursor position with ASCII code P, which was either the code that was there before, or is the new code being used to draw on the screen.

Lines 200 and 210 reposition the cursor if it was about to move off the screen.

Line 220 moves the cursor in direction D and increments the cursor position. The whole cycle then repeats from line 40.

Now type these lines:

```
297 REM
298 REM--------NEW ASCII CODE--------
299 REM
300 B$="ASCII OF NEW GRAPHICS:     "
310 GOSUB 900:M=Y+24:A=0
320 GOSUB 2000
330 IF A$<"0" OR A$>"2" THEN 320
340 POKEM,ASC(A$):A=A+100*VAL(A$):M=M+1
350 GOSUB 2000
360 IF A$<"0" OR A$>"9" THEN 350
370 POKE M,ASC(A$):A=A+10*VAL(A$):M=M+1
380 GOSUB 2000
390 IF A$<"0" OR A$>"9" THEN 380
400 POKE M,ASC(A$):A=A+VAL(A$)
410 GOSUB 950:IF A>255 THEN 300
420 GOTO 60
```

When the program is running the user types an A to indicate he wants to change the ASCII code of the graphics being used to draw the picture. The program stops and gets a new value for variable A. Normally, all we would need is a single line such as:

300 INPUT"NEW ASCII CODE";A

But this would destroy any images that happened to be on that area of the screen. It would spoil the picture. Also, the INPUT statement reads the whole of two screen lines, which may contain graphics and other characters when this program is running. So we can't use INPUT.

Changing Shapes and Colors

Instead, there's a routine (on lines 900 through 980, which we'll get to later) which memorizes the contents of a screen line, then displays a message (in this case, "ASCII OF NEW GRAPHICS:"), then GETs the ASCII code one digit at a time. Codes under 100 must be preceded with 0. Codes under 10 must be preceded with 00.

The program rejects ASCII codes less than 0 or more than 255 because they would cause error messages which would stop the program and disrupt the video picture.

After getting the new ASCII code, the program replaces the strip of the picture that was there before and continues drawing the picture.

Now type these lines:

```
497 REM
498 REM---------NEW COLOR CODE---------
499 REM
500 B$="CODE OF NEW COLOR:    "
510 GOSUB 900:M=Y+20:C=0
520 GOSUB 2000
530 IF A$<"0" OR A$>"1" THEN 520
540 POKE M,ASC(A$):C=C+10*VAL(A$):M=M+1
550 GOSUB 2000
560 IF A$<"0" OR A$>"9" THEN 550
570 POKE M,ASC(A$):C=C+VAL(A$)
580 GOSUB 950:IF C>15 THEN 500
590 GOTO 60
597 REM
598 REM---------HELP MESSAGE----------
599 REM
600 B$="U=UP:D=DOWN:L=LEFT:R=RIGHT"
610 GOSUB 900:GOSUB 2000:GOSUB 950
620 B$="I=INSERT:E=ERASE:H=HELP"
630 GOSUB 900:GOSUB 2000:GOSUB 950
640 B$="A=ASCII:C=COLOR:S=SAVE"
650 GOSUB 900:GOSUB 2000:GOSUB 950
660 GOTO 60
```

The NEW COLOR CODE section works just like the NEW ASCII CODE. The user types a C when he wants to specify a new color, then types the color number as two digits. Color numbers under 10 must be preceded with a 0.

The HELP MESSAGE is selected by typing H, and is displayed in three parts. The first part displays the cursor-control commands; the second, those for Insert, Erase, and Help; and the third, those to change graphics symbols and colors, and to Save the program. Each stays on the screen until you touch any key. After the third message, the display disappears and the program continues.

Saving Your Picture

Now we get to the save routine:

```
797 REM
798 REM---------SAVE PICTURE----------
799 REM
800 B$="READY TO SAVE?":GOSUB 900
810 GOSUB 2000
820 IF A$<>"Y" AND A$<>"N" THEN 810
830 GOSUB 950:IF A$="N" THEN 60
835 POKE X,P:POKE X+CC,Q
840 OPEN 2,8,2,"@0:"+F$+",S,W"
850 FOR N=VA TO VA+999
860 PRINT#2,CHR$(PEEK(N+CC));
870 PRINT#2,CHR$(PEEK(N));
880 NEXT N
890 CLOSE 2:GOTO 40
```

First the program asks "READY TO SAVE?" just in case the user has typed an S by mistake. Then line 835 erases the cursor, since you don't want to save it as part of the picture. Line 840 OPENs a sequential disk file whose name has already been established as F$. If you use a cassette recorder, you need to type a different line 840:

840 OPEN 2,1,2,F$

You use a 1 in this statement instead of an 8 because the cassette recorder is Device #1 whereas the disk drive is Device #8. The ",S,W" used with a disk are not needed.

Lines 850 through 880 methodically PEEK the color and graphics of each video location, and PRINT them as a CHR$ (single character) to file #2, which you opened with the OPEN statement. Don't leave out the semicolons at the ends of lines 860 and 870!

Line 890 CLOSEs the file, and the program continues, in case you want to work on your picture some more. The only way to stop this program, when you've done all you want to do, is with the RUN/STOP key.

Displaying a Message

Now here's the subroutine that memorizes an area of the screen, displays a message, then replaces the message with the picture that was there before:

```
897 REM
898 REM--------DISPLAY A MESSAGE-------
899 REM
900 FOR N=1 TO LEN(B$)
910 A(N)=PEEK(N+Y):B(N)=PEEK(N+Y+CC)
920 POKE N+Y+CC,0
925 M=ASC(MID$(B$,N,1))
930 IF M>SF THEN M=M-SF
935 POKE N+Y,M
940 NEXT N:RETURN
950 FOR N=1 TO LEN(B$)
960 POKE N+Y,A(N)
970 POKE N+Y+CC,B(N)
980 NEXT N:RETURN
```

Line 910 assigns to A( ) and B( ) the graphics and colors in the line of the screen beginning at video address Y.

Line 920 POKEs the color in this line to black, so that the message will appear in black.

Line 925 takes the ASCII value of one letter at a time in the message, which has been assigned to B$. Because of the differences between CHR$ and POKE codes, SF (a constant of value 64) must be subtracted from the CHR$ value of characters whose value exceeds 64 before they're POKEd into video memory.

Lines 950 through 980 are the subroutine that puts back the line of the picture that the first subroutine erased with its message.

Loading Your Picture

Only one thing remains, which is the routine for loading your picture from your disk or tape onto the screen:

```
1797 REM
1798 REM---------LOAD PICTURE----------
1799 REM
1800 INPUT"FILE NAME";F$
1810 OPEN 2,8,2,"0:"+F$+",S,R"
1820 FOR N=VA TO VA+999
1830 GET#2,A$
1840 POKE N+CC,ASC(A$+CHR$(0))
1850 GET#2,A$
1860 POKE N,ASC(A$+CHR$(0))
1870 NEXT N
1880 CLOSE 2:GOTO 40
1999 REM
2000 GET A$:IF A$="" THEN 2000
2010 RETURN
```

Use this exact same routine in any program where you want to load and display a picture that the Graphics Generator has created and stored on tape or disk. (Leave out lines 1999 through 2010 which are a separate "GET keyboard entry" routine, not part of the load routine.)

Line 1810 opens the file. You must have previously assigned a file name to variable F$. If you use a cassette recorder, retype line 1810 like this:

1810 OPEN 2,1,0,F$

Lines 1830 through 1860 methodically GET each single character that you previously saved, and POKE them alternately into color and video memory. The expression:

ASC(A$ + CHR$(0))

is needed to avoid an error message when A$ has a code value of 0.

If you use lines 1800 through 1880 as a subroutine in your own programs, you can of course change the line numbers to suit yourself, and end the routine with RETURN instead of GOTO 40.

So much for the Graphics Generator. If you play with it, remember that you must have a disk or tape ready to store your picture. For reference, Figure 5.1 is a summary of the keyboard commands used in the Graphics Generator.

Image-control commands

    A : Set ASCII code. Following the A, type the three-digit code (000–255).

    C : Set color code. Following the C, type the two-digit code (00–15).

    I : Insert the image where the cursor appears.

    E : Erase the image where the cursor appears.

Cursor-control commands

    U : Move cursor Up.

    D : Move cursor Down.

    L : Move cursor Left.

    R : Move cursor Right.

Other commands

    S : Save your picture on tape or disk.

    H : Help. If you forget any command codes, type H and the program will remind you.

Figure 5.1: Keyboard commands for the Graphics Generator program.

It's easier to draw your picture in pencil first, on a photocopy of the video memory map, and then transfer it onto the screen, rather than try to create a screen picture from scratch.

You may want to enhance Air Attack by drawing a landscape and adding a routine to load that picture onto the screen before the game begins. But before you do this, I strongly suggest you read the next two chapters about sprites. There's no point in creating good-looking scenery so long as your airplane is a mere X mark. The next chapters show how to make the airplane actually look like an airplane. For reference, the complete listing of the Graphics Generator appears in Appendix X.

Summary

This chapter has explained:

- How to fill the screen with graphics characters using DATA and POKE statements.
- How the Graphics Generator program works.
- How sequential files work.
- How to use the Graphics Generator program.

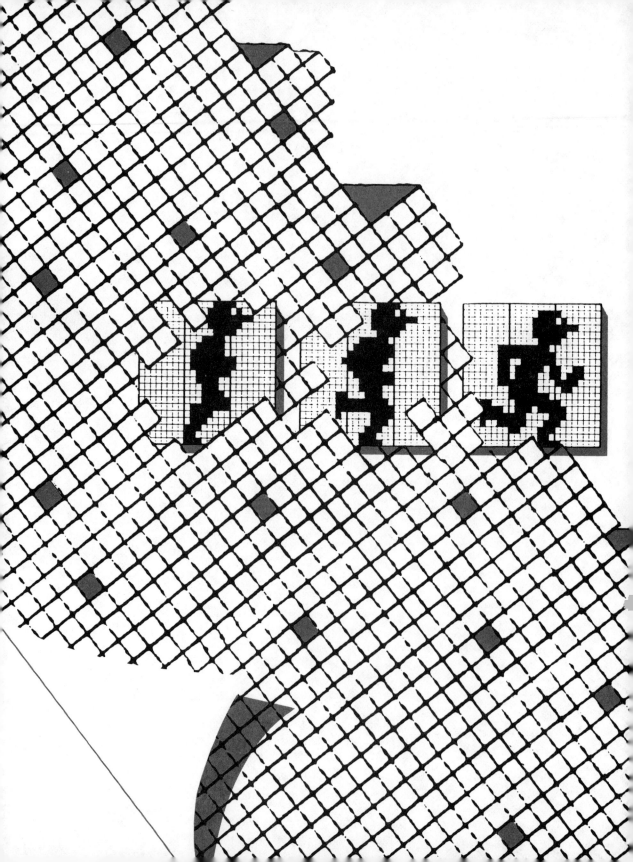

SIX
Specifying Sprites

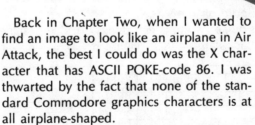

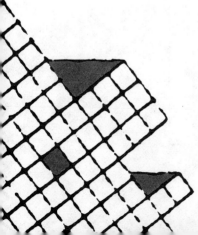

Back in Chapter Two, when I wanted to find an image to look like an airplane in Air Attack, the best I could do was the X character that has ASCII POKE-code 86. I was thwarted by the fact that none of the standard Commodore graphics characters is at all airplane-shaped.

Of course, I could have assembled a few of the graphics shapes like building blocks, so they formed a bigger image that looked like an airplane. But then I would have had to move all of these characters across the screen, to make the airplane appear to move. The program would have repositioned each character one at a time, so the image of the plane would have been taken apart and rebuilt, piece by piece, and the whole business would have taken much, much too long.

It would be nice, wouldn't it, if we could design our own airplane image? And it would be even nicer if the image could be larger than one pixel, but movable with a single command, instead of piece by piece.

Building Sprites from Dots

Well, this is exactly what a *sprite* is and does.

If you look at Appendix C, or if you have a good black and white video monitor, you'll be able to see that each Commodore character is made up of little dots. Each pixel, in fact, is 8 dots high and 8 dots wide.

A sprite, likewise, is composed of these dots. But we draw it ourselves—*we* decide where the dots go. And the image is 24 dots wide by 21 dots high. Since one pixel is 8 × 8 dots, you can see that a sprite is exactly three pixels wide and almost three pixels high.

And when we want to move this image around, we can shift it in very small increments—one dot at a time, instead of one pixel at a time. This results in a smooth, gliding effect.

In Figure 6.1 you'll see a grid, which we will be using for building sprites. It also appears in Appendix M for reference. You should make photocopies of this grid whenever you want to design sprites of your own. Fill in squares of the grid to form the picture you want. Then, using a system I'll describe in a moment, you can convert your drawing into a series of 63 numbers, which define your sprite. You then write these numbers into your program, which POKEs them into a reserved section of computer memory, which the computer refers to in order to display the sprite on the screen.

To save you some trouble and to speed things up, I've designed the sprites for our Air Attack game myself. Figure 6.2 shows an airplane

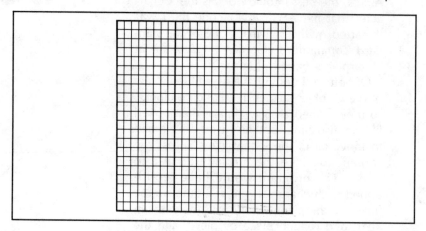

Figure 6.1: Sprite grid.

3	128	0
3	192	0
1	224	0
1	240	0
0	248	0
0	252	0
192	126	0
224	127	0
240	127	128
255	255	254
255	255	255
255	255	254
240	127	128
224	127	0
192	126	0
0	252	0
0	248	0
1	240	0
1	224	0
3	192	0
3	128	0

12	3	0
28	3	0
60	7	0
124	7	0
254	15	0
255	15	0
15	159	0
7	223	0
3	255	0
1	255	0
0	255	0
3	255	0
15	255	0
63	255	0
255	255	128
255	255	192
0	3	224
0	1	240
0	0	248
0	0	120
0	0	56

0	192	48
0	192	56
0	224	60
0	224	62
0	240	127
0	240	255
0	249	240
0	251	224
0	255	192
0	255	128
0	255	0
0	255	192
0	255	240
0	255	252
1	255	255
3	255	255
7	192	0
15	128	0
31	0	0
30	0	0
28	0	0

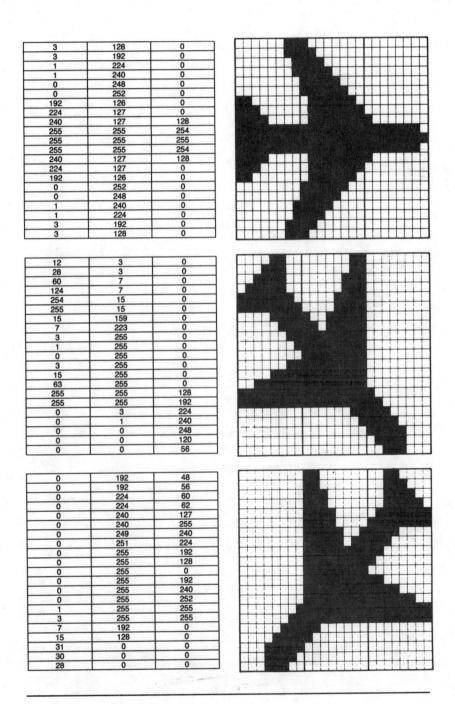

Figure 6.2: Airplane sprites.

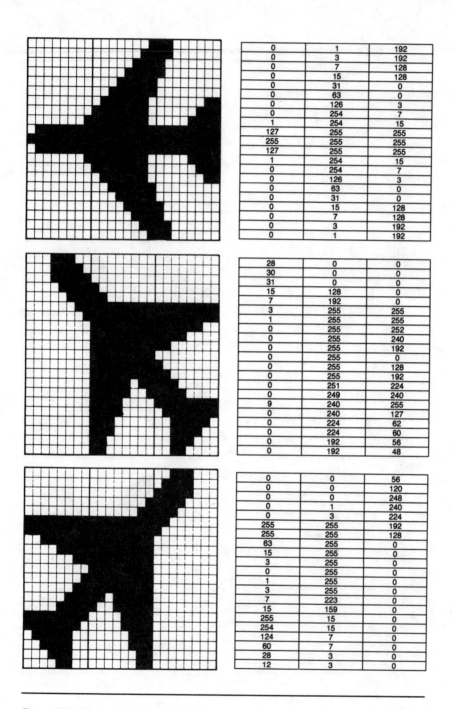

0	1	192
0	3	192
0	7	128
0	15	128
0	31	0
0	63	0
0	126	3
0	254	7
1	254	15
127	255	255
255	255	255
127	255	255
1	254	15
0	254	7
0	126	3
0	63	0
0	31	0
0	15	128
0	7	128
0	3	192
0	1	192

28	0	0
30	0	0
31	0	0
15	128	0
7	192	0
3	255	255
1	255	255
0	255	252
0	255	240
0	255	192
0	255	0
0	255	128
0	255	192
0	251	224
0	249	240
9	240	255
0	240	127
0	224	62
0	224	60
0	192	56
0	192	48

0	0	56
0	0	120
0	0	248
0	1	240
0	3	224
255	255	192
255	255	128
63	255	0
15	255	0
3	255	0
0	255	0
1	255	0
3	255	0
7	223	0
15	159	0
255	15	0
254	15	0
124	7	0
60	7	0
28	3	0
12	3	0

Figure 6.2: Airplane sprites (continued).

pointing in various different directions. Figure 6.3 is the image which I'll use as the gun at the bottom of the screen, and a blob which is the bullet. Figure 6.4 shows three more pictures which will be used as the explosion when the plane is blown up.

Beside each picture is a chart which shows how the sprite is coded as a series of 63 numbers. Note that two of the vertical lines in the sprite grid are thicker, splitting it into three columns, each eight squares wide. Consider the top horizontal row of squares. Start with the first eight squares, beginning at the top left corner. In the first picture of the airplane, six squares are blank, and then two are filled in. Now turn to Appendix N. This shows every possible way that eight

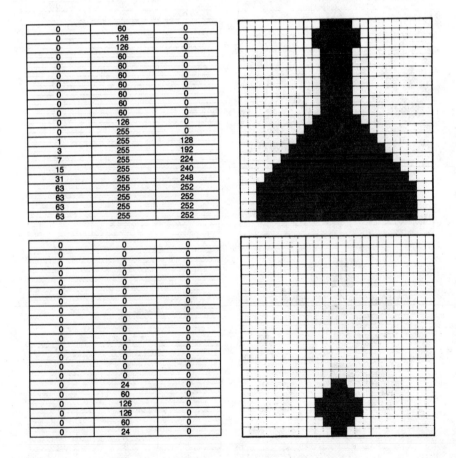

0	60	0
0	126	0
0	126	0
0	60	0
0	60	0
0	60	0
0	60	0
0	60	0
0	60	0
0	60	0
0	126	0
0	255	0
1	255	128
3	255	192
7	255	224
15	255	240
31	255	248
63	255	252
63	255	252
63	255	252
63	255	252

0	0	0
0	0	0
0	0	0
0	0	0
0	0	0
0	0	0
0	0	0
0	0	0
0	0	0
0	0	0
0	0	0
0	0	0
0	0	0
0	0	0
0	0	0
0	24	0
0	60	0
0	126	0
0	126	0
0	60	0
0	24	0

Figure 6.3: Gun and bullet sprites.

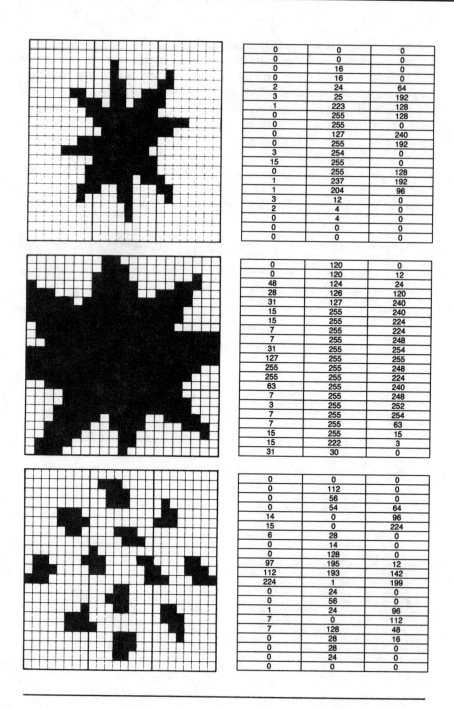

Figure 6.4: Explosion Sprites.

squares can be filled in—256 permutations altogether. You'll see that six blanks followed by two solid squares is the pattern numbered 3.

Now turn back to the picture of the airplane, and you'll see that the chart below it has a 3 entered in the space that corresponds with the first eight squares.

The rest of the numbers are derived in exactly the same way. You just have to be careful when you match each pattern of eight squares with a pattern in Appendix N.

Turning Sprites into Data

Having defined our sprites this way, the next step is to incorporate their numbers in our game program. This requires a lot of boring typing. Well, no one ever said programming would all be fun, fun, fun! The sprite code numbers must be entered as DATA statements, at the end of the program.

Tackle the task one sprite at a time. Start at the top-left corner of the first sprite chart. Type that number, then the top-middle number, then the top-right number. Then move down to the next row and repeat the process, like reading a book, from left to right, top to bottom. Use a comma to separate each number from the next in your DATA statements.

To make things as easy as possible for you, here are the sprite DATA statements as they should appear in the new, sprite version of Air Attack. Load the previous version of that program (the one we perfected in Chapter Four), list it to make sure you have the right one, then clear the screen, and type the following new lines:

```
2997 REM
2998 REM-------- Airplane Data --------
2999 REM
3000 DATA 3,128,0,3,192,0,1,224,0,1,240
3010 DATA 0,0,248,0,0,252,0,192,126,0
3020 DATA 224,127,0,240,127,128,255,255
3030 DATA 254,255,255,255,255,255,254
3040 DATA 240,127,128,224,127,0,192,126
3050 DATA 0,0,252,0,0,248,0,1,240,0,1
3060 DATA 224,0,3,192,0,3,128,0
3099 REM
3100 DATA 12,3,0,28,3,0,60,7,0,124,7,0
3110 DATA 254,15,0,255,15,0,15,159,0,7
3120 DATA 223,0,3,255,0,1,255,0,0,255,0
3130 DATA 3,255,0,15,255,0,63,255,0,255
3140 DATA 255,128,255,255,192,0,3,224,0
3150 DATA 1,240,0,0,248,0,0,120,0,0,56
3199 REM
3200 DATA 0,192,48,0,192,56,0,224,60
3210 DATA 0,224,62,0,240,127,0,240,255
3220 DATA 0,249,240,0,251,224,0,255,192
3230 DATA 0,255,128,0,255,0,0,255,192,0
```

```
3240 DATA 255,240,0,255,252,1,255,255,3
3250 DATA 255,255,7,192,0,15,128,0,31,0
3260 DATA 0,30,0,0,28,0,0
3299 REM
3300 DATA 0,1,192,0,3,192,0,7,128,0,15
3310 DATA 128,0,31,0,0,63,0,0,126,3,0
3320 DATA 254,7,1,254,15,127,255,255
3330 DATA 255,255,255,127,255,255,1,254
3340 DATA 15,0,254,7,0,126,3,0,63,0,0
3350 DATA 31,0,0,15,128,0,7,128,0,3,192
3360 DATA 0,1,192
3399 REM
3400 DATA 28,0,0,30,0,0,31,0,0,15,128,0
3410 DATA 7,192,0,3,255,255,1,255,255,0
3420 DATA 255,252,0,255,240,0,255,192,0
3430 DATA 255,0,0,255,128,0,255,192,0
3440 DATA 251,224,0,249,240,0,240,255,0
3450 DATA 240,127,0,224,62,0,224,60,0
3460 DATA 192,56,0,192,48
3499 REM
3500 DATA 0,0,56,0,0,120,0,0,248,0,1
3510 DATA 240,0,3,224,255,255,192,255
3520 DATA 255,128,63,255,0,15,255,0,3
3530 DATA 255,0,0,255,0,1,255,0,3,255,0
3540 DATA 7,223,0,15,159,0,255,15,0,254
3550 DATA 15,0,124,7,0,60,7,0,28,3,0,12
3560 DATA 3,0
3597 REM
3598 REM---------- Gun Data -----------
3599 REM
3600 DATA 0,60,0,0,126,0,0,126,0,0,60,0
3610 DATA 0,60,0,0,60,0,0,60,0,0,60,0
3620 DATA 0,60,0,0,60,0,0,126,0,0,255,0
3630 DATA 1,255,128,3,255,192,7,255,224
3640 DATA 15,255,240,31,255,248,63,255
3650 DATA 252,63,255,252,63,255,252,63
3660 DATA 255,252
3697 REM
3698 REM--------- Bullet Data ---------
3699 REM
3700 DATA 0,0,0,0,0,0,0,0,0,0,0,0,0,0,0,0
3710 DATA 0,0,0,0,0,0,0,0,0,0,0,0,0,0,0,0
3720 DATA 0,0,0,0,0,0,0,0,0,0,0,0,0,0,0,0
3730 DATA 0,24,0,0,60,0,0,126,0,0,126,0
3740 DATA 0,60,0,0,24,0
3797 REM
3798 REM------- Explosion Data --------
3799 REM
3800 DATA 0,0,0,0,0,0,0,16,0,0,16,0,2
3810 DATA 24,64,3,25,192,1,223,128,0
3820 DATA 255,128,0,255,0,0,127,240,0
3830 DATA 255,192,3,254,0,15,255,0,0
3840 DATA 255,128,1,237,192,1,204,96,3
3850 DATA 12,0,2,4,0,0,4,0,0,0,0,0,0,0
3899 REM
3900 DATA 0,120,0,0,120,12,48,124,24,28
3910 DATA 126,120,31,127,240,15,255,240
3920 DATA 15,255,224,7,255,224,7,255
3930 DATA 248,31,255,254,127,255,255
3940 DATA 255,255,248,255,255,224,63
3950 DATA 255,240,7,255,248,3,255,252,7
```

```
3960 DATA 255,254,7,255,63,15,255,15,15
3970 DATA 222,3,31,30,0
3999 REM
4000 DATA 0,0,0,0,112,0,0,56,0,0,56,64
4010 DATA 14,0,96,15,0,224,6,28,0,0,14
4020 DATA 0,0,128,0,97,195,12,112,193
4030 DATA 142,224,1,199,0,24,0,0,56,0,1
4040 DATA 24,96,7,0,112,7,128,48,0,28
4050 DATA 16,0,28,0,0,24,0,0,0,0
```

Compare any one of these blocks of data with the sprite pictures and charts on the preceding pages, and you'll see how I transcribed the sprite data into the program.

How the Computer Finds its Sprites

Is this all you need to do? By no means! After you've added all these extra DATA lines to your program, you must add instructions to READ the DATA and POKE it into memory. Once the data has been POKEd into memory, the computer can refer to it as a blueprint for building and displaying each sprite. It does this so fast, the sprites seem to appear on the screen instantly, like PRINTed text.

Here are the new lines to READ and POKE the data. Clear the screen and type:

```
2597 REM
2598 REM------ Read & Poke Data -------
2599 REM
2600 FOR A=15680 TO 16320 STEP 64
2610 FOR B=A TO A+62
2620 READ C:POKE B,C
2630 NEXT B
2640 NEXT A
```

Sprite Pointers

But how does the computer know where to find the sprite data after your program has POKEd it into memory? This is where things start to get a little complicated. The computer refers to something called a *pointer*, which tells it where the data for each sprite is to be found.

It works like this. The computer can display up to eight sprites at a time. They are numbered 0 through 7. The pointer to the data for sprite 0 is stored in memory address 2040. The pointer to the data for sprite 1 is stored in 2041, and so on. Figure 6.5 is a complete list (which you will also find, for reference, in Appendix K).

To find the data for sprite 0, the computer PEEKs 2040, takes the number it finds there, and multiplies it by 64. Assuming that the data resides in the first quarter of memory (which is what we're using right now), 64 × PEEK(2040) gives the address of the beginning of the data that define sprite 0. The sequence of events is shown in Figure 6.6.

ADDRESS	POINTER TO
2040	Data for sprite 0
2041	Data for sprite 1
2042	Data for sprite 2
2043	Data for sprite 3
2044	Data for sprite 4
2045	Data for sprite 5
2046	Data for sprite 6
2047	Data for sprite 7

Figure 6.5: Addresses of sprite data pointers.

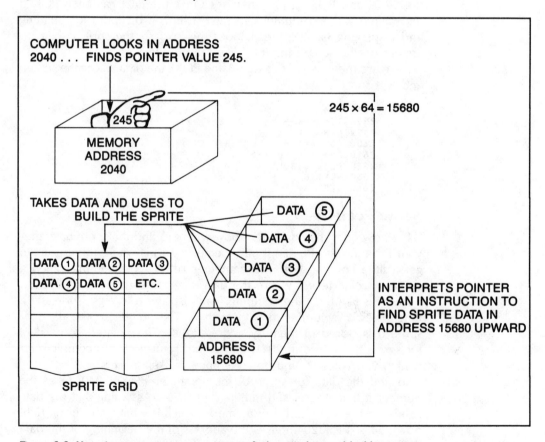

Figure 6.6: How the computer uses a pointer to find sprite data and build a sprite.

This sounds like a roundabout way of doing things. It's complicated to program, because first we have to decide where to store our sprite data in memory (beginning at an address which must be evenly divisible by 64). Then we divide this address by 64, and POKE the result into 2040, to tell the computer what we've done.

But this system has a great advantage. To tell the computer to use a new set of data to build sprite 0, all we have to do is POKE a new number into 2040. In other words, we change the pointer so that it points elsewhere. Instantly, the computer decodes the new pointer, finds the new set of data, and displays that as sprite 0. On the screen, sprite 0 changes shape in a flash.

This will be useful when our airplane changes direction. When it's flying toward the right, we want its image to face rightward. When it starts flying in a different direction, we want to substitute the leftward-pointing image accordingly. Otherwise, the airplane will seem to move backward or sideways.

All we have to do is adjust the pointer for sprite 0 so that it points to the set of airplane data that corresponds to the direction the plane is moving. In a moment, I'll explain how we keep track of where each block of sprite data is stored, and how we give the computer this information.

Choosing a Stretch of Memory

There's one thing I haven't dealt with, and that is, how do we decide which part of memory to use to store sprite data? Until now, I've said it was unwise to POKE data into any address outside of video memory. Are there other parts of memory which are safe to POKE?

Look at the complete memory map in Appendix H. It isn't divided into squares representing single addresses, like the video memory map, because the complete Commodore computer memory contains 65536 addresses, and there isn't room to show them all. So the map shows the whole stretch, or "street," of memory divided into four main sections, called *banks*, and each bank is marked off at intervals of 1024, just as city streets are divided into blocks.

There are 1024 bytes in a kilobyte, so we can say the memory map is marked off at intervals of 1K.

Your actual program listing resides in the BASIC workspace, from 2048 upward, just above video memory. Ignore the "Character Set (ROM Image)" for now—it doesn't concern us. The Air Attack program will never be longer than 3K even in its final version, so there's a lot of room in the top part of bank 0 for our sprite data. POKEing the data there won't interfere with anything, and nothing will interfere with it.

So our sprite data will reside in the stretch of memory from 15680 to 16383.

Data for the first airplane image, flying horizontally to the right ("due East"), will begin at 15680. Since 15680 divided by 64 equals 245, this is the number we POKE into 2040, the pointer for sprite 0, when the airplane flies toward the right.

This is exactly what the new version of the program does. Edit lines 2800 and 2810 so that they now look like this:

```
2800 POKE SP,245
2810 POKE SP+1,251:POKE SP+2,252
```

SP is a constant which the new version of the program will define as having the value of 2040. SP stands for Sprite Pointer. You can see that the pointer for sprite 0 is given its initial value on line 2800, while pointers for sprites 1 and 2 are given their values on line 2810.

In the program, sprite 0 is the airplane, sprite 1 is the gun, and sprite 2 is the bullet. When the bullet hits the airplane, do we need another sprite to show the explosion? No, because the explosion takes the place of the airplane. All we have to do is point sprite 0 at the explosion data instead of the airplane data.

Figure 6.7 will help you keep track of the addresses of the blocks of sprite data, and the pointer values that guide the computer to those addresses.

Is this all there is to know about sprites? We've hardly begun!

Sprite Registers

Next you need to know how the computer turns sprites on and off, colors them, moves them around, and detects collisions between them.

These things are controlled by *registers*. A register is a fancy name for a memory address that the computer refers to, and updates, to keep track of what's happening someplace else. Sprite registers begin at address 53248, which is the start of memory in a "video chip" that controls all events on the video screen. To avoid typing a lot of big numbers that all look much the same, it's convenient to use VC to stand for Video Chip. We state that VC = 53248, and then give the addresses of the subsequent registers as VC + 1, VC + 2, and so on.

Sprite Position

In Figure 6.8 you'll find a list of the registers that control the positions of sprites on the video screen. You'll see that two registers are required for each sprite: an "X distance register" and a "Y distance register." This is because the position of a sprite is defined by counting its horizontal distance in dots (the "X distance") from the left edge of the screen, and its vertical distance in dots (the "Y distance") down from the top edge of the screen. Remember, each dot is one-eighth the width or height of a pixel.

You move a sprite by POKEing its X distance and Y distance into the registers. If you want to move it horizontally, without altering its vertical position, you need to change only the number in the X register. The opposite applies if you want to move it vertically. To move it diagonally, you have to POKE both registers.

	IMAGE	FIRST BYTE OF DATA STORED AT:	DIVIDE BY 64 TO GET POINTER VALUE:	TO BE POKED INTO POINTER ADDRESS:
EXPLOSION		16320	255	2040
		16256	254	2040
		16192	253	2040
BULLET		16128	252	2042
GUN		16064	251	2041
AIRPLANE		16000	250	2040
		15936	249	2040
		15872	248	2040
		15808	247	2040
		15744	246	2040
		15680	245	2040

Figure 6.7: The sprite images in Air Attack, and where their addresses are stored in memory.

ADDRESS	FUNCTION
VC + 0	X distance of sprite 0
VC + 1	Y distance of sprite 0
VC + 2	X distance of sprite 1
VC + 3	Y distance of sprite 1
VC + 4	X distance of sprite 2
VC + 5	Y distance of sprite 2
VC + 6	X distance of sprite 3
VC + 7	Y distance of sprite 3
VC + 8	X distance of sprite 4
VC + 9	Y distance of sprite 4
VC + 10	X distance of sprite 5
VC + 11	Y distance of sprite 5
VC + 12	X distance of sprite 6
VC + 13	Y distance of sprite 6
VC + 14	X distance of sprite 7
VC + 15	Y distance of sprite 7

53248 (the starting address of the Video Chip) is represented by the constant VC. Thus VC + 1 is 53249, VC + 2 is 53250, and so on.

Figure 6.8: Sprite position registers.

The X distance and Y distance of the sprite are measured to the top-left dot of the sprite image area. Does this mean that when a sprite is at the top-left corner of the screen, its X distance and its Y distance are both zero? No, because Commodore designed the system so that sprites can travel off the screen. Therefore, the numbering of positions begins in an imaginary area "outside" the video area. The sprite video memory map in Figure 6.9 will make things clearer.

If you're particularly observant, you may have noticed that since the video screen is 40 pixels wide, and each pixel is 8 dots wide, the total screen width contains 320 dots. Thus the X distance of a sprite can be 320—or more, since the distance is measured out from beyond the left edge of the screen.

But you can't POKE the X distance register with 320, because you can't POKE any memory address with a number larger than 255. So how do sprites ever move past the point where the X distance reaches 255?

In the sprite version of Air Attack, there's a simple answer: the airplane and gun *don't* ever move past the 255 line! Oh, it can be done, and I will explain how, but it's complicated, and first I have to explain how sprites are turned on and off.

Sprite On/Off

I've said that each sprite is numbered, from 0 through 7. Each sprite also has what I will call a *bit value*, as follows:

Sprite 0: Bit value 1

Sprite 1: Bit value 2

Sprite 2: Bit value 4

Sprite 3: Bit value 8

Sprite 4: Bit value 16

Sprite 5: Bit value 32

Sprite 6: Bit value 64

Sprite 7: Bit value 128

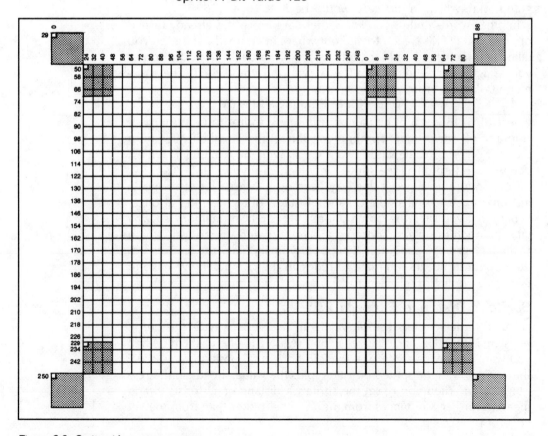

Figure 6.9: Sprite video memory map.

Note that the bit value of each sprite is twice the bit value of the preceding sprite. Mathematical readers will see that the bit value is 2 raised to the power of the sprite number. Non-mathematical readers needn't trouble themselves with this irrelevant fact.

One register turns all the sprites on and off. It is at VC+21. To turn on one sprite, you POKE VC+21 with the bit value of that sprite. To turn on more than one sprite, you POKE VC+21 with their bit values added together. To turn on sprite 4 and sprite 7, for instance, you would POKE VC+21 with 16 + 128, or 144.

But this only works if you start from a situation where all sprites are turned off, i.e., if VC+21 originally contains 0. Suppose one sprite has been previously activated—sprite 3, for instance. VC+21 will already contain its bit value, namely 8. Now, if you want to turn on sprites 4 and 7 as well as sprite 3 you have to add their bit values to the value that is already in the register, and then POKE the register with the grand total, which in this case would be 8 + 16 + 128.

In other words, unless you *know* there are no sprites already turned on, first you PEEK(VC+21) to find out what's in it already, and then you take that number, add it to the total of the bit values of the extra sprites you're activating, and POKE VC+21 with the grand total. The statement looks like this:

POKE VC+21,PEEK(VC+21)+BV

where BV is the total of bit values of the new sprites to be turned on.

To turn off one or more sprites, you subtract their total bit value from the PEEK(VC+21) value, and POKE VC+21 with the remainder—unless you want to turn off *all* the sprites, in which case you POKE VC+21,0.

Commodore arranged it this way because it saves a lot of memory: just one register controls the on and off status of eight sprites at once. What's that you say? The Commodore 64 has 64K of memory, so why take so much trouble to conserve a byte here and there? Well, if you really feel strongly about this, I suppose you should write to Commodore about it. But it's a bit late to redesign the computer. We have to take it as we find it.

Sprite X Distance Exceeds 255

Other sprite registers use bit values in the same way as the on/off register. The "X Distance Exceeds 255" register is one of them. When you want to move a sprite past the 255 horizontal position, you POKE this register with the sprite's bit value (plus the value already in the register, if any). Then you re-set the sprite's X distance register to 0, and measure further X distances from the 255 line, rather than from the left edge of the screen.

Sprite Collisions

The sprite-to-sprite collision register is another one that uses bit values. The register is at VC + 32. Normally it contains a 0, but if two or more sprites touch each other, their combined bit values will be found when you PEEK(VC+32), as Figure 6.10 illustrates. PEEKing this register resets it to 0, provided the sprites are no longer touching.

For the purposes of Air Attack, the only collision that can occur is between the bullet and the airplane, so all we need to know is whether PEEK(VC+32) is greater than 0. If it is, the player has scored a hit.

Sprite Color

Color, I'm glad to say, is a simple matter. There is one color register for each sprite, and you POKE it with the number of the color that you want that sprite to be. The register for sprite 0 is at VC+39, for sprite 1 is at VC+40, and so on. They're all listed in Appendix K. As before, we'll color the airplane red, the gun green, and the bullet black.

Of course, I'm assuming we're using single-color sprites. There are such things as multicolor sprites, and multicolor control registers. . . . But I'm not even going to think about that, at least until Chapter Ten. And I advise you to do likewise.

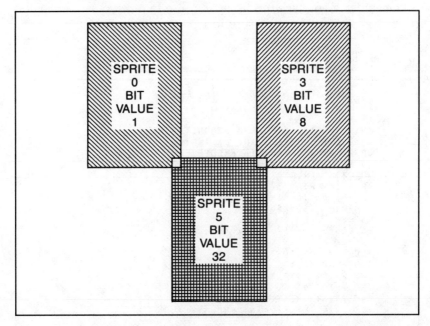

Figure 6.10: When three sprites collide, the sum of their bit values appears in the sprite-to-sprite collision register, so that in this case PEEK(VC+32) = 41.

Sprite Demonstration Program

The easiest way to understand sprite control registers is to see sprites on the video screen actually responding to the program statements that control them. How is this possible? With the Sprite Demonstration Program in Figure 6.11. If you're willing to take the time to type and run this program, first save the new version of Air Attack that we've been working on. Save it in a new file, called GAME VERSION 4 or something similar. You can retrieve it later, and we'll finish it in the next chapter.

If you're reluctant to type the following listing, you have two choices. You can buy it from me, pre-recorded on a tape or disk—see the ordering instructions in Appendix Y. Or you can simply read through the program listing to see how it works.

VC is the starting address of the video chip, where the sprite control registers are. On lines 200 through 530 you'll see a series of program statements, POKEing various registers in the video chip. After each statement is a description of what that statement does. If you run the program, you will see the statements displayed on the screen, one at a time. Simultaneously, the computer obeys each statement and manipulates a sprite before your very eyes.

Remember, if you type this listing, be sure to save your new version of Air Attack first. Then, be sure to type:

NEW

and press RETURN.

```
10 GOSUB 5000
18 REM------------- Intro -------------
19 REM
20 PRINT"THIS PROGRAM DEMONSTRATES"
30 PRINT"SPRITES, AND LISTS THE"
40 PRINT"PROGRAM STATEMENTS"
50 PRINT"AS THEY ARE BEING EXECUTED."
60 PRINT:PRINT
70 PRINT"READY?"
80 GET A$:IF A$="" THEN 80
90 PRINT C$D$D$D$D$D$
95 REM
96 REM------- Read/Execute Data -------
97 REM
100 FOR N=1 TO 17
110 READ X$,Y$
120 PRINT B$X$
130 PRINT Y$
140 PRINT:PRINT G$" CONT"
145 PRINT B$L$:PRINT"PRESS RETURN ";
```

Figure 6.11: Sprite Demonstration Program.

```
150 PRINT"KEY TO CONTINUE."
160 PRINT L$G$U$U$U$U$U$U$U$U$U$
166 REM
167 REM:NEXT LINE LOADS KEYBD BUFFER
168 REM:WITH A CARRIAGE RETURN
169 REM
170 POKE 198,1:POKE 631,13
180 STOP
190 PRINT D$D$D$D$:NEXT N
195 PRINT B$"END OF DEMO.":END
197 REM
198 REM--------- Data/Instrs ----------
199 REM
200 DATA "POKE VC+21,1"
210 DATA"<THIS TURNS ON SPRITE 0>"
220 DATA"POKE VC,24:POKE VC+1,50"
230 DATA"<MOVES IT TO X=24, Y=50>"
240 DATA"POKE VC+39,5"
250 DATA"<CHANGES COLOR TO GREEN>"
260 DATA"POKE 2040,255"
270 DATA"<SETS POINTER TO SPRITE DATA>"
280 DATA"POKE VC+29,1"
290 DATA"<EXPANDS IT HORIZONTALLY>"
300 DATA"POKE VC+23,1"
310 DATA"<EXPANDS IT VERTICALLY>"
320 DATA"FOR C=24 TO 255:POKEVC,C:NEXT"
330 DATA"<MOVES IT ACROSS THE SCREEN>"
340 DATA"POKE VC+16,1:POKE VC,40
350 DATA"<MOVES IT PAST X=255 LINE>"
360 DATA"FOR C=50TO208:POKEVC+1,C:NEXT"
370 DATA"<MOVES IT VERTICALLY>"
380 DATA"POKE VC+16,0:POKE VC,150"
390 DATA"<BACK TO LEFT OF X=255 LINE>"
400 DATA"POKE VC+27,1"
410 DATA"<PUTS IT BEHIND VIDEO TEXT>"
420 DATA"POKE VC+37,2"
430 DATA"<SELECTS RED, MULTICOLOR #1>"
440 DATA"POKE VC+38,6"
450 DATA"<SELECTS BLUE, MULTICOLOR #2>"
460 DATA"POKE VC+28,1"
470 DATA"<SWITCHES ON MULTICOLOR>"
480 DATA"POKE VC+29,0"
490 DATA"<SHRINKS IT HORIZONTALLY>"
500 DATA"POKE VC+23,0"
510 DATA"<SHRINKS IT VERTICALLY>"
520 DATA"POKE VC+21,0"
530 DATA"<TURNS IT OFF>"
4997 REM
4998 REM------ Set Up Sprite Etc ------
4999 REM
5000 VA=1024
5010 VC=53248
5040 L$="============================="
5050 C$=CHR$(147)
5060 B$=CHR$(144)
```

Figure 6.11: Sprite Demonstration Program (continued).

```
5070 G$=CHR$(155)
5080 U$=CHR$(145)
5090 D$=CHR$(17)
5100 POKE 53280,12:POKE 53281,15
5110 PRINT B$C$;
5150 FOR N=16320 TO 16331
5160 POKE N,255:POKE N+51,255
5170 NEXT N
5180 FOR N=16332 TO 16368 STEP 3
5190 POKE N,245:POKE N+1,66:POKEN+2,175
5195 NEXT N
5200 RETURN
```

Figure 6.11: Sprite Demonstration Program (continued).

In the next chapter, we'll finish the sprite version of Air Attack. First, here's a summary of what this chapter has covered.

Summary

Chapter Six has attempted to explain:

- How a sprite is composed of 24 × 21 dots.
- How to draw a sprite and convert its dot patterns into numbers.
- How to incorporate these numbers into a program, as DATA statements.
- How to get your program to read these DATA statements and POKE the numbers into a stretch of memory.
- How to choose that stretch of memory.
- How to tell the computer where the sprite data is, using pointers.
- How to switch a pointer from one set of data to another, to switch the appearance of a sprite.
- How the video chip turns sprites on and off, colors them, moves them, and detects collisions.
- How to use bit values in the registers that require them.

SEVEN
Making Sprites Move

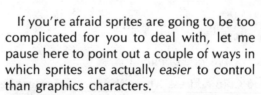

If you're afraid sprites are going to be too complicated for you to deal with, let me pause here to point out a couple of ways in which sprites are actually *easier* to control than graphics characters.

Sprites are easier to move. Before you can POKE a graphics character into its new address, you have to erase it from its old address by POKEing a blank space into that location. But to move a sprite, we simply POKE its X and Y distance registers with its new distances from the left edge and the top edge of the screen, respectively. The sprite instantly appears in its new location, and automatically disappears from its old location. Also, it takes its color with it, so we don't need to keep POKEing color memory.

Sprites make it easier to specify limits to the screen. We no longer need to POKE special blanks (ASCII 96) down the left and right edges, and then PEEK to see if the airplane is trying to enter this forbidden zone. Instead, we simply stop the X distance of the sprite from becoming too large or small. We limit the Y distance the same way.

Now, here are the modifications we need to make in the "Establish Constants" and the "Establish Variables" sections of the Air Attack program. Load the most recent version, the fourth one, which we were working on in the last chapter, and list lines 1000 through 1070. Edit the lines marked with an E below, but don't alter any of the lines marked with a hyphen (-). Then clear the screen and type the new lines that are marked here with asterisks (*).

```
E 1000 VA=1024:CA=55296:CC=CA-VA:VC=53248
E 1005 SX=16:TH=30:SP=2040
- 1006 T=10:FT=15:BS=32
E 1010 VU=58:VD=150:VL=24:VR=255
* 1015 A(0)=246:A(1)=247:A(2)=249
* 1016 A(3)=250:A(4)=248:A(5)=245
* 1017 A(6)=245:A(7)=248
E 1020 D(0)=3:D(1)=-3:D(2)=-1:D(3)=1
E 1021 D(4)=-2:D(5)=2:D(6)=2:D(7)=-2
- 1040 POKE 650,128
E 1050 A=0:B=0:C=0:D=0:E=0
E 1060 H=0:L=0:N=0:X=0:SC=0
- 1070 AA=0:AB=0:AG=0
* 1080 XA=0:YA=0:XG=0:XB=0:YB=0
```

In addition, you need to type new lines 2140 and 2150, and edit old line 2160:

```
* 2140 PRINT:PRINT
* 2150 PRINT"LOADING SPRITE DATA..."
E 2160 GOSUB 2600
```

Several new constants have been defined:

VC is the Video Chip address where the sprite registers begin.

SP is where the Sprite Pointers begin.

Constants that we once needed, defining the ASCII codes of airplane, gun, etc, are gone, because we're using sprites to represent them now.

VU is the Video Up limit.

VD is the Video Down limit. VU and VD are now sprite distances measured in dots (see Appendix L).

VL is the Video Left Limit.

VR is the Video Right Limit.

On new lines 1015 through 1017, you'll find a new set of subscripted variables, using letter A (for Airplane). In the old game, the airplane was the same X symbol no matter which direction it moved, but now we have to keep changing its image so that it points in the same direction that it flies. For instance, when it moves in direction D(6), which is "due East" just as it was in the previous version of the program, we want the computer to build the airplane from the sprite data which show the airplane pointing to the right. From the chart in the previous chapter, you can see this means we need to POKE the sprite pointer with 245. The simplest way of doing this is to set things up so that A(6) = 245. Then when the direction is D(6), the program POKEs the sprite Pointer with A(6). The rest of the A( ) values are set up the same way, so when the airplane flies in direction D(N), the sprite pointer is simply POKEd with A(N). Thus the airplane image always automatically matches the direction in which it's flying.

New values for D(0) through D(7) are established on lines 1020 and 1021. I'll explain how they work in a moment.

On line 1080, several new variables are introduced:

> XA is the X position of the Airplane.
>
> YA is the Y position of the Airplane.
>
> XG is the X position of the Gun. (Its Y position is always the same—at the bottom of the screen—so once it has been established, we don't need a variable to keep track of it.)
>
> XB is the X position of the Bullet.
>
> YB is the Y position of the Bullet.

Moving the Airplane

Here are the program lines that control the movements of the airplane, now that it's represented by a sprite instead of by a single character:

```
E 100 L=L+1
(Delete Old Line 110)
E 120 IF  YA+IY<VU THEN  L=0:N=3-N
E 130 IF  YA+IY>VD THEN  L=0:N=3-N
E 140 IF  XA+IX<VL  ORXA+IX>VRTHENL=0:N=N+4
- 150 IF  N>7 THEN  N=N-8
- 160 IF  L>T THEN  L=0:N=INT(RND(1)*8)
E 170 IX=SGN(D(N)):IY=ABS(D(N))-2
* 175 XA=XA+IX: YA=YA+IY
E 180 POKE SP,A(N)
```

Old line 110 should be deleted. To do this, clear the screen, type

110

and press RETURN.

Variable K has been eliminated. We used it previously to count from

0 to 3 over and over again, so that the airplane moved one step for each three steps that a bullet moved. Now, we simply change the airplane's position by smaller steps than the bullet, in every cycle of the program, and we don't need K.

Figure 7.1 shows increments that must be added to distances XA and YA, defining the horizontal and vertical position of the airplane, to move it in its six possible directions. IX is the Increment of the X distance, and IY is the Increment of the Y distance. For instance, when the airplane is flying horizontally to the right, its X increment is +1, and its Y increment is 0. In other words, IX = 1 and IY = 0.

Lines 120 and 130 test whether adding increment IY will take the vertical position of the Airplane, YA, above the Video Up limit or below the Video Down limit. If so, N = 3 − N, just as in the previous listing of the program.

Line 140 tests whether adding increment IX will move the airplane

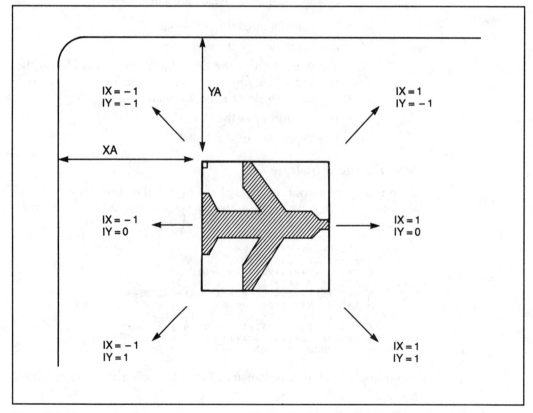

Figure 7.1: The position of the airplane is given by XA and YA. To move it in the directions shown, increments IX and IY must have these values.

beyond the Video Left limit or the Video Right limit. If so, N = N + 4, as in the previous version of the program. Note that I had to leave out some spaces in line 140 to keep it less than 39 characters long.

Line 170 calculates new values for IX and IY, in case the airplane has had to change direction. D(N) is still used as the subscripted variable that tells the program the airplane's direction, but the new values of D(0) through D(7) that are specified on lines 1020 and 1021 enable increments IX and IY to be derived from them, on line 170.

For instance, if the airplane is flying up and to the right, that's direction number 3, just as it was in the previous version of the program. But D(3) now has a value of 1, so that IX and IY will work out correctly. Line 170 says that IX = SGN(D(N)), and IY = ABS(D(N)) − 2. If you insert the various values of D(N) into these formulas, for N = 0 through N = 7, you'll find that IX and IY work out right every time.

Line 175 adds the increments to the airplane X and Y distances, and line 190 POKEs the X and Y registers with the new values.

Moving the Gun

Moving the gun is a much simpler affair. First, delete old line 260 in the same way that you deleted old line 110. Then list old lines 220 through 250 and edit them as follows:

```
E 220 IF A$="1" AND XG-3=>VL THEN IG=-3
E 230 IF A$="2" AND XG+3<=VR THEN IG=3
E 240 XG=XG+IG
E 250 POKE VC+2,XG
```

IG is the increment added to the horizontal position of the gun, XG. IG is 0, 3, or − 3, according to whether the player wants to leave the gun where it is or move it right or left. VC+2 is the address of the X distance register for sprite 1.

Moving the Bullet

The logic of this routine is the same as before, but changes are necessary to control sprites instead of characters. List lines 300 through 390 and edit them as follows:

```
- 300 IF A$=CHR$(BS) THEN 370
E 310 IF YB=0 THEN 50
E 320 YB=YB-2
E 330 IF YB<VU THEN YB=0
E 340 POKE VC+5,YB
E 350 IF PEEK(VC+TH)>0 THEN 800
- 360 GOTO 50
- 365 REM---------- Fire Gun
E 370 XB=XG
E 380 YB=208
E 390 POKE VC+4,XB:POKE VC+5,YB:GOTO 50
```

When the gun is fired (lines 370 through 390), the X (horizontal) distance of the Bullet, XB, is set equal to the X distance of the Gun, XG. After this, the X position of the bullet won't change, because it moves vertically up the screen, and doesn't move horizontally at all.

Line 380 starts the bullet's (vertical) Y position, YB, at 208, which is just above the gun. Line 390 POKEs the X and Y distance registers with these initial values for sprite 2, the bullet.

Once the bullet has been fired, the routine on lines 320 through 360 takes care of moving it in each subsequent cycle of the program. YB, the Y position of the Bullet, is decremented by 2 on line 320. In the last version of Air Attack, the bullet moved three times as fast as the airplane, but the airplane image is bigger now, making it easier to hit. So I've reduced the speed of the bullet, from three times to twice the speed of the airplane. Otherwise, the game would be too easy.

Line 330 checks to see whether the bullet has gone above the Video Up limit. If so, YB = 0. Either way, the value of YB is POKEd into the Y position register for the bullet, on line 340. If YB = 0, this places the bullet off the top of the screen, out of sight, waiting to be called back onto the screen the next time the player fires the gun.

Lastly, line 350 PEEKs the sprite collision register to see if the bullet has hit the airplane. Note that a hit is registered only if the actual colored image of the bullet overlaps, by one dot or more, the image of the airplane. The bullet image is a small blob that occupies only part of the total 24 × 21 dot area of sprite 2. The rest of that area is not filled in—is "empty." If that empty area overlaps the area of the airplane sprite, the collision register does not respond. It only indicates a hit when the actual colored images touch, as Figure 7.2 shows.

Scoring a Hit

A new routine is needed when the bullet hits the target, so that we can make use of the three-step explosion that is part of the sprite data. List lines 800 through 890, edit those with E beside them, then clear the screen and type the new line 870.

```
E 800 POKE VC+TH,0:POKE VC+21,3
E 810 A=7:B=253:GOSUB 860
E 820 A=8:B=254:GOSUB 860
E 830 A=9:B=255:GOSUB 860
E 840 POKE VC+21,2:SC=SC+1
E 845 GOSUB 880
- 850 GOSUB 2800:GOTO 50
- 855 REM---------- Delay Loop
E 860 POKE VC+39,A
* 870 POKE SP,B
- 880 FOR C=1 TO 100:NEXT C
- 890 RETURN
```

Line 800 resets the collision register to 0, then POKEs the sprite on/off register with a 3, thus turning off sprite 2 (the bullet) but leaving sprites 0 and 1 (the airplane and gun) turned on. Remember, sprite 0 has a bit value of 1, sprite 1 has a bit value of 2, and sprite 3 has a bit value of 4, and we POKE the on/off register with the total of bit values of sprites that are to be turned on.

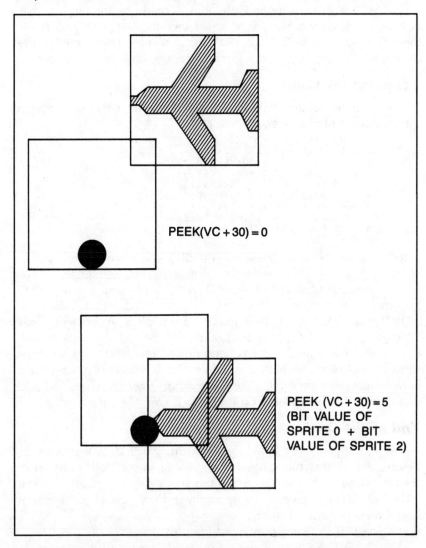

PEEK(VC + 30) = 0

PEEK (VC + 30) = 5
(BIT VALUE OF
SPRITE 0 + BIT
VALUE OF SPRITE 2)

Figure 7.2: The sprite-to-sprite collision register at VC + 30 shows a collision only when colored areas of the sprites touch—not when "transparent" sprite areas overlap.

Lines 810 through 830 set a series of colors—yellow, orange, and bright red—and a series of pointer values, for the three stages of the explosion, which will take the place of the airplane image. Subroutine 860 through 890 POKEs the colors into the color register for sprite 0, POKEs the pointer for sprite 0, and then runs the delay loop so that the explosion develops slowly enough.

Line 840 leaves only sprite 1, the gun, turned on—the airplane has now been vaporized. SC, the score, is incremented. Line 850 resets the video picture with GOSUB 2800: the airplane is resurrected in the middle of the screen, and the game continues until time runs out.

Resetting the Game

The subroutine at line 2800 is very different now, because it sets up sprites instead of character graphics.

```
E 2800 POKE SP,245
E 2810 POKE SP+1,251:POKE SP+2,252
E 2820 XA=160: YA=100:XG=160: YB=0
E 2830 POKE VC,XA:POKE VC+1,YA
* 2840 POKE VC+2,XG:POKE VC+3,229
* 2850 POKE VC+5,YB:POKE VC+16,0
* 2860 POKE VC+39,2:POKE VC+40,5
* 2870 POKE VC+41,0:POKE VC+30,0
* 2880 POKE VC+21,7
- 2890 RETURN
```

You've already edited lines 2800 and 2810 in the previous chapter; I list them again simply to show the complete set-up sequence.

After lines 2800 and 2810 have POKEd the sprite pointers, line 2820 sets the starting positions for airplane, gun, and bullet, and lines 2830 through 2850 POKE these into the sprite position registers. Lines 2860 and 2970 set the sprite colors, and reset the collision register to 0. Lastly—after everything else has been done—line 2880 turns all three sprites on. Always establish the colors and positions of your sprites before you turn them on. It's like giving actors their costumes and putting them in the right places on the stage before the curtain goes up.

End of the Game

The end-of-game routine, beginning on line 900, is the same as before, except that the sprites must now be turned off. Otherwise, they'd still be on the screen while the score is being displayed. The PRINT CHR$(147) screen-clearing command only clears video memory. It does not erase sprites.

Edit line 910 so that it now looks like this:

```
910 PRINT C$:POKE VC+21,0
```

And that's the last of the changes that need to be made. Save your new listing as GAME VERSION 4, and then run it. There's a moment's pause while the program reads its DATA statements and POKEs the numbers into memory. And then you see, on the screen, an airplane that really looks like an airplane, cruising to and fro.

Adjusting the Speed

There's only one little snag, and that is . . . the program now moves at an absolute snail's pace!

Did you do all this work for nothing? Not at all. The program is slow now because the images that were previously moved in increments of one pixel are now being shifted in increments of one or two dots. There are eight dots to a pixel, so the airplane is actually moving at one-eighth of its previous speed.

There are two simple ways to fix this. The obvious way is to move the airplane, gun, and bullet in bigger steps. In other words, use different values for their increments. Hardly any retyping is needed, to make these adjustments.

Edit lines 170, 220, 230, 320, 1020, and 1021, as shown here:

```
170 IX=SGN(D(N))*8:IY=ABS(D(N))-SX
220 IF A$="1" AND XG-SX=>VL THEN IG=-SX
230 IF A$="2" AND XG+SX<=VR THEN IG=SX
320 YB=YB-T
1020 D(0)=24:D(1)=-24:D(2)=-8:D(3)=8
1021 D(4)=-16:D(5)=16:D(6)=16:D(7)=-16
```

The constant SX, which has value 16, is used in the airplane and gun routines. This constant has already been defined on line 1005, which you typed previously. When you retype lines 220 and 230, note that SX occurs *twice* on each line.

After you make these small changes, the game will run at the right speed. But you can tinker with its speed some more if you like, by varying the sprite increments. Use different numbers instead of T on line 320, and instead of SX on lines 220 and 230.

When you alter the speed of the airplane, you'll have to adjust lines 170, 1020, and 1021 so that each constant remains in the same ratio to the others. Right now, all the numbers are multiples of 8. You can change that, to multiples of 6, for instance. You must keep all the plus and minus signs the same in lines 1020 and 1021.

The disadvantage of making the sprites move in larger increments is that they take little jumps instead of gliding smoothly. Well, this is one of the limitations of BASIC programming. The game still looks pretty good.

Compiling Your Program

I mentioned that there is one other way of speeding up the program. This way allows you to keep the old, small values for the increments.

The images don't jump; they simply glide much faster.

How do you work this magic trick? Simple. You compile your BASIC program. And how do you do this? Simple. You buy a compiler. And what, pray, is a compiler? All right, I'll tell you.

When the computer runs a BASIC program, it has to interpret each statement before it can obey. This takes time, and it's why BASIC moves so slowly. If you compile the program, you pre-convert it into a code which is much easier for the computer to understand, so the interpreting process is speeded up by a factor of 5 to 10. The game runs at least five times as fast.

The "compiler" that makes this happen is itself a program, sold on a disk. First, you load the compiler program into your computer. Then, you load your BASIC program, which the compiler converts into compiled code, instead of BASIC code. Then, you save your new, compiled program into a new file. Once you have compiled the program, the process doesn't have to be repeated. You simply load and run your compiled program like any BASIC program.

There are a couple of disadvantages. (There always are, aren't there?) First, you cannot LIST the compiled version of your program, because it is no longer in BASIC code. So if you decide, at a later date, that you want to make any changes, you have to go back to your original BASIC program (which is referred to as the "source code"), make the changes in that, then compile it all over again. Compiling takes fifteen or twenty minutes, so you don't want to have to do it any more often than necessary. For this reason, don't compile a program until you're certain it is fully functional and finished.

The second disadvantage is that you have to have a disk drive to compile your program. The compiler needs a disk to save temporary files while it does its job.

But if you don't have a disk drive, don't despair. Go to your local Commodore user group (ask your dealer for the phone number or address) and see if you can make temporary use of someone else's disk drive. After you have compiled your program, you can save it back onto tape like any other program, take the tape home, and then use it on your own system. You'll find that the compiled version takes much longer to load than the old BASIC version, because the compiled version includes its own interpreter. However, this is the only real snag, and it's a small one.

The compiler that I use is called Petspeed, and you can get your Commodore dealer to order it for you. It comes with a very brief instruction manual, and a little gadget you plug into one of the joystick sockets at the side of your computer.

If you want to compile Air Attack, you'll have to change the timing of the delay loop on line 880. Since a compiled program runs about five times as fast, the delay loop needs to be five times as slow if it is to produce the same observed delay when the program is running.

But before you go ahead and compile your program, there's just one more modification I want to make to Air Attack: a big, impressive display heading. Then, our game program will be truly complete.

Summary

In this chapter, my crash course in sprite graphics has attempted to explain:

- Why sprites are easier to move and to color than graphics characters.
- How the X and Y distances of a sprite are incremented to move it in various directions.
- How the sprite-to-sprite collision detector responds.
- How to set up the various sprite parameters in the correct sequence.
- How to adjust running speed by changing the increments by which the sprites move.
- How to compile your program, to overcome the slowness of the BASIC interpreter.

EIGHT
A Handsome Heading

To me, a program isn't finished until it displays a proper title on the screen at the beginning, in large, well-designed letters.

There are two ways to accomplish this. The best way is to use sprites, one sprite for each letter. This allows you to custom-design your alphabet, in sharp detail, with elegant angles and curves. Plates 2 and 5 show examples, one in shaded block letters and the other in script. However, the Commodore 64 can only display eight sprites at a time, so if the title of a program has more than eight letters in it, you're out of luck.

Well, AIR ATTACK contains nine letters, so we have to use the second method for generating big letters on the screen, which is by assembling standard graphics characters. The result isn't quite as elegant, but it's simpler if we go about it the right way.

Assembling Graphics Characters

The POKEable characters that are most useful for our purpose have ASCII codes 160 and 32 (the solid and blank pixels), codes 95, 105, 223, and 233 (the four wedge shapes), and codes 98 and 226 (the half-filled pixels). These characters are shown in Figure 8.1.

From these, we can build some quite good-looking display letters. Appendix R shows a complete display alphabet that was built this way, and gives the code numbers of the graphics characters that were used.

To display the title of Air Attack, I'll use a larger display alphabet, which is not included in this book. But Figures 8.2–8.4 show the letters we'll be using.

The first step is to make a photocopy of the video memory map in Appendix E and pencil in the letters where they should appear. I prefer headings centered on the screen, so I think the AIR ATTACK title should look like Plate 7. Of course, you can position the words differently if you like. Figure 8.5 shows the filled-in video memory map on which it is based.

The next step is to POKE each pixel with its appropriate character code. There are two ways of doing this: the slow, simple way and the fast, complicated way.

The simple way is to take each pixel in turn, and write down the code that must be POKEd into it. Put all these numbers in DATA statements, and then have the program READ the DATA one number at a time, POKE that number into the appropriate pixel, go on to the next number and POKE it into the next pixel, and so on. This is a slow process and entails a lot of typing, since the AIR ATTACK heading covers about 250 pixels. Also, the DATA statements occupy a lot of program space.

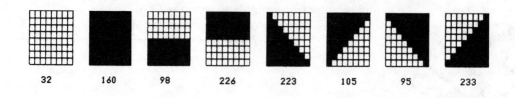

Figure 8.1: These are the characters used to build display letters in the Headline Generator program.

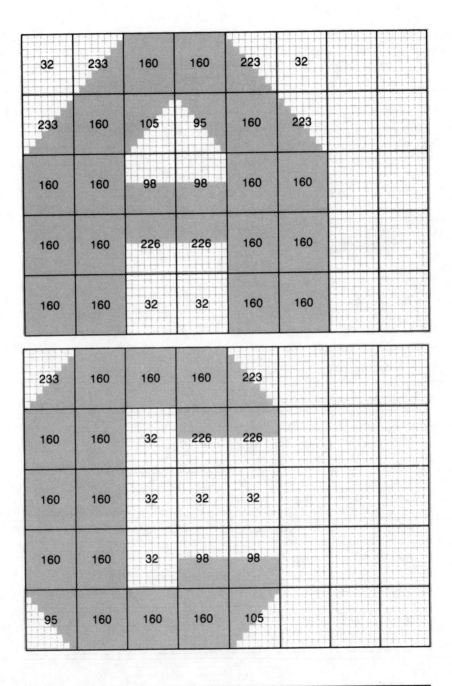

Figure 8.2: Headline letters for Air Attack.

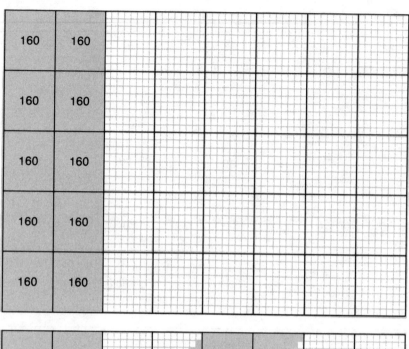

Figure 8.3: Headline letters for Air Attack.

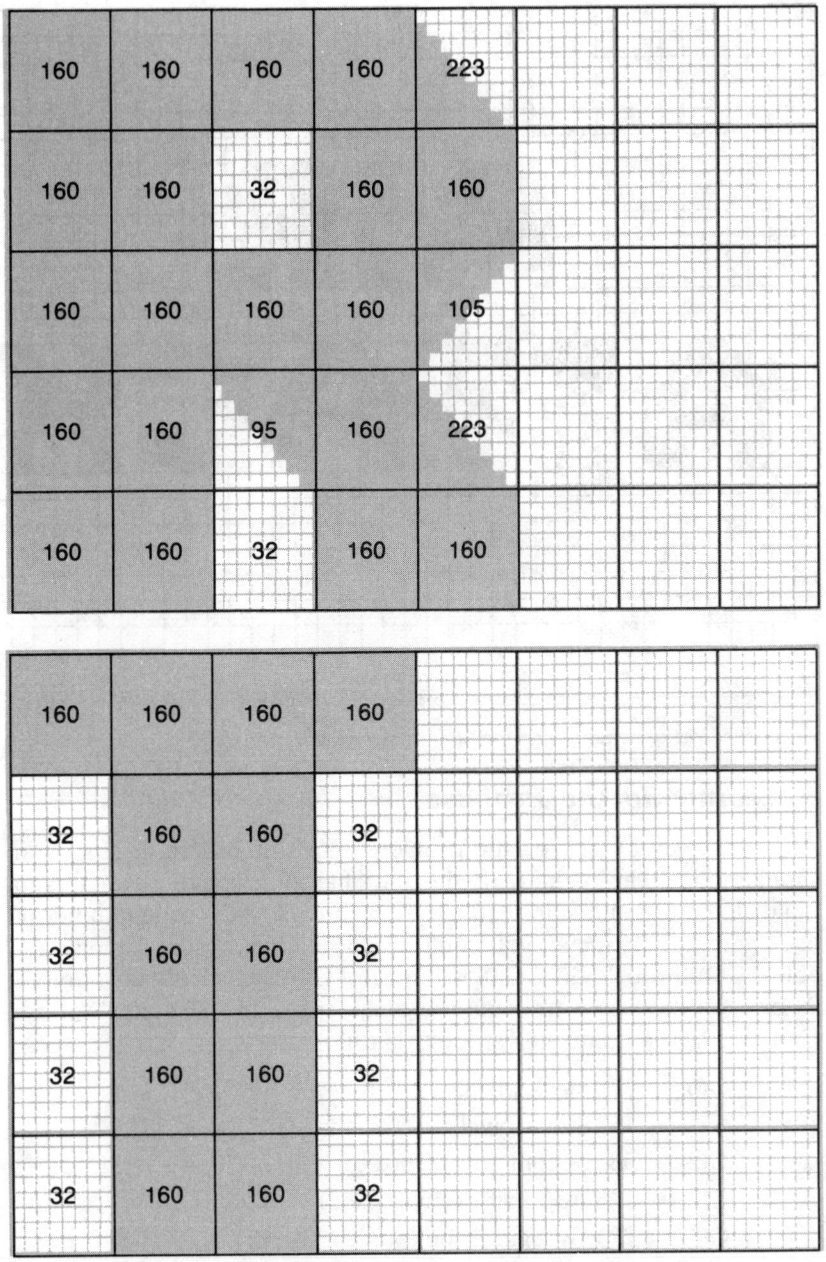

Figure 8.4: Headline letters for Air Attack.

Figure 8.5: Video memory map for Air Attack headline.

Speeding Up the Process

The fast way of tackling the problem is to systematize it. First, you should notice that I've only used eight different graphics characters to build all the big letters. Instead of typing the full ASCII code number of each graphics character, you could use a new set of subscripted variables, G(0) through G(7). G(0) will mean "Graphics character number 0" and we can use it to mean the blank space of ASCII 32. We say: G(0) = 32. The complete list looks like this:

G(0) = 32 (blank pixel)

G(1) = 160 (solid pixel)

G(2) = 98 (bottom half of pixel filled)

G(3) = 226 (top half of pixel filled)

G(4) = 223 (wedge, in bottom-left corner)

G(5) = 105 (wedge, in top-left corner)

G(6) = 95 (wedge, in top-right corner)

G(7) = 233 (wedge, in bottom-right corner)

Now our DATA statements can consist of a series of single numbers. Instead of:

DATA 32,160,98

we can write:

DATA 0,1,2

to be interpreted by the program as an instruction to POKE graphics characters G(0), G(1), and G(2) into successive video addresses.

But we can simplify things even more. Rather than POKE a series of whole lines of graphics characters and spaces, we can generate each big letter separately, one at a time. This way, we don't have to bother inserting spaces between letters, and we can use the same letter-building routine repeatedly when a letter appears more than once (such as letter A, which appears three times in AIR ATTACK).

We can define each big display letter with a single string of numbers. Then, whenever we want this program—or any other program—to build a big letter, we simply specify the first pixel where the letter is to begin, and let the letter-bulding routine do the rest.

The string of numbers that defines big letter A looks like this:

07111711115230162304111104111

The computer will interpret this string as follows:

Start at the left end of the string. Take the first single digit, which is a zero. POKE graphics character G(0) into the top-left pixel of the part of the screen where the big A is to appear. G(0) has been assigned the value 32, so POKEing G(0) into video memory results in a space being placed. Check display letter A in Figure 8.A and you will see that its top left pixel is indeed blank.

Now go to the next single digit in the string of numbers. It's a 7. This means, POKE graphics character G(7) (a wedge shape, ASCII code 233) into the next pixel, and so on.

For a couple of reasons, I'm building each big letter from its top-left corner down to its bottom-left corner, then moving one pixel to the right and again scanning from top to bottom, and so on, till I get to the end of the big letter. The letters "grow" more nicely on the screen this way, in vertical slices. And because all the letters are the same height (five pixels), but they vary in width (two to six pixels), it's easier to devise the program. All we need to do is add an extra numeral at the beginning of the string, to tell the computer how wide each letter is going to be. Since big-letter A is six pixels wide, we need to put the numeral 6 at the beginning of its string of digits.

There's one small snag, though. If you ask the computer to look at:

607111711115230162304111104111

it will see it as one giant number, rather than as a series of single digits. To avoid this, we have to put the series of digits within quote marks. This tells the computer to consider the digits a *string*, not a big number. Then we can use a MID$ operation to take each digit in the string in turn, figure its value, and insert it as a subscript in the G( ) system.

The new (final!) listing of Air Attack can be modified to include a heading in big letters. Load the fourth version of the program (which we completed in the last chapter). Clear the screen and type these new lines, 1025 and 1026, defining G(0) through G(7):

```
1025 G(0)=32:G(1)=160:G(2)=98:G(3)=226
1026 G(4)=223:G(5)=105:G(6)=95:G(7)=233
```

Now type these new lines, 1100 through 1120, establishing the strings that define the big display letters:

```
1100 DIM L$(26)
1101 L$(1)="6071117111111152301623041111"
1102 L$(1)=L$(1)+"041111"
1103 L$(3)="5711161111111100011302143025"
1109 L$(9)="21111111111"
1111 L$(11)="61111111111107150711601541"
1112 L$(11)=L$(11)+"150041"
1118 L$(18)="51111111111101601111141541"
1120 L$(20)="41000011111111110000"
```

I've used subscripts 1, 3, 9, 11, 18, and 20 to identify the strings defining the big letters. Why these numbers? Because I want this part of the program to be *portable*. AIR ATTACK doesn't contain all the letters of the alphabet, and in fact uses only six big letters (A, C, I, K, R, T). I want to be able to lift out the new subroutines I've added, and use them in other programs, without changing anything except, perhaps, the line numbers. This system of numbering leaves room for the rest of the alphabet. Also, it's less confusing if L$(3) means the third letter of the alphabet, C, rather than the third letter that happens to be in AIR ATTACK. Making subroutines generalized and portable—and easy to understand!—saves a lot of time when you write other programs later.

When a variable will be followed by a subscript greater than 10, we have to *dimension* that subscripted variable in Commodore BASIC. So line 1100 says:

DIM L$(26)

which tells the computer to reserve space for an array of L$ values of that size.

Now, lastly, type these lines, all of which are new:

```
1797 REM
1798 REM-------- Show Headline --------
1799 REM
1800 H=5:POKE 53280,3:POKE 53281,3
1810 PRINT C$
1820 A$="AIR":X=VA+172:GOSUB 2500
```

```
1830 A$="ATTACK":X=VA+442:GOSUB 2500
1840 FOR A=1 TO 19
1850 PRINT
1860 NEXT A
1870 PRINT TAB(9)"PRESS ANY KEY ";
1880 PRINT"TO BEGIN"
1890 GET A$:IF A$="" THEN 1890
2497 REM
2498 REM----- Headline Subroutine -----
2499 REM
2500 FOR A=1 TO LEN(A$)
2510 B=ASC(MID$(A$,A,1))-64
2520 C=2
2530 FOR D=X TO X+VAL(LEFT$(L$(B),1))-1
2540 FOR E=D TO D+(H-1)*40 STEP 40
2550 POKE E+CC,2
2560 POKE E,G(VAL(MID$(L$(B),C,1)))
2570 C=C+1
2575 NEXT E
2580 NEXT D
2585 X=D+1
2590 NEXT A
2595 RETURN
```

Line 1820 says: Assign to the temporary variable A$ the word "AIR"
and go to subroutine 2500, which will display *any* A$ on the screen in
big letters, beginning from video pixel number X.

Subroutine 2500 works like this. It uses several loops. The first, using
variable A, keeps track of which letter in A$ is being displayed. The
loop increments A from 1, meaning the first letter, to LEN(A$), meaning
the last letter.

Line 2510 says, "What's the ASCII code of letter number A in A$?"
Having learned the answer, it subtracts 64 from that ASCII value, and
assigns the result to variable B. It has to subtract 64, because if you ask
the computer for ASC("A") it will tell you the answer is 65, which is the
CHR$ code for "A". But in our scheme of things "A" is letter number
1. This value is assigned to variable B.

Line 2520 now sets C equal to 2. This means, we start with the second digit in the string that identifies L$(B). The first digit in L$(B) merely
defines how wide the big letter will be; the second digit is where the
graphics numbers start.

Lines 2530 and 2540 begin two more loops. The first steps across the
top row of pixels in which the display letter will appear, starting from
the pixel at address X. The second loop steps down each column of
five pixels, and uses E to keep track of the address of each pixel. Line
2550 POKEs E plus the Color Constant (CC) with the letter color, which
is 2 (red) in this case. Line 2560 POKEs pixel E with the appropriate
graphics character, G(?), where ? is found by taking the value of the
Cth digit in L$(B).

C is then incremented, and the loops are incremented. After each big letter has been displayed, a new value is calculated for X, so that the next big letter will be drawn on the screen starting one pixel further along from the last big letter.

The Advantage of Portability

Does this seem complicated? It is. But it has two enormous advantages as a system for displaying large letters. First, instead of hundreds of DATA statements, we have to type just six strings of numbers. Second, those same numbers can be used again and again, in different programs, any time you want to display those large letters. And subroutine 2500 can be used in any program, so long as the program doesn't already make special use of variables A, B, C, D, E, and X, and so long as CC has previously been defined as the Color Constant, and G(0) through G(7) have been given their proper ASCII values.

Storing Large Letters

Lastly, consider this. If you really want to save time, you can design a complete alphabet (a somewhat smaller-scale one is shown in Appendix P), and store strings L$(1) through L$(26), identifying all the big letters of the alphabet, on a disk or tape as a sequential file. Then you don't even have to retype the strings from one program to the next. You simply get your program to load that file.

In the next chapter, I'll provide and explain a program which lets you create, save, and reload your own display alphabets, without typing any ASCII or graphics codes at all. You do it all on the screen, with simple cursor control.

In the meantime, we've finished with Air Attack. I suppose it could be converted for two-player action, we could build in a high-score chart which would be saved on tape or disk along with the program, and so on and so forth . . . but the main purpose of the program was to demonstrate how a game is developed, from simple concept to finished product, using POKE, PRINT, and sprite techniques along the way. We've accomplished this purpose, so it's time now to explore other possibilities.

Summary

The chapter has dealt with the following topics:
- How large letters can be made from sprites, or by putting graphics characters together.
- How to sketch your heading first.

- How to systematize the process of building a heading, by using subscripted variables and building one large letter at a time.
- How to install a large-letters routine in a game program.
- How to store on disk or tape the strings that define your large letter.

NINE
Headings With Fewer Headaches

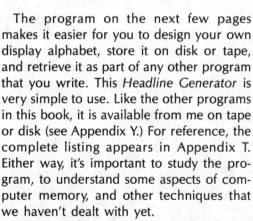

The program on the next few pages makes it easier for you to design your own display alphabet, store it on disk or tape, and retrieve it as part of any other program that you write. This *Headline Generator* is very simple to use. Like the other programs in this book, it is available from me on tape or disk (see Appendix Y.) For reference, the complete listing appears in Appendix T. Either way, it's important to study the program, to understand some aspects of computer memory, and other techniques that we haven't dealt with yet.

If you're going to type this program yourself, remember to save any other program you have been working on, then type:

NEW

and press RETURN, and clear the screen.

The beginning of the Headline Generator controls the creation and modification of large display letters in response to the user's keyboard commands. This is the only part of the program where running speed is important, which is why it has been placed at the top where line numbers are lowest.

When you run the program, execution actually begins with the set-up section commencing at line 5000. I'll explain these lines first.

```
4997 REM
4998 REM-------- Set Variables --------
4999 REM
5000 POKE 650,128:POKE 56,128:CLR
5100 VA=1024:CC=55296-VA:GM=36864
5110 F=48:TH=32:T=10:FT=15
5120 F1=133:F3=134:F5=135:F7=136
5200 B$=CHR$(144)
5201 C$=CHR$(147)
5202 D$=CHR$(17)
5203 G$=CHR$(155)
5204 H$=CHR$(19)
5206 R$=CHR$(18)
5207 U$=CHR$(145)
5210 W$=CHR$(5)
```

Lines 5200 through 5210 are all cursor commands and other special-effects CHR$s. Check Appendix B if you're unsure about any of them. Line 5120 defines the ASCII-CHR$ values of the four function keys. GM is the starting address of Graphics Memory, where the graphics data you create with this program will be stored. You are already familiar with VA and CC from Air Attack.

The first POKE statement on line 5000 makes all the keys repeat, as it did in the Air Attack game. This will make cursor control more convenient. The second POKE statement requires a bit more explanation.

Some Words About Workspace

POKE 56,128 resets the end of the workspace. What does this mean? Explaining it isn't simple, but it's important. First, look again at the memory map in Appendix H. Remember that any BASIC program you write or load resides from 2048 upward, in the BASIC workspace.

This workspace is large—it contains 38 kilobytes of memory. No program will ever fill that space. Most will use about 3K. The longest will occupy perhaps 10K. So what's the rest of the workspace used for?

It's *string space.* Now, the identities of some strings can be contained within the program listing itself—for instance, the strings defined on lines 5200 through 5210 of the Headline Generator program. But if a program GETs or INPUTs a string, or makes a new string by putting together two old ones, or does a MID$ operation, or redefines an old string (i.e. gives an old variable a new identity), it has to store the new string someplace outside of the program listing. It starts storing such strings at the "top" of the BASIC workspace (address 40960), and works down, gradually filling available memory. Some programs, such as word-processing programs, create a great many strings, which make active use of the large BASIC workspace.

The Headline Generator doesn't create a lot of strings. However, it does need to store data which define the large display letters it builds— just as we needed to store data to define sprites in Air Attack. The Headline Generator needs 4K of memory for this purpose, and this is too large a chunk to fit above the program in Bank 0 of memory, where we put the sprite data. So what's the answer?

There is a stretch that's normally not used for anything, and happens to be exactly 4K long, from 49152 to 53247. But, as you can see from the memory map in Appendix H, 1K of this is sometimes occupied by a special program called C-64 WEDGE, an aid for people who have disk drives. Since I want my program to function on every Commodore 64, I can't put my data where some users may want to store the WEDGE program.

The only answer is to store my data somewhere in the BASIC work-space. But if I put it at the top of the workspace, any time a string is redefined, my data will be *overwritten* by the new strings. And if I use 4K of memory somewhere in the middle of the workspace, between the end of the program and the beginning of the addresses being used for string storage, my data won't be absolutely safe there, either. Every time the computer stores a new string, it works downward, so that in the end, if the program runs for a long time, my data will once again be overwritten.

The answer to this problem is simple: reset the BASIC workspace so that it ends at a lower address. If we tell the computer its workspace ends at, say, 32768, then that's where it will start storing its strings, working downward, leaving the memory from above this address, all the way up to 40960, safe and untouched.

The computer must have its new workspace limit defined right at the start, before it generates any strings. This is done with POKE 56,128 on line 5000. The number stored in address 56 is a *pointer* which tells the computer the end of its workspace.

$$256 \times PEEK(56) + PEEK(55)$$

is the exact formula it uses to find the end of its workspace. Normally, PEEK(56) yields 160, and PEEK(55) yields 0. Since $256 \times 160 + 0 =$

40960, that's the usual end of the workspace. We simply change things by POKEing 56 with 128, so that the workspace now ends at 128 × 256, which is 32768.

One more thing needs to be done. The statement CLR is needed on line 5000 to clear all variable values and make the computer take note of the new workspace limit.

Taking Out the "Garbage"

Before I explain the rest of the program, a few more words on string storage. You may have wondered: what if a program creates so many new strings that they are stored lower and lower in the workspace, until they bump up against the program itself?

At this point, the computer does what is called *garbage collection*. The Headline Generator program uses the expression GET A$ over and over, to get keyboard instructions, to control cursor position. (It GETs many more keyboard instructions than Air Attack, in which I judged there was no risk of strings moving so low in memory that they would overwrite sprite data in bank 0.) Even though the GET statement uses the same string name, A$, every time, the computer keeps a separate record of every value for A$ whenever A$ is of more than zero length. The first value of A$ is recorded at the end of the workspace, the second value in the next available memory address below that, the next value below that, and so on.

The computer goes back and throws out all those old values for A$ when the workspace finally becomes totally cluttered. This garbage collection can take quite a while—several minutes, if there are a great many very short strings. During garbage collection, all other operations are suspended, and the computer seems to go completely dead. We do *not* want this to happen while a program is running.

Well, each GET A$ operation only records one character, which occupies only one byte, and there are perhaps 30,000 bytes available. But if a program is used repeatedly, it's just possible that the workspace could become filled.

One way around this is to use the word RUN in the program, each time the user wants to re-start it without turning the computer off. RUN resets all variables to zero, and clears the workspace of everything except the program itself.

However, RUN re-starts the program right from the beginning, including title, instructions, and other things that the user doesn't need to see over and over again. To get around this we can use the word RUN followed by a line number; this starts program execution at the specified line.

But this means we have to make sure to redefine all constants in subsequent lines, since RUN sets them to zero. Also, RUN followed by a line number is not a valid statement in a program that will be compiled, because a compiled program doesn't have BASIC line numbers any more.

The way to deal with this problem is to avoid using RUN altogether. Instead, we reset another pointer any time the workspace is likely to become full of strings. This is the "lowest string" pointer, which tells the computer where it placed its last string. Address 52 holds the "high byte" of that pointer, and 51 holds the "low byte."

$$256 \times PEEK(52) + PEEK(51)$$

gives the actual address of the lowest string stored so far. Garbage collection is triggered when the value of the lowest-string pointer descends dangerously close to the top of the program listing.

We can re-set the string pointer and thus avoid garbage collection. If we re-set it all the way up at the end of the workspace with POKE 52,128 that will erase the computer's memory of *all* its strings, and there are some that we don't want to lose, because they are constants that are referred to during the program. So the Headline Generator program actually POKEs 52 with 120, on line 990, if the user wants to re-start after creating or editing an alphabet. This resets the string pointer high enough to avoid garbage collection, but not so high that it might interfere with strings that we want to keep on a permanent basis. If you want to avoid garbage collection in any program you write yourself that creates surplus strings during program execution, you should use this principle.

This has been a long digression, but it's important to get acquainted with the way the computer uses its memory. It gives you more control, and also helps you understand certain kinds of faults that may occur.

Variables and Constants

Now, I'll explain some more of the Headline Generator listing. Type the following lines, continuing the set-up routine:

```
5500 DIM G(10),VM(9,7),L$(26)
5510 L=VA+204
5520 FOR M=1 TO 7
5530 FOR N=1 TO 9
5540 VM(N,M)=L+N
5550 NEXT N
5560 L=L+40
5570 NEXT M
5750 G(0)=32:G(1)=160:G(2)=98:G(3)=226
5751 G(4)=223:G(5)=105:G(6)=95:G(7)=233
5752 G(8)=97:G(9)=225:G(10)=100
5800 L$(1)="3711110104111"
5801 L$(4)="3111110014115"
5802 L$(5)="3111112311001"
```

```
5803  L$(7)="3711610011011"
5804  L$(8)="3111102301111"
5805  L$(9)="11111"
5806  L$(12)="3111100010001"
5807  L$(14)="41111416004161111"
5808  L$(15)="3711610014115"
5809  L$(18)="3111110164154"
5810  L$(20)="3100011111000"
```

G(0) through G(10) are subscripted variables, dimensioned on line 5500. They are used to represent the ASCII graphics codes. Their values are assigned on lines 5750 through 5752.

VM(9,7) defines the address of each pixel in a 7 × 9 grid of Video Memory which will be drawn on the screen, and which will be used to create display alphabets. Instead of POKEing each graphics character into a numbered memory address, the program assigns those addresses to VM(1,1) (the top-left corner of the grid), VM(1,2) (the next pixel to the right on the top row), and so on, as shown in Figure 9.1. This makes it much easier to visualize and control the building of letters.

Lastly, the DIMension statement L$(26) has the same function as in the headline-generating opener we added to the Air Attack program. You'll find various L$s defined on lines 5800 through 5810. This time, they define letters in the display typeface in Appendix P. The letters spell out HEADLINE GENERATOR, the title of this program (see Figure 9.2).

VM(1,1)	VM(2,1)	VM(3,1)	VM(4,1)	VM(5,1)	VM(6,1)	VM(7,1)	VM(8,1)	VM(9,1)
VM(1,2)	VM(2,2)	VM(3,2)	VM(4,2)	VM(5,2)	VM(6,2)	VM(7,2)	VM(8,2)	VM(9,2)
VM(1,3)	VM(2,3)	VM(3,3)	VM(4,3)	VM(5,3)	VM(6,3)	VM(7,3)	VM(8,3)	VM(9,3)
VM(1,4)	VM(2,4)	VM(3,4)	VM(4,4)	VM(5,4)	VM(6,4)	VM(7,4)	VM(8,4)	VM(9,4)
VM(1,5)	VM(2,5)	VM(3,5)	VM(4,5)	VM(5,5)	VM(6,5)	VM(7,5)	VM(8,5)	VM(9,5)
VM(1,6)	VM(2,6)	VM(3,6)	VM(4,6)	VM(5,6)	VM(6,6)	VM(7,6)	VM(8,6)	VM(9,6)
VM(1,7)	VM(2,7)	VM(3,7)	VM(4,7)	VM(5,7)	VM(6,7)	VM(7,7)	VM(8,7)	VM(9,7)

Figure 9.1: Subscripted variable VM is assigned the values of these memory addresses.

Figure 9.2: The Headline Generator headline, using the smaller display alphabet from Appendix P.

A Quick Way to Set Color Memory

Having set all the constants and variables, the program displays its heading from line 6000 onward.

```
5997 REM
5998 REM----- Title & Instructions ----
5999 REM
6000 POKE 53280,3:POKE 53281,1
6010 PRINTC$CHR$(28)
6020 FOR N=1 TO 15
6030 PRINT "(24 spaces)"
6040 NEXT N:PRINTB$D$D$D$D$
6050 H=4
6060 A$="HEADLINE":X=VA+45:GOSUB 6900
6070 A$="GENERATOR":X=VA+242:GOSUB 6900
6080 PRINT"     1. RETRIEVE AN OLD ";
6085 PRINT"ALPHABET?":PRINT
6090 PRINT"     2. START A NEW ";
6095 PRINT"ALPHABET?"D$D$D$
6100 GOSUB 9000
6110 IF A<49 OR A>50 THEN 6100
6120 IF A=50 THEN 6300
6200 GOSUB 2000:GOSUB 2300
6210 GOSUB 7000:GOSUB 7500:GOTO 900
6300 PRINT"   HEIGHT OF ";
6305 PRINT"LETTERS (2-7 PIXELS):";
```

```
6310 GOSUB 9000
6320 IF A<50 OR A>55 THEN 6310
6330 H=A-48:PRINT H:GOSUB 9200
6340 GOSUB 7000:GOSUB 7500
6350 FOR N=GM TO GM+4032 STEP 64
6360 POKE N,T
6370 NEXT N
6380 GOTO 100
6897 REM
6898 REM------ Display Subroutine -----
6899 REM
6900 FOR J=1 TO LEN(A$)
6910 K=ASC(MID$(A$,J,1))-64:L=2
6920 FOR M=X TO X+VAL(LEFT$(L$(K),1))-1
6930 FOR N=M TO M+(H-1)*40 STEP 40
6940 POKE N,G(VAL(MID$(L$(K),L,1)))
6950 L=L+1
6960 NEXT N
6970 NEXT M
6980 X=M+1:NEXT J
6990 RETURN
```

First, the loop on lines 6020 through 6040 prints a string of 24 spaces, 15 times. So you can see how many spaces I mean, I have written "(24 spaces)" in the listing. If you type this program, instead of actually typing the words "(24 spaces)" you should type a quote mark, hit the space bar 24 times, then type another quote mark.

Printing spaces is a super-speedy, sneaky way to set a whole lot of addresses in color memory. Line 6010 sets text color to red with the PRINT CHR$(28) statement. Then the spaces are PRINTed onto the screen. As spaces, they are "transparent" and show no color. But they do reset color memory to red, so that characters subsequently POKEd into video memory will appear red. This eliminates having to make separate POKEs to add color, and speeds up the display of the headline.

The headline is now displayed using exactly the same routine that was added to Air Attack. First, the temporary variable A$ has the word "HEADLINE" assigned to it, and a starting video address, X, is established, on line 6060. Then the subroutine at 6900 takes care of putting the word on the screen. You should recognize this subroutine from the one we used in the Air Attack game.

Then, line 6070 assigns the word "GENERATOR" to A$, a new value is given for X, and the routine is repeated.

Lines 6080 through 6095 ask the user whether he wants to retrieve previous lettering (to edit it), or start a new alphabet. Depending on the user's choice, various subroutines are executed. We'll deal with them in a moment, or you can sneak a look at them in Appendix T.

If the user is starting a new alphabet, lines 6300 through 6310 find out how many pixels tall the letters are going to be. Then lines 6350 through 6370 POKE the constant T into the addresses in Graphics Memory (from GM onward) where the data for each headline letter will begin. T is used as to indicate that no headline letter has yet been created.

Displaying the Directory

If an existing alphabet is to be retrieved, GOSUB 2000 brings the disk directory onto the screen. Here's the section that handles this:

```
1997 REM
1998 REM----- Get Disk Directory ------
1999 REM
2000 M=0:POKE 53280,15:PRINT C$
2005 PRINT" SEE THE DIRECTORY?"
2010 GOSUB 9000:IF A$="N" THEN 2200
2015 PRINT:PRINT" ";
2020 OPEN 2,8,2,"$"
2030 FOR N=1 TO 254:GET#2,A$:NEXT N
2040 K=13:M=M+1:IF M=8 THEN K=11:M=0
2050 GET#2,A$
2060 IF ST>0 THEN CLOSE 2:GOTO 2200
2070 IF A$<>"" THEN A=ASC(A$):GOTO 2100
2080 FOR N=1 TO 18+K:GET#2,A$
2090 NEXT N:GOTO 2040
2100 GET#2,A$,A$
2110 FOR N=1 TO 16:GET#2,A$
2120 PRINT A$;:NEXT N
2130 PRINT" "CHR$(83-(A-129)*3)"  ";
2140 FOR N=1 TO K:GET#2,A$:NEXT N
2150 GOTO 2040
2199 REM-----------------
2200 PRINT:PRINT:PRINT" ";
2210 INPUT"WHICH FILE";F$
2220 RETURN
```

If you don't have a disk drive, renumber line 2210 as line 2000, then omit lines 2005 through 2200 completely, because a tape does not have a directory to be displayed. However, if you do have a disk, you can use subroutine 2000 in *any* program where you want to display the disk directory before choosing a file name. This subroutine is shorter than the one that Commodore includes in the manual for the disk drive. It puts a P beside each program, an S beside each sequential file. Sequential files will be used to store the headline data.

One snag: if you load the Headline Generator program from one disk, then switch to a different disk that holds your sequential files, the disk drive will give you an error message if you try to read the directory—unless the identification titles of the two disks are exactly the same. So, either give all your disks the same titles when you format them, or store your sequential files of display alphabets on the same disk as you store the Headline Generator program itself.

Loading a File

Here's the section of the program that handles this little operation:

```
2297 REM
2298 REM--------- Load File -----------
2299 REM
2300 OPEN 2,8,2,"0:"+F$+",S,R"
2310 INPUT#2,H
2320 FOR M=GM TO GM+4032 STEP 64
2330 GET#2,A$:W=ASC(A$)
2340 POKE M,W:IF W=T THEN 2400
2350 FOR N=M+1 TO M+W*H
2370 GET#2,A$
2380 POKE N,ASC(A$)
2390 NEXT N
2400 NEXT M
2410 CLOSE 2:RETURN
```

If you have tape, not disk, you will have to rewrite line 2300 as follows:

2300 OPEN 2,1,0, + F$

Note that the first of the three digits after OPEN remains the same. The second digit was 8, which is the "device number" of the disk drive; we have to replace that with a 1, the "device number" of the cassette recorder, to tell the computer where the data is coming from. The third number has to be changed to a 0, which means, for cassette users, data is being loaded rather than saved. The ",S,R" expression which is necessary for disk users is eliminated, for cassette use. But we keep the file name, F$, in case you have a series of sequential files on tape, and you don't necessarily want to load the first one. The cassette recorder will scan through till it finds the file whose name corresponds with F$. If you omit F$, the cassette recorder will simply load the first data file it finds.

Note the form in which the program stores its data—on tape and on disk. The first item in the sequential file is a number representing the height of all the letters, measured in pixels. This is INPUT from disk or tape and assigned to variable H. Then the data for each letter of the alphabet is loaded. The first character will be a number from 1 to 10, representing the width W, in pixels, of that particular headline letter. If it's 10, this means the letter has not yet been defined. I could have signified this with a 0, but the expression ASC(A$) causes an error message on the Commodore 64 when A$ has ASCII value of 0. So I used 10 instead. When a headline letter *has* been defined, its maximum width is 9.

If a headline letter hasn't been defined, the computer skips on to the next one, until the whole file is loaded. Program execution then shifts to the main menu (line 900) to allow the options of reviewing, editing, or saving the display alphabet.

Saving a File

Subroutine 2500 puts the data defining the display alphabet onto tape or disk, after the alphabet has been created or edited:

```
2497 REM
2498 REM--------- Save File -----------
2499 REM
2500 OPEN 2,8,2,"@0:"+F$+",S,W"
2510 PRINT#2,H
2520 FOR M=GM TO GM+4032 STEP 64
2530 W=PEEK(M):PRINT#2,CHR$(W);
2540 IF W=T THEN 2600
2550 FOR N=M+1 TO M+W*H
2560 A=PEEK(N)
2570 PRINT#2,CHR$(A);
2580 NEXT N
2600 NEXT M
2610 CLOSE 2:RETURN
```

Cassette users will have to modify line 2500 so it looks like this:

2500 OPEN 2,1,2, + F$

The third digit is now a 2, which tells the computer that this is a save operation, which should terminate in an end-of-file marker.

After a data-saving operation, the program automatically restarts. When you want to quit it altogether, you must turn off the computer, or hit RUN/STOP. Turning the computer off and then on again is better practice, because that resets the workspace to its usual limit, and restores any other POKEs to their usual status. The RUN/STOP key does not do this, with the result that subsequent programs that you try to run will misbehave, or do nothing at all.

Other Subroutines

This program is written in "structured form," which means that each operation, such as loading or saving, or even resetting the basic screen layout, has been put in its own little section as a subroutine. The advantage of this is that you can see what each separate piece of the program does. Also, as a programmer, I can string together any sequence of operations such as load, display a letter, edit it, and save, simply by writing a series of GOSUB commands—such as those on lines 6200 and 6210, which you have already typed.

The disadvantage of this system is that, to you, GOSUB 7000 doesn't mean much. You have to check the full listing to discover that the subroutine starting on line 7000 creates the main screen layout of the program. This is why we're including the whole listing in Appendix T, to help you find your way around. And this is why I've included a lot of REM lines to remind you what each part of the program does.

Time now to type the remaining subroutines, before we finally deal with the main part of the program, which controls everything (lines 10 through 1510).

First, the main screen layout:

```
6997 REM
6998 REM--------- Main Layout ---------
6999 REM
7000 POKE 53280,15
7010 POKE 53281,1
7020 PRINT C$G$
7030 FOR N=1 TO 15:PRINT:NEXT N
7040 FOR N=1 TO 17
7050 PRINT R$"(21 spaces)"
7060 NEXT N
7070 PRINT R$"  "U$U$U$
7080 POKE VA+999,160:POKE VA+CC+999,15
7090 L=48:FOR N=2 TO 38 STEP 4
7100 PRINT TAB(N)R$CHR$(L);
7110 L=L+1:NEXT N
7120 FOR M=VA+721 TO VA+801 STEP 40
7130 READ A$
7140 A$="000111"+A$:L=1
7150 FOR N=M TO M+38
7160 IF N/4=INT(N/4) THEN N=N+1
7170 POKE N+CC,0
7180 POKE N,G(VAL(MID$(A$,L,1)))
7190 L=L+1
7200 NEXT N:NEXT M
7210 PRINTH$B$;
7220 RETURN
7300 DATA "00011140011561100718 0091"
7310 DATA "22233314015006107118 0091"
7320 DATA "11100011450000671118 0091"
```

This produces the screen design shown in Figure 9.3. At the bottom of the picture, three times normal size, are the ten possible graphics characters that can be combined to form each display letter. These shapes are numbered 0 through 9. Their ASCII values have already been defined in the program set-up as G(0) through G(9). When the program is running, you type any number from 0 through 9 to identify the graphics shape that you want to use.

Now here's a subroutine that clears only the "window" part of the screen where headline letters are displayed.

```
7497 REM
7498 REM------ Letter Grid Layout -----
7499 REM
7500 PRINT:PRINTH$G$;
7510 FOR N=1 TO 16
7520 PRINT R$"(21 spaces)"
7530 NEXT N
7540 FOR M=1 TO 9
7550 FOR N=1 TO H-1
7560 POKE VM(M,N),G(T)
7570 NEXT N
7580 POKE VM(M,H),G(0)
7590 NEXT M
7600 PRINT B$;:RETURN
```

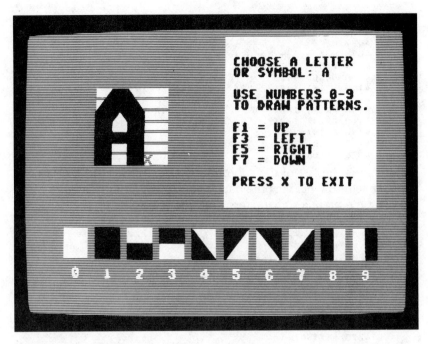

Figure 9.3: The Headline Generator program at work.

And here are some general-purpose subroutines, for GETting a keyboard entry, clearing an area of the screen, and inserting a delay loop.

```
8997 REM
8998 REM-------- Subroutines ---------
8999 REM
9000 GET A$:IF A$="" THEN 9000
9010 A=ASC(A$):RETURN
9100 PRINTH$:FOR N=1 TO 14
9110 PRINT TAB (22)"(17 spaces)"
9120 NEXT N
9130 PRINT H$:PRINT
9140 RETURN
9200 FOR DY=1 TO 200:NEXT DY:RETURN
```

Next, two subroutines which display menus of options on the screen,
and GET the user's choice.

```
3997 REM
3998 REM------ Menu for Editing -------
3999 REM
4000 PRINT TAB(22)"USE NUMBERS 0-9"
4010 PRINT TAB(22)"TO DRAW PATTERNS."
4020 PRINT
4030 PRINT TAB(22)"F1 = UP"
4040 PRINT TAB(22)"F3 = LEFT"
4050 PRINT TAB(22)"F5 = RIGHT"
4060 PRINT TAB(22)"F7 = DOWN"
4070 PRINT
```

```
4080 PRINT TAB(22)"PRESS X TO EXIT"
4090 RETURN
4097 REM
4098 REM----- Menu for Reviewing -----
4099 REM
4100 GOSUB 9100
4110 PRINT TAB(22)"1. CONTINUE":PRINT
4120 PRINT TAB(22)"2. GO BACK":PRINT
4130 PRINT TAB(22)"3. EDIT":PRINT
4140 PRINT TAB(22)"4. ABORT"
4150 PRINT:PRINT
4160 PRINT TAB(22)"CHARACTER:  "
4170 RETURN
```

And here's the last of the subroutines. Its purpose is to display one headline letter by PEEKing the data defining that letter in memory, and POKEing the graphics characters onto the screen.

```
4197 REM
4198 REM----- Display a Character -----
4199 REM
4200 K=1:W=PEEK(CM)
4210 FOR M=1 TO W
4220 FOR N=1 TO H
4230 POKE VM(M,N)+CC,0
4240 POKE VM(M,N),PEEK(CM+K)
4250 K=K+1
4260 NEXT N
4270 NEXT M
4280 RETURN
```

Reviewing Headline Letters

Once you have defined a few headline letters using this program, or loaded a file of existing letters, the program allows you to review your whole alphabet one letter at a time. Each letter is displayed in the screen "window;" you can edit it some more, or move on to the next. The following section handles this operation:

```
997 REM
998 REM------------ Review ------------
999 REM
1000 GOSUB 4100
1100 CN=0:S=1:V=1
1110 POKE VA+473,CN
1120 CM=GM+(64*CN)
1130 IF PEEK(CM)=T THEN 1300
1140 GOSUB 4200:IF W=>V THEN 1190
1150 FOR M=W+1 TO V
1155 FOR N=1 TO H-1
1160 POKE VM(M,N)+CC,FT
1165 POKE VM(M,N),G(T)
1170 NEXT N
1175 POKE VM(M,N),TH
1180 NEXT M
1190 V=W:POKE 198,0:GOSUB 9000
1200 IF A<49 OR A>52 THEN 1140
1210 IF A=49 THEN S=1
```

```
1220 IF A=50 THEN S=-1
1230 IF A=51 THEN GOSUB 1500
1240 IF A=52 THEN 1330
1250 PRINT H$
1260 PRINT D$D$D$D$D$D$D$D$D$TAB(33);
1300 CN=CN+S
1310 IF CN<0 THEN S=1:CN=0
1320 IF CN<64 THEN 1110
1330 GOSUB 7500:GOTO 900
1499 REM---------------
1500 GOSUB 9100:GOSUB 300:GOSUB 7500
1510 GOSUB 4100:RETURN
```

These are the variables defined in this section:

CN stands for Character Number.

CM is Character Memory—the address where data for that character begins.

W is the letter width.

V is the width of the previous character displayed.

M and N are loop variables.

Lines 1190 through 1240 GET the user's instruction (e.g. go on to the next letter, go back to the previous letter, edit, etc.) and take appropriate action. S is the Step through the alphabet, either 1 (next character) or −1 (previous character).

After you've reviewed your alphabet, the program shows you its main menu:

```
897 REM
898 REM---------- Main Menu ----------
899 REM
900 GOSUB 9100
910 PRINT TAB(22)"1. REVIEW":PRINT
920 PRINT TAB(22)"2. EDIT":PRINT
930 PRINT TAB(22)"3. SAVE":PRINT:PRINT
940 PRINT TAB(22)"...YOUR CHOICE?"
950 GOSUB 9000
960 IF A<49 OR A>51 THEN 950
970 ON A-48 GOTO 1000,100,980
980 RESTORE:GOSUB 2000:GOSUB 2500
990 POKE 52,120:PRINT C$:GOTO 6080
```

Note line 990, which restarts the program after you have saved an alphabet that you've created. POKE 52,120 resets the string pointer, as I described earlier in this chapter.

Selecting and Editing Headline Letters

Lastly, here's the beginning part of the program. The first few lines ask you to type on the keyboard the letter or symbol that you want to create in headline size. The program only accepts CHR$ codes 32 through 95 (see line 140). Since it uses POKE codes to number the characters, A is character number 1 rather than character number 65, and line 150 is needed to convert the CHR$ code to a POKE code.

Line 170 calculates the address where the data defining that character will reside. Line 180 looks to see if that character has already been defined, in which case it is displayed via subroutine 4200. Then line 200 allows you to create a character, or modify an existing one, via lines 300 through 890, which are one big subroutine.

```
10 GOTO 5000
97 REM
98 REM------- Select a Character ------
99 REM
100 GOSUB 9100
110 PRINT TAB(22)"CHOOSE A LETTER"
130 PRINT TAB(22)"OR SYMBOL: ":PRINT
140 GOSUB 9000:IF A<32 OR A>95 THEN 140
150 IF A>63 THEN A=A-64
160 POKE VA+153,A
170 CM=GM+(A*64)
180 IF PEEK(CM)<T THEN GOSUB 4200
200 GOSUB 300
210 PRINT TAB(22)"CHOOSE ANOTHER?"
220 GOSUB 9000
230 GOSUB 7500
240 IF A=89 THEN 100
250 GOTO 900
297 REM
298 REM------- Edit a Character -------
299 REM
300 GOSUB 4000
310 X=1:Y=1
320 P=PEEK(VM(X,Y)):M=0
330 POKE VM(X,Y),86:GOSUB 550
340 IF M=1 THEN 400
350 POKE VM(X,Y),P:GOSUB 550
360 IF M=0 THEN 330
400 A=ASC(A$):IF A>57 OR A<F THEN 420
410 L=0:IF A=F THEN L=15
412 POKE VM(X,Y)+CC,L
414 POKE VM(X,Y),G(A-F)
416 X=X+1:GOTO 490
420 POKE VM(X,Y),P:IF A=88 THEN 600
430 IF A<F1 OR A>F7 THEN M=0:GOTO 330
440 IF A=F1 THEN IF Y>1 THEN Y=Y-1
450 IF A=F7 THEN IF Y<H THEN Y=Y+1
460 IF A=F3 THEN X=X-1
470 IF A=F5 THEN X=X+1
480 IF X=OTHEN X=9:Y=Y-1:IF Y=OTHEN Y=H
490 IF X=T THENX=1:Y=Y+1:IFY>H THEN Y=1
500 GOTO 320
540 REM------------------------
550 FOR N=1 TO 50
560 GET A$:IF A$<>""THEN N=50:M=1
570 NEXT N
580 RETURN
590 REM------------------------
600 GOSUB 9100
610 PRINT TAB(22)"DO YOU WANT TO"
620 PRINT TAB(22)"MEMORIZE THIS?"
```

```
630 PRINT
640 GOSUB 9000
650 IF A=78 THEN RETURN
660 IF A<>89 THEN 640
670 PRINT TAB(22)"SCANNING"
680 PRINT TAB(22)".";
690 REM---------- First Find Width
700 W=10
710 FOR M=9 TO 1 STEP -1
720 FOR N=1 TO H
730 P=PEEK(VM(M,N))
740 IF P<>G(T) AND P>TH THEN W=M
750 NEXT N
760 PRINT".";:IF W=M THEN M=1
770 NEXT M
780 POKE CM,W
790 IF W=10 THEN 890
795 REM-------- Now Scan Letter
800 L=CM
810 FOR M=1 TO W
820 FOR N=1 TO H
830 P=PEEK(VM(M,N))
840 IF P=G(T) THEN P=TH
850 L=L+1:POKE L,P
860 NEXT N
870 PRINT".";
880 NEXT M
890 PRINT:PRINT:RETURN
```

The program uses its own cursor, rather than the Commodore cursor, to mark the part of the character being edited on the screen. There are various reasons for doing this, such as avoiding errors that would occur if the operator pressed the RETURN key while the Commodore cursor was flashing in INPUT mode, while graphics characters are on the screen. I wanted my cursor to flash, which is accomplished by lines 310 through 360, and lines 550 through 580.

Lines 400 through 500 interpret any keyboard entry as a cursor-control command, and move the cursor accordingly, making sure it doesn't stray beyond the "window" where the letter is being built or edited. When the user has refined the headline letter to his satisfaction, lines 700 through 790 scan the screen "window" to find how wide this letter is (remember, your headline letters can be from 1 to 9 pixels wide), and then lines 800 through 890 scan the letter and record its graphics data in memory.

Using the Headline Generator

When you RUN this program, it asks you if you want to start a new alphabet or load and edit an old one. If you load and edit, you are shown the disk directory, and you choose an alphabet file that you've previously created. You are then given the options of review, edit, or save.

If you start a new alphabet, you must first define the height of its letters in pixels. This is the maximum height; you can make some letters smaller if you wish. The program then puts you straight into create/edit mode, so you can start creating headline letters on the screen.

You do this by typing numbers 0 through 9, to select the graphics shapes you want and insert them. The position where they will appear is marked by the flashing X of the cursor. You can move the cursor around by pressing function keys f1, f3, f5, and f7, which have been defined as Up, Left, Right, and Down, respectively. I find this easier to use than Commodore's cursor-control keys.

Rather than try to create headline letters straight onto the screen, it's easiest to sketch them on squared paper first, then transfer them from your sketch to the screen. When you've created all the letters you want (including, if you like, symbols such as a comma, quote mark, or exclamation point), you type X to exit from the Create/Edit mode. You can now review, edit some more, or save your work on disk or tape.

Using Headline Files in Your Programs

The whole purpose of the Headline Generator is to create files of headline letters which you can then load into programs you write yourself. Your programs can then display headlines.

Pieces of the Headline Generator can be incorporated into your programs for this purpose. To load a file of headline letters, use the subroutine on lines 2300 through 2410. (Cassette users, remember to modify line 2300 as already described.)

You can change the line numbers to suit your program, but be sure your program does not use variables named W or H for anything other than the Width and Height of headline letters. Your program must define T = 10 and CC as the Color Constant and must establish GM as the start of Graphics Memory where your headline data will reside. Reset your workspace below this area of memory.

Do not use variables A$, K, M, or N in your program for anything other than transient values. Do not use them as constants, for instance, because this subroutine will change their values.

To display a headline letter after you have loaded the headline alphabet into memory, use the following subroutine (which is derived from line 170, line 180, and subroutine 4200 of the Headline Generator):

```
50000 CM=GM+(A*64)
50010 W=PEEK(CM):IF W=T THEN RETURN
50020 K=1
50030 FOR M=X TO X+W-1
50040 FOR N=M TO M+40*(H-1) STEP 40
50050 POKE N+CC,C
```

```
50060 POKE N,PEEK(CM+K)
50070 K=K+1
50080 NEXT N
50090 NEXT M:RETURN
```

In the subroutine, as in the Headline Generator, A stands for the ASCII code of the character you want to display. H is the Height of your display letters; your routine for loading your display alphabet should have established this. Define C as the Color of the headline letters. K, M, and N are loop variables.

X must be defined as the video address where you want the top-left corner of your headline letter to appear on the screen. If you forget to define X, the subroutine will POKE addresses that will make your program come to a sudden halt.

If you tell the subroutine to display a letter for which data does not exist (because you forgot to define that headline letter with the Headline Generator), line 50010 detects the fact that there is no data for that letter, and RETURNs you out of the subroutine before it can attempt to produce that letter.

Summary

Most of this chapter has dealt with the Headline Generator, but other topics have included:

- How to reset the end of BASIC workspace, to reserve memory for special purposes.
- How strings are stored.
- How the string pointer operates.
- How to reset the string pointer to avoid avoid "garbage collection."
- How to display a disk directory.
- How to read and write sequential files on disk or tape.
- How to use files created by the Headline Generator.

TEN
Unforgettable Characters

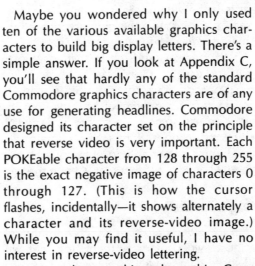

Maybe you wondered why I only used ten of the various available graphics characters to build big display letters. There's a simple answer. If you look at Appendix C, you'll see that hardly any of the standard Commodore graphics characters are of any use for generating headlines. Commodore designed its character set on the principle that reverse video is very important. Each POKEable character from 128 through 255 is the exact negative image of characters 0 through 127. (This is how the cursor flashes, incidentally—it shows alternately a character and its reverse-video image.) While you may find it useful, I have no interest in reverse-video lettering.

We can do something about this. Commodore has very kindly allowed us to modify its character set, or even to design our own from scratch. The system for doing this is a bit inconvenient, but if you've tackled sprite-building in Chapters Six and Seven, you should be an old hand at this sort of thing by now.

The Video Chip and Memory Banks

Look once again at the memory map in Appendix H. I've mentioned that it is divided into four sections called banks 0, 1, 2, and 3. What I didn't mention is that the video chip, which controls everything you see on the screen, can only "look at" data in one of these banks of memory at a time.

When you turn on the computer, the video chip is pre-set to "look at" bank 0 of memory, which extends from address 0 to address 16383. Therefore, video memory lies in this bank, and when we used sprites I stored their data in this bank, too. If their data had been POKEd into a different bank, the video chip wouldn't have been able to "see" them.

Bank 0 also contains a "ROM image" of the character set—a representation of all the characters that the computer can display. This may seem confusing, because it overlaps the area of memory where programs normally reside. How can two things be in the same location?

The answer is that two sets of data, the program and the character set, are switched into memory one at a time, very, very fast. When the video chip needs to refer to its character set to display characters on the screen, the character set is there. When the CPU chip needs to look at the program, the program is there.

There's a pointer that tells the video chip where to look to find the data for its character set. This is just like the pointers that tell the chip where to find data to build sprites. All we need to do is POKE data for our new character set into memory, and tell the video chip to look for it *there*, instead of at the usual "ROM image."

But we're apt to run out of room if we try to do this in bank 0. Commodore offers us two character sets, remember, and together they will occupy 4K. We may want to use some sprites as well, in which case their data will take up still more room. Bank 0 also contains any program that we use, plus video memory, and part of the operating system in addresses 0 through 1023. All in all, there isn't enough space.

Switching Memory Banks

The answer is to switch the video chip so it looks at a different bank of memory. We can relocate video memory there, together with our new character set, and sprite data as well, if necessary. Our program, of course, will still be back in bank 0, where it usually is. But the video chip doesn't need to refer to the program. It only needs data for the video display.

The most convenient way to store all this data is to reduce the size of the BASIC workspace (by POKEing the pointers in 55 and 56, remember?) and then put all our video data where the top of workspace used to be, in bank 2.

The only snag is, there's a "ROM image" of the old Commodore character set in bank 2 as well as in bank 0, and we can't put our new character set, or any other video data, where this "ROM image" is. From the video chip's point of view, the "ROM image" will "hide" any video data we POKE into memory "beneath" it. Even so, we still have enough room left if we convert only one of the two Commodore character sets into our new character set. If we do the job right, we should only need one character set. It can contain upper-case letters, lower-case letters, and all the most ideal graphics characters, instead of the less useful reverse-video characters.

The way I usually set up memory, after switching to bank 2, is shown in Figure 10.1.

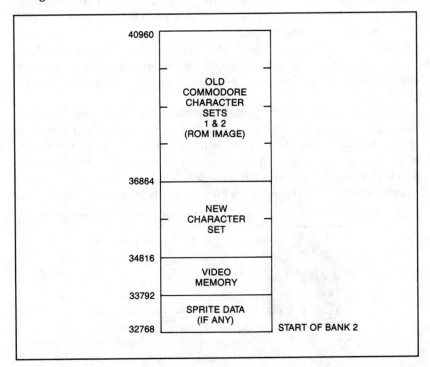

Figure 10.1: A recommended way to make use of computer memory, after relocating the end of the BASIC workspace and switching the video chip to bank 2.

How Characters are Coded

There's one little detail I haven't explained, and that is how characters are coded. This is very similar to the way that sprites are coded. Each character is constructed in an 8 × 8 grid of dots, just as each sprite occupies a 24 × 21 grid of dots. The 8 × 8 grid of a single character should be considered as eight rows, each one of which is a pattern that can be numbered using the pattern-matching chart in Appendix N. For instance, the Commodore standard character set uses a letter A which looks, and is coded, as in Figure 10.2.

Note that there is a blank line underneath the A. Otherwise, there would be no space between it and characters on the screen below it. For the same reason, there is space on either side of the A, to separate it from preceding and subsequent characters.

There are two ways of building a new character, whether it's a letter such as A, or a graphics symbol. The slow way is to draw each letter or symbol with pencil and paper, using an 8 × 8 grid, then look up the corresponding code numbers on the pattern-matching chart, then type those numbers into DATA statements (just as we did to construct sprites), and then have a program READ the DATA statements and POKE the numbers into memory.

Coding one letter doesn't take long. But there are 256 possible characters. A labor-saving process would be an advantage, and there is one. It consists of a *Character Generator* program, which I've listed in full in Appendix U.

This program works very much like the Headline Generator. You move a cursor across a grid on the screen, filling the grid with the character pattern you want. Then you save all the patterns onto tape or disk, and reload them as part of any other program you write, which will use the revised character set.

If you don't want to type such a long program, it's available from me,

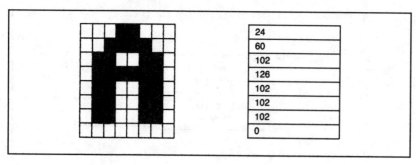

Figure 10.2: One number identifies each row of eight dots in a standard Commodore character.

with the others in this book, on tape or disk. But you must understand some of the things that the program does. In particular, you need to know how to switch banks, and how to store and retrieve a new character set in memory. Otherwise, you won't be able to write programs which take advantage of your new character set.

Six Steps for Building an Alternate Character Set

1. First, choose the addresses you'll use for the character set and video memory in the bank you're switching to.
2. Second, shift the end of the BASIC workspace below these addresses.
3. Third, copy the old Commodore character set into the area of memory where you'll build your new character set. This way, you'll only have to modify those particular characters that you want to look different.
4. Fourth, tell the video chip which bank of memory you're using.
5. Fifth, reset a pointer to shift video memory into the new memory bank.
6. Sixth, tell the video chip the addresses where video memory and the character set have been moved to.

When choosing memory addresses for the character set and video memory, bear in mind that:

7. the character set *must* begin at an address that is evenly divisible by 2048, and there must be 2K of memory above this address, not used for anything else;
8. the new video memory *must* begin at an address which is evenly divisible by 1024, and there must be 1K of memory above this address, not used for anything else;
9. video memory and character memory *must* both be in the same bank.

Character Set Demonstration Program

Here's a short demonstration program which uses these steps very simply, to show how easy they are. I'm using D as a constant identifying the memory address from which the old Commodore character set is to be copied. This address is always 53248. (This address normally contains other data, but during the copying operation, the Commodore character set is superimposed in the 4K of memory from 53248 upward.)

Insert your own values for the variables as desired. EW must be an address evenly divisible by 256.

```
10 EW=(NEW END OF WORKSPACE)
20 POKE 56,(EW/256):CLR
30 D=53248
40 B=(YOUR CHOICE OF MEMORY BANK: 0, 1, 2, OR 3)
50 C=(STARTING ADDRESS FOR NEW CHARACTER SET)
60 VA=(STARTING ADDRESS FOR NEW VIDEO MEMORY)
70 POKE 56334,0
80 POKE 1,PEEK(1) AND 251
90 FOR N=0 TO 2047
100 POKE C+N,PEEK(D+N)
110 NEXT N
120 POKE 1,PEEK(1) OR 4
130 POKE 56334,1
140 POKE 56576,(23-B)
150 POKE 648,(VA/256)
160 POKE 53272,(VA/64)+(C/1024)-(B*272)
170 PRINT CHR$(147)CHR$(8)
```

In my memory setup, in Figure 9.1, EW = 32768, B = 2, C = 34816, and VA = 33792. You can use these values if you like.

Line 70 switches off the computer keyboard, which is necessary before copying the old character set to the new location. Line 130 switches the keyboard back on again.

Lines 80 and 120 use a kind of statement we haven't dealt with before. Type these lines exactly as they appear. Line 80 makes the Commodore character set available for copying. Line 120 terminates this copying mode.

Lines 90, 100, and 110 do the copying, by POKEing into memory each value of the Commodore character set that the program PEEKs from address D upward.

Line 140 tells the video chip to look at the new bank you have chosen.

Line 150 shifts video memory.

Line 160 tells the video chip where video memory and the new character set have been relocated. Take VA, divide it by 64, add C divided by 1024, and subtract B multiplied by 272. POKE the result into 53272.

The *Commodore 64 Programmer's Reference Guide* will give you a different procedure for doing all this. But I think the method I have described is much simpler.

Lastly, line 170 clears the screen and stops the user from selecting the second character set, since only one of the two Commodore sets has been copied into memory.

Using the Demonstration Program

First save this program, in case you made any typing errors, and then run it. Nothing will happen for about twenty seconds, while the program copies the Commodore character set. Then the screen blinks and clears. You're now ready to modify the character set.

If the screen doesn't clear, or if no letters appear on the screen when you type on the keyboard, you made a programming error. Turn off the computer, turn it back on, reload your program, and look for mistakes.

If the program has run correctly, you can now modify Commodore characters and see the result instantly. For instance, to modify letter A, type, in immediate mode:

FOR N = C + 8 TO C + 17:POKE N,255:NEXT

(I'm assuming you have just run the demonstration program, so the computer still knows what value you assigned to C. If in doubt, type:

PRINT C

and press RETURN, to make sure that C has not been reset to 0. If it has been reset, you should substitute for C, in the above line, the numerical value you established for it on line 50 of the demonstration program.)

You will see the result immediately in the A of the computer's READY prompt. Its eight rows of dots have all been changed to code 255, which means, all-dots-filled-in. A has become a solid rectangle! But it still *functions* as an A.

Adding to the Program

Add the following lines to the demonstration program, so you can properly redefine any characters you choose and then save your revised alphabet on disk or tape:

```
200 INPUT"MODIFY CHARACTER NUMBER";CN
210 CX=C+8*CN
220 FOR N=0 TO 7
230 PRINT"NEW CODE (0-255) FOR ROW"N;
240 INPUT K
250 POKE CX+N,K
260 NEXT N
270 POKE 55296+199,0
280 POKE VA+199,CN
300 PRINT:PRINT"MODIFY ANOTHER?":PRINT
310 GET A$:IF A$="" THEN 310
320 IF A$<>"Y" AND A$<>"N" THEN 310
330 IF A$="Y" THEN 200
400 INPUT"FILE NAME FOR CHARACTERS";F$
410 OPEN 2,8,2,"@0:"+F$+",S,W"
420 FOR N=C TO C+2047
430 PRINT#2,CHR$(PEEK(N));
440 NEXT N
450 CLOSE 2
```

Cassette users must use a different line 410:

410 OPEN 2,1,2, + F$

This is a very primitive program. It makes you look up the ASCII POKE code of each character you want to modify, as listed in Appendix C. Then, you have to figure out, and type in, the number for the dot-pattern of each of the eight rows defining the new character. (Use the pattern-matching chart in Appendix N to find your code numbers.) The character is then POKEd in at the side of the screen, so you can see what you've done—after you've done it.

The Character Generator program in Appendix U enables you to forget all about code numbers, and manipulate a video image till it looks the way you want it. The program is much longer, but much easier to use. At the same time, you can still find in it the same bank-switching and character-set-copying routines, on lines 5000 and 6300, respectively.

If you want to use your new character set in some other program that you write, you should include the following routine in your program, to load your character set and switch banks.

(Do not add these new lines to the end of the demonstration program. Save that if you wish, then type NEW.)

```
50000 EW=(NEW END OF WORKSPACE)
50010 POKE 56,(EW/256):CLR
50020 D=53248
50030 B=(YOUR CHOICE OF MEMORY BANK: 0, 1, 2, OR 3)
50040 C=(STARTING ADDRESS FOR NEW CHARACTER SET)
50050 VA=(STARTING ADDRESS FOR NEW VIDEO MEMORY)
50060 INPUT"FILE NAME";F$
50100 OPEN 2,8,2,"0:"+F$+",S,R"
50110 FOR N=0 TO 2047
50120 GET#2,A$
50130 POKE C+N,ASC(A$+CHR$(0))
50140 NEXT N
50150 CLOSE 2
50200 POKE 56576,(23-B)
50210 POKE 648,(VA/256)
50220 POKE 53272,(VA/64)+(C/1024)-(B*272)
50230 PRINT CHR$(147)CHR$(8)
```

As before, cassette users must substitute a different OPEN statement:

50100 OPEN 2,1,0,+F$

Note that the variable set-up and the bank-switching are identical to lines 10 through 60 and 140 through 170 in the character set demonstration program. This time, however, we're loading the new character set instead of copying the old Commodore characters into the new location to be modified.

I've used high line numbers because I assume you'll put this routine out of the way at the bottom of your programs. Naturally, you can use whatever line numbers you like.

You can't make this routine a subroutine, ending in RETURN, because the statement CLR clears the computer's memory of any preceding GOSUB statement. So you get to the start of this routine with GOTO 50000, and end it with another GOTO. Also, remember CLR clears all variables, so define your variables and constants in program lines that are executed *after* this routine, not before it.

The strange expression, ASC(A$+CHR$(0)) is necessary, instead of the simpler form ASC(A$), because when the computer GETs an A$ whose ASCII value is 0, it converts that A$ into ""—a string of zero length. If you try to take the ASCII value of such a string, you get an error message.

A Few Words of Caution

First, remember that, having repositioned video memory, you won't see any results if you POKE addresses in the old location of video memory. POKE 1024 won't do a thing, because video memory doesn't begin at 1024 any more. However, as mentioned, it is good practice always to define the start of video memory with a constant such as VA, and then specify all video locations by adding a number to that constant; e.g., POKE VA+400 or POKE VA+X. This way, to transfer your routines to a different program, you'll only have to change the value of VA, instead of retyping a whole lot of numbers.

Second, if you change the start of video memory, you must change the "color constant" too. In other words, to find the color address that corresponds with a video address, you don't add 54272 any more. To figure the new value for the Color Constant, simply perform the calculation CC = CA − VA, where CA is 55296, as always, and VA is the starting address of your new video memory.

Remember to include in any program with your new characters the PRINT CHR$(8) statement, to prevent the user from selecting the second optional character set, which has not been copied or loaded into memory.

When modifying characters, you'll suffer less eyestrain if you use a black and white monitor, rather than a color monitor. Also, bear in mind that characters whose vertical lines are two dots wide will look better on a color monitor than characters whose vertical lines are only one dot wide.

Avoid redefining characters 32 (blank space) and 160 (solid pixel). The Commodore 64 uses these characters for its flashing cursor. Change them, and the cursor will look very strange. The Character Generator program includes a trap to prevent you from changing these characters accidentally, on lines 3230 and 3240.

Lastly, after you run any program that switches banks or uses redefined characters, you *must* turn off the computer and then turn it on again, before you run any other program, to reset your changes to normal. As with the Headline Generator, things may be left behind in memory that will get in your way if you don't do this.

The Character Generator Program

The listing for the Character Generator which is shown in action in Figure 10.3, appears in Appendix U. Compare it with the listing for the Headline Generator in Appendix T. You'll see many similarities.

In Appendix Q you'll find my suggestion for a complete new character set, including lowercase letters with proper ascenders and descenders, uppercase letters with standard ASCII codes instead of Commodore's non-standard POKE codes, and useful graphics symbols.

These symbols include curves and varying wedge shapes that allow you to build a truly elegant display alphabet. I've included such an alphabet in Appendix R, of big letters composed of the new graphics characters. It's a great improvement over display alphabets that can be built with the old Commodore graphics characters.

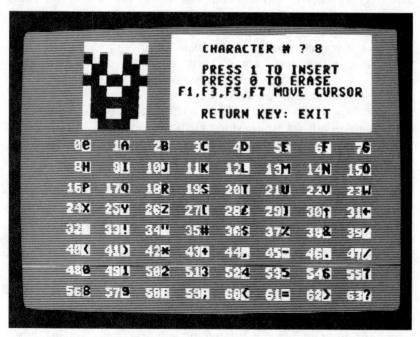

Figure 10.3: The Character Generator at work, creating an alien from the letter H.

Summary

This chapter has explained:

- How the video chip "looks" at one bank of memory at a time.
- How to switch banks and copy the Commodore character set.
- How to create your own character set.
- How to save and reload your character set.

ELEVEN
Sprites: The Final Confusing Facts Explained

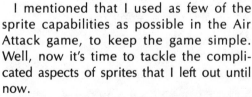

I mentioned that I used as few of the sprite capabilities as possible in the Air Attack game, to keep the game simple. Well, now it's time to tackle the complicated aspects of sprites that I left out until now.

Figure 11.1 is a complete listing of all the addresses that control sprites or are used as sprite registers that I have not yet discussed. I'm going to go through these addresses one by one.

After I've dealt with them all, I'll explain how sprites can produce actual Disney-style cartoon-character animation on your video screen. Would you believe a little running man, with moving arms and legs? The principles are simple, and the programming is simple, too.

Doubling Height and Width

I've already explained the X Distance Exceeds 255 register, and the on/off register. But how about the double-height register, at VC + 23? (Remember that I'm defining VC as 53248, the start of the Video Chip.)

Sprites can be doubled in height if you POKE the sum of their bit values into VC + 23. You can also double their width, by POKEing the sum of their bit values into VC + 29. Or, you can POKE both registers, and double height and width both at once.

Doubling the height of a sprite distorts its image, of course—it stretches it vertically. Each bit of data that used to define one dot now defines two dots. If you double the width, the same kind of thing occurs, and if you double both height and width, each bit of data that defined one dot now defines *four* dots. This means the image isn't as detailed, but that's only noticeable in a monochrome display. You won't be bothered by the loss of detail on a color video screen.

When a sprite is doubled in height and width, it becomes six pixels wide and slightly more than five pixels high. If you put all eight sprites

ADDRESS	FUNCTION
VC + 16	X Distance Exceeds 255 register
VC + 21	Sprite on/off register
VC + 23	Double-height register
VC + 27	Sprite-to-pixel priority register
VC + 28	Multicolor sprite on/off register
VC + 29	Double-width register
VC + 30	Sprite-to-sprite collision register
VC + 31	Sprite-to-pixel collision register
VC + 37	Color #1 of multicolor sprites
VC + 38	Color #2 of multicolor sprites
VC + 39	Main color of sprite 0
VC + 40	Main color of sprite 1
VC + 41	Main color of sprite 2
VC + 42	Main color of sprite 3
VC + 43	Main color of sprite 4
VC + 44	Main color of sprite 5
VC + 45	Main color of sprite 6
VC + 46	Main color of sprite 7

Figure 11.1: Special-purpose sprite registers and their addresses.

together, you can cover about a quarter of the total screen area with them. They could be used, for instance, to create a custom-designed, highly colored landscape at the bottom of the screen, which would be easier than using the high-res mode described in Chapter Twelve, and probably easier than defining a different character set.

Sprite-to-Pixel Priorities

The next important address is VC + 27, the sprite-to-pixel priority register. Remember, back in Chapter One, I suggested you should think of characters in pixels as being "in front of" screen background color. Well, sprites usually appear "in front of" characters in pixels. In other words, when you move a sprite across an area of the screen where characters are displayed, the sprite will obscure the characters (see Figure 11.2). However, if you POKE the bit value of the sprite into

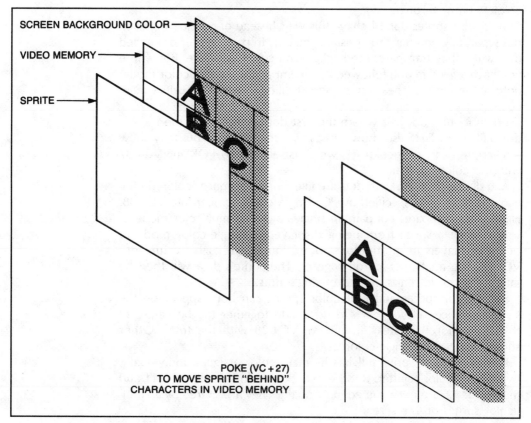

Figure 11.2: Sprites can move in front of or behind pixel.

VC+27, it will then appear to move behind characters in pixels on the screen. This means, for example, you could create a simple picture of a house in character graphics (perhaps using your own character set), and then have a sprite in the shape of a man "walk into" the house— i.e. disappear behind the wall of POKEd graphics characters. He could then appear at a window, if there is one; "transparent" areas of the pixels will allow the sprite to show through.

Multicolor Sprites

With multicolor sprites, things become unpleasantly complicated. You'll recall that each sprite in Air Attack was given one color by POKEing a number into its color register, these registers being at VC+39 through VC+46. Solid dots of the sprite appear in that color on the screen. "Empty" dots are "transparent" and allow background color to show through.

Multicolor sprites don't behave this way. Instead of considering each dot separately, you have to consider the dots in pairs. A pair of unfilled dots will still be transparent to background color, as before. But where you have a filled-in dot, followed by an empty dot, in multicolor mode, *both* of these dots appear on the screen filled in with the sprite's main color.

What about a dot pair where the first dot is empty, and the second dot is filled in? That also shows up as two colored dots, but they show a different color: multicolor #1, which is selected by POKEing VC+37 with the color number.

And dot pairs where both dots are filled in? They appear colored multicolor #2, which is specified by POKEing a color number into VC+38. Figure 11.3 compares dot-pairs in single-color and multicolor mode.

To change a sprite from being displayed in single-color mode to being displayed in multicolor mode, you POKE its bit value into VC+28, the multicolor on/off register. The sprite's data will then be interpreted in dot pairs instead of single dots.

Single-color sprites and multicolor sprites can both appear on the screen at once; all you have to do is add together the bit values of the multicolored sprites, and POKE VC+28 with the total. Other sprites will remain single-colored.

Each multicolor sprite still has its main color assigned individually, by its usual color register. But the two extra colors, multicolor #1 and multicolor #2, are not assigned individually. They are shared by *all* multicolor sprites on the screen.

The advantage of using multicolor sprites is obvious: you can have three colors on each sprite, instead of one. However, you lose horizontal detail, because the data is now interpreted and displayed as colored *pairs* of dots. Single dots cannot be displayed.

This doesn't matter so long as your sprite can have a boxy, angular appearance. But when you want curves or diagonal lines, the multicolor mode gives a low-resolution "staircase" effect, especially if you double the height or width of the sprite.

The Sprite Generator Program

Personally, I find it difficult to draw multicolor sprites on paper and have them look the way I expect when they appear on the screen.

My answer to this problem was to create a program to handle it for me. You'll find its listing in Appendix V, and it's called—guess what?—a Sprite Generator.

Now, there are lots of sprite control programs advertised in the computer magazines, but I like to think mine's a bit better than most of them. It is shown in action in Plate 8. It allows you to draw and edit

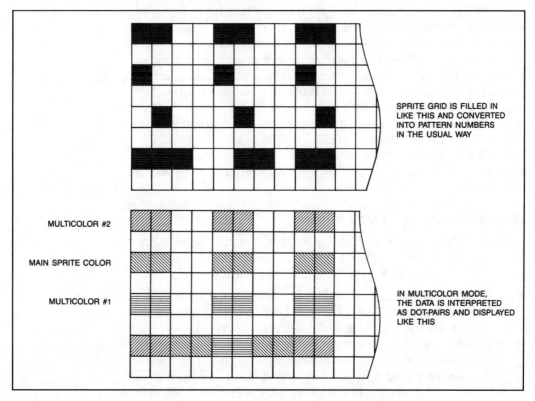

SPRITE GRID IS FILLED IN
LIKE THIS AND CONVERTED
INTO PATTERN NUMBERS
IN THE USUAL WAY

MULTICOLOR #2

MAIN SPRITE COLOR

MULTICOLOR #1

IN MULTICOLOR MODE,
THE DATA IS INTERPRETED
AS DOT-PAIRS AND DISPLAYED
LIKE THIS

Figure 11.3: How dot pairs are colored on the screen in sprite multicolor mode.

your sprite eight times actual size, in whatever colors you want (multi-color or single color). You can change colors and have them copied into the display very quickly. As you edit this display, using cursor-control commands, you also see your actual sprite in the corner of the screen in its normal size, and expanded-normal size, continuously updated. (Most sprite-building programs don't show you the actual sprite until after you've finished creating it, and they make you wait while the big image is "scanned" to create the little image.)

The program allows you to merge sprite data files, delete data sets, change background color, and mix single-color and multicolor sprites. You can build a total of 48 sets of sprite data, and save them on tape or disk as a series of bytes, rather than as decimal numbers, which take much more file space and are slower to load and save.

You can reload your sprite data into future programs. At the beginning of each file of sprite data, the program places a number indicating how many sets of data are in that file, so you know how many data sets to load. Since the 64th byte of data for each sprite is not normally used for anything, my program makes it a 1 if the sprite is to be displayed in single-color mode, and a 2 if the sprite is to be multicolored. Any program that uses the data can include a statement for interpreting the 64th byte and POKEing the multicolor on/off register accordingly.

I created the Sprite Generator for my own purposes, before I even thought of writing this book. So this program is not listed in exactly the same format as the others that I have supplied. The names of the constants aren't the same, and some of the program lines are much longer than 39 characters. It's such a complicated program that I don't have space to explain every detail of it, so you can either type it yourself in blind faith, or order it ready-recorded from me on tape or disk (see Appendix Y).

Accessing Sprite Data Files

To write programs that load the sprite data files created by the program, you need something like the load routine in the Character Generator and Headline Generator programs. Specifically:

1. Open the file and use INPUT#2,N where N is the number of sprite data sets. The numbering begins with Set #0, so if there is a 0 at the beginning of the file, that means in fact there is a single set of sprite data in the file. If a 5 is at the beginning of a file, there are six sets of data, and so on.
2. Use the GET#2,A$ statement to load the rest of the file. Each sprite consists of 64 bytes, so you GET#2,A$ 64 times to load one sprite, 128 times for two sprites, and so on.

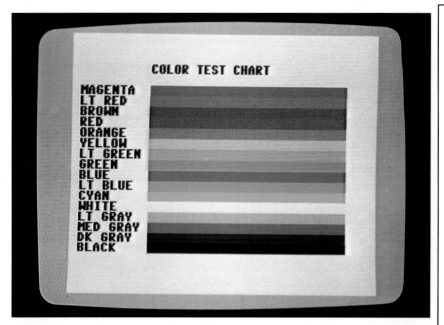

Plate 1. Color Test Chart
A test chart is very little trouble to program, and allows you to adjust a color monitor or TV properly so that a game will look its best.

Plate 2. Sprite Headline
Each letter is one sprite, in multicolor mode, double size, created with the Sprite Generator program listed in Chapter Eleven. The rainbow bands of color are created by POKEing addresses in video memory with ASCII 160 (solid pixel) and then POKEing color memory with colors 6, 14, 3, 7, 8, 2, and 9.

Plate 3. House
The standard Commodore graphics characters can produce lifelike pictures of objects composed of straight lines. This house was drawn with the Graphics Generator program described in Chapter Five. The screen background is white; everything else is superimposed. The man running in the front door is one of the sprites shown in Chapter eleven.

Plate 4. Rocket
True high-res graphics are complicated to program. As a shortcut, sprites can be put together like this. The range of colors is limited in that no sprite can have more than three colors, and two of those colors must be the same for all the multicolor sprites. However, solid pixels can be POKEd into video memory behind the sprites and colored by POKEing color memory, as was done here to create the gray smoke and the white highlights.

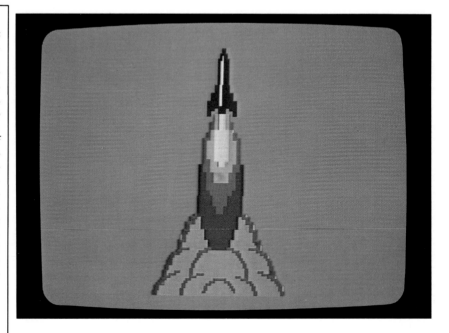

Plate 5. Script
Sprites allow you to produce curved shapes that are impossible using standard Commodore graphics characters. Here, each letter is a double-size sprite, created with the Sprite Generator program described in Chapter Eleven. Placing the sprites accurately on the screen produces the illusion of continuity, although the changes in color show where one sprite ends and the next begins.

HEADINGS IN...

script

...USING SPRITES

1:38 TIME   12 HITS

Plate 6. Air Attack landscape
This optional enhancement of the Air Attack program adds a city landscape and streamers of cloud behind the airplane, gun, and bullet. The landscape serves merely to make the screen look more interesting; it does not affect the game. The gun, bullet, and airplane are the sprites described in Chapter Six. Here, their size has been doubled for the sake of clarity.

Plate 7. Air Attack heading
The Character Generator program described in Chapter Eight makes it easy to create bold headlines using standard Commodore graphics characters.

Plate 8. Sprite Generator in action
Using the Sprite Generator program described in Chapter Eleven, the picture of the running man is being edited on the right-hand side of the screen, while the four small pictures on the left instantly show how the actual sprite looks as each change is made. This program can hold up to 48 sprites, in multicolor and/or single color mode, and can edit and chain together files of sprites on disk or tape.

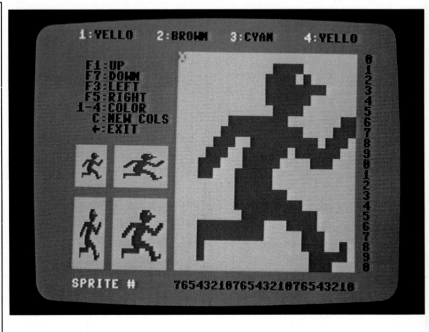

3. Each time you GET#2, A$, POKE the ASC of each A$ into the memory you have chosen for sprite data, byte by byte. Remember to use the expression:

ASC(A$ + CHR$(0))

rather than simply ASC(A$) so you don't get an error message if the ASCII value of A$ is zero.

The load routine on lines 600 through 660 of the Sprite Aid program described below will serve the purpose quite well. This program creates exactly the same kind of sprite data files on tape or disk as the Sprite Generator, so the load routine is basically the same, and you can use it as a model if you write your own programs that load sprite data.

```
597 REM
598 REM---------- Load Data -----------
599 REM
600 PRINT C$:INPUT"FILE NAME";F$
610 OPEN 2,8,2,"0:"+F$+",S,R"
620 INPUT#2,S
630 FOR A=SD TO SD+64*S
640 GET#2,A$:POKE A,ASC(A$+CHR$(0))
650 NEXT A
660 CLOSE 2:RETURN
```

The Sprite Aid Program

If my Sprite Generator looks too big and elaborate for your needs, you can experiment with a much simpler program that I am listing here, in Figure 11.4, called Sprite Aid. It doesn't do as much as the Sprite Generator, and isn't quite as easy to use. But Sprite Aid is much shorter, and it *will* display the animated, running figure that I promised at the beginning of this chapter.

In Sprite Aid, S is the number of sets of sprite data. S can range from

```
10 GOTO 1000
97 REM
98 REM--------- Create Sprite ---------
99 REM
100 PRINT C$:POKE SP,S+240:GOSUB 800
110 FOR A=0 TO 60 STEP 3
120 FOR B=0 TO 2
130 PRINT"WHAT'S THE DOT-PATTERN NUMBER
140 PRINT"FOR THE "S$(B)" SEGMENT
150 PRINT"OF ROW";(A/3)+1;
160 GOSUB 900:NEXT B:NEXT A
170 PRINT:PRINT"EDIT THE SPRITE?"
180 GOSUB 5000:IF YN$="N" THEN 300
190 GOSUB 200:GOTO 300
197 REM
198 REM---------- Edit --------------
```

Figure 11.4: The Sprite Aid Program.

```
199 REM
200 PRINT C$:B=0:FOR A=0 TO 62
210 X=SD+S*64+A:P=PEEK(X):Q=255-P
220 FOR D=1 TO 2
230 POKE X,Q:FOR E=1 TO 50:NEXT E
240 POKE X,P:FOR E=1 TO 50:NEXT E
250 NEXT D:A$="":PRINT"EDIT: SPRITE"S
260 PRINT:PRINT"X=EXIT    RTN=NEXT"
265 INPUT"OR NEW VALUE";A$
270 IF A$="" THEN PRINT:GOTO 290
280 IF A$="X" THEN A=62:PRINT:GOTO 290
285 C=VAL(A$):GOSUB 910
290 NEXT A:A$="":PRINT:PRINT:RETURN
297 REM
298 REM---------- Review ? ----------
299 REM
300 PRINT C$:IF S<15 THEN 330
310 PRINT"NO ROOM FOR MORE SPRITES."
320 GOTO 360
330 PRINT"CREATE A NEW SPRITE?":PRINT
340 GOSUB 5000: IF YN$="N" THEN 360
350 S=S+1:GOTO 100
360 PRINT"REVIEW YOUR SPRITES?":PRINT
370 GOSUB 5000:IF YN$="N" THEN 500
400 R=S:S=0
410 PRINT C$"REVIEW SPRITE DATA":PRINT
420 PRINT"E=EDIT    X=EXIT    SPC=NEXT"
430 POKE SP,240+S
440 GET A$:IF A$="" THEN 440
450 IF A$="E"THENPRINT:GOSUB200:GOTO410
460 IF A$="X" THEN S=R:PRINT:GOTO 300
470 S=S+1:IF S>R THEN S=0
480 GOTO 430
497 REM
498 REM--------- Save Data ---------
499 REM
500 PRINT"SAVE YOUR SPRITES?":PRINT
510 GOSUB 5000:IF YN$="N" THEN END
520 INPUT"FILE NAME";F$
530 OPEN 2,8,2,"@0:"+F$+",S,W"
540 PRINT#2,S
550 FOR A=SD TO SD+64*S
560 PRINT#2,CHR$(PEEK(A));
570 NEXT A
580 CLOSE 2:END
597 REM
598 REM---------- Load Data -----------
599 REM
600 PRINT C$:INPUT"FILE NAME";F$
610 OPEN 2,8,2,"0:"+F$+",S,R"
620 INPUT#2,S
630 FOR A=SD TO SD+64*S
640 GET#2,A$:POKE A,ASC(A$+CHR$(0))
650 NEXT A
660 CLOSE 2:RETURN
797 REM
798 REM------- Erase Sprite Data ------
799 REM
```

Figure 11.4: The Sprite Aid Program (continued).

```
800 FOR A=SD+64*S TO SD+64*S+62
810 POKE A,255
820 NEXT A:POKE A,0:RETURN
897 REM
898 REM--------- Get Code # -----------
899 REM
900 INPUT C
910 IF C<=255 AND C=>0 THEN 960
920 PRINT"THE NUMBER MUST BE NO LESS
930 PRINT"THAN 0, NO GREATER THAN 255.
940 PRINT:PRINT"WHAT'S THE NUMBER";
950 GOTO 900
960 POKE SD+S*64+A+B,C
970 PRINT:RETURN
997 REM
998 REM---------- Constants -----------
999 REM
1000 VA=1024:VC=53248:SP=2040
1010 SD=15360
1050 S$(0)="LEFT"
1051 S$(1)="MIDDLE"
1052 S$(2)="RIGHT"
1060 C$=CHR$(147)
1097 REM
1098 REM--------- Variables -----------
1099 REM
1100 A=0:B=0:C=0:D=0:E=0:P=0:Q=0
1110 R=0:S=0
1150 A$="":YN$="":F$=""
1197 REM
1198 REM-------- Set Up Sprite --------
1199 REM
1200 PRINT C$;CHR$(144)
1210 POKE 53280,1:POKE 53281,1
1220 POKE VC,40:POKE VC+1,50
1230 POKE VC+16,1:POKE VC+23,1
1240 POKE VC+29,1:POKE VC+39,0
1250 POKE 2040,240
1997 REM
1998 REM-------- Instructions ---------
1999 REM
2100 PRINT"THIS IS A PRIMITIVE PROGRAM
2110 PRINT"FOR BUILDING SINGLE-COLOR
2120 PRINT"SPRITES.":PRINT:PRINT
2130 PRINT"YOU WILL BE ASKED TO TYPE
2140 PRINT"THE 63 NUMBERS THAT DEFINE
2150 PRINT"EACH SPRITE, AND YOU'LL SEE
2160 PRINT"THE SPRITE GROW AS YOU TYPE
2170 PRINT:PRINT
2200 PRINT"DO YOU WANT TO RETRIEVE
2210 PRINT"AN OLD FILE OF SPRITES?
2220 GOSUB 5000:POKE VC+21,1
2230 IF YN$="Y" THEN GOSUB 600:GOTO 300
2240 GOTO 100
4999 REM-------- Get Yes or No
5000 GET YN$:IF YN$="" THEN 5000
5010 IF YN$<>"Y" AND YN$<>"N" THEN 5000
5020 RETURN
```

Figure 11.4: The Sprite Aid Program (continued).

0 to 15. SD is the Sprite Data starting address in computer memory, defined on line 1010. To avoid the fuss of bank switching, I'm using the top kilobyte of bank 0 for this data.

Lines 1200 through 1250 prepare the sprite display, before a sprite is actually turned on. The sprite position is set (at the top-right corner of the screen), the sprite is made double-height and double-width (to be as easy as possible to see in detail), the color is set to black, and the pointer for sprite 0 is POKEd with 240, which identifies the first (zero) set of sprite data.

The program shows its instructions, then asks you whether to load an old file, or start a new sprite. At this point, on line 2220, sprite 0 is turned on. No data has yet been put in memory, so sprite 0 is displayed as a random jumble of dots. If you now load a file of sprite data, you'll see the sprite pattern "fill up" as the data is loaded and POKEd into memory. On the other hand, if you create a new sprite, the sprite image is initialized solid black, to define its edges, and the program executes the "create sprite" routine on lines 100 through 190.

This routine requires you to type the code number for each set of 8 dots in the sprite. Screen prompts help you to keep track of which row of numbers you're entering from the sprite grid, and which of the three grid columns you're dealing with—left, middle, or right.

If you use this program and type a wrong number by mistake, continue with the rest of the numbers. After you've entered all of them, the program lets you go back and edit your mistakes. It flashes each sprite segment in turn, and lets you revise it by typing in a new number, or move on to the next segment by pressing the RETURN key. You'll find all this easier on a monochrome monitor, which shows more detail than a color screen. If you only have a color monitor or TV, turn the color control down. At any time, you can exit from the edit mode by typing X and pressing RETURN.

You can then type data for another sprite, or you can review your sprites. When you review, the data pointer is simply switched from one set of data to the next each time you touch the space bar. If you hold the space bar down, it starts to repeat, so the switching occurs fairly fast. When the pointer reaches the last set of data that you've defined, it resets back to the first set. So you see the images flash over and over again, in quick succession, in the top-right corner of the screen.

Now, what are you reminded of, when images flash in succession in one place on a screen? Did anyone say "animated movies"?

Principles of Animation

If you define several sets of sprite data so that each one shows a picture slightly different from the one before, and if you display those pictures in succession by switching the data pointer quickly, you'll get the illusion of motion.

Figure 11.5 shows five pictures of a running man, which will come to life when viewed in succession. I've included the pattern numbers that correspond with each picture; all you have to do is get the Sprite Aid program running (or the Sprite Generator, if you're more ambitious), and then type the numbers (or use cursor-control to draw the running man on the screen, if you have the Sprite Generator).

Review the sprite pictures and you'll see the little fellow running quite realistically. He's running in one place, of course, but you could write a program to move him along, simply by incrementing his X distance each time you reset the data pointer. An increment of 2 or 3 dots works well. I've used this running man in a video game of my own, to

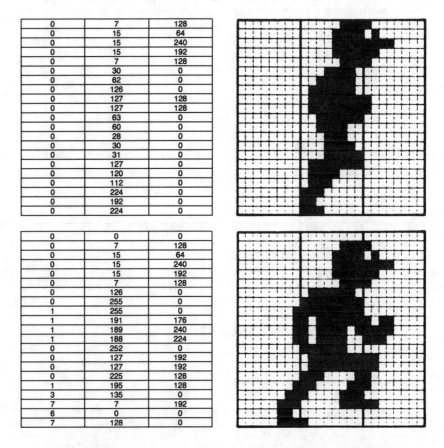

0	7	128
0	15	64
0	15	240
0	15	192
0	7	128
0	30	0
0	62	0
0	126	0
0	127	128
0	127	128
0	63	0
0	60	0
0	28	0
0	30	0
0	31	0
0	127	0
0	120	0
0	112	0
0	224	0
0	192	0
0	224	0

0	0	0
0	7	128
0	15	64
0	15	240
0	15	192
0	7	128
0	126	0
0	255	0
1	255	0
1	191	176
1	189	240
1	188	224
0	252	0
0	127	192
0	127	192
0	225	128
1	195	128
3	135	0
7	7	192
6	0	0
7	128	0

Figures 11.5: Running sprite.

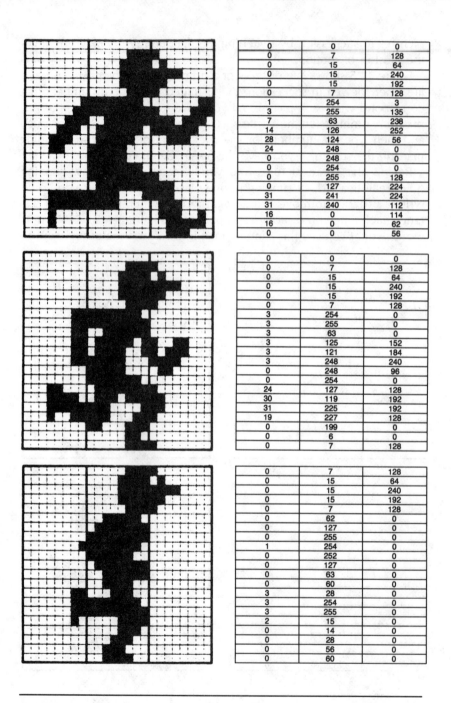

0	0	0
0	7	128
0	15	64
0	15	240
0	15	192
0	7	128
1	254	3
3	255	135
7	63	238
14	126	252
28	124	56
24	248	0
0	248	0
0	254	0
0	255	128
0	127	224
31	241	224
31	240	112
16	0	114
16	0	62
0	0	56

0	0	0
0	7	128
0	15	64
0	15	240
0	15	192
0	7	128
3	254	0
3	255	0
3	63	0
3	125	152
3	121	184
3	248	240
0	248	96
0	254	0
24	127	128
30	119	192
31	225	192
19	227	128
0	199	0
0	6	0
0	7	128

0	7	128
0	15	64
0	15	240
0	15	192
0	7	128
0	62	0
0	127	0
0	255	0
1	254	0
0	252	0
0	127	0
0	63	0
0	60	0
3	28	0
3	254	0
3	255	0
2	15	0
0	14	0
0	28	0
0	56	0
0	60	0

Figures 11.5: Running sprite (continued).

teach people to type. You're welcome to use him in any game that you make up youself.

How did I create his image? I made a few photocopies of the sprite grid, and sketched a running figure lightly in pencil on each. I saw which squares my sketch covered, and inked them with a felt-tip marker. Then I used the Sprite Generator program to transfer the inked images onto the screen, one grid-square at a time. Since the program eliminates all typing of numbers, this was very quick.

Then I reviewed the images in succession, to see if they looked realistic. I had never attempted any animation before, so I was doing everything by guesswork. I had to modify my sprite somewhat—he flung his arms out too quickly, and his leg movements weren't quite right. I discovered that his foot touching the ground should move back by an equal increment between each frame and the next. I also realized that when people run, their heads bob up and down, so I added that feature.

You can develop animated figures in the same way. Remember, I had no experience at all when I did mine. Just give it a try; the results could be much more impressive than you expect.

Summary

This final chapter on the subject of sprites has explained:

- How to double height and width.
- How to make sprites move behind characters that are in video memory.
- How to program multicolored sprites.
- How to load and save files of sprite data.
- How to use sprites for animation.

TWELVE
Beyond BASIC

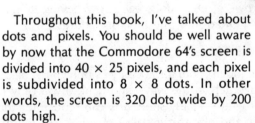

Throughout this book, I've talked about dots and pixels. You should be well aware by now that the Commodore 64's screen is divided into 40 × 25 pixels, and each pixel is subdivided into 8 × 8 dots. In other words, the screen is 320 dots wide by 200 dots high.

Using sprites and alternate character sets, I've suggested techniques to turn individual dots on and off. Always, we've considered dots in rows of eight at a time, the pattern of each eight dots being defined by a number from 0 to 255. The pattern chart in Appendix N shows these patterns and their numbers.

High-Res Graphics

Wouldn't it be nice if we could write simple commands to turn on individual dots, or strings of them, anywhere in the whole screen? This is what's usually meant by *high-res* (high resolution) *graphics:* a system where you control the contents and color of the video picture in dot detail.

Well, the Commodore 64 does offer this kind of system . . . in its own fashion. You'll be unsurprised to hear that it is not very easy to control.

To turn on high-res mode:

POKE 53265,PEEK(53265) OR 32

which tells the computer not to get its video data from ordinary video memory any more. Also:

POKE 53272,PEEK(53272) OR N

where N × 1024 is the starting address in memory at which you'll store your high-res graphics data, and N is a multiple of 8.

Standard high-res mode is very much like having the screen completely filled with programmable graphics characters. You'll remember that to devise your own character set, you POKE its data into a stretch of memory, and tell the video chip where to look for it. Well, you do much the same thing in high-res graphics, except that you need not just 2048 bytes, but *8000* bytes of video memory, to create 1000 "characters," one filling each pixel of the screen. As before, each "character" consists of eight rows of eight dots, each row having its pattern specified by a number POKEd into one memory address.

Limits of Space and Time

Bank 2 doesn't have enough room for 8000 bytes of high-res data (the character set ROM image gets in the way), and bank 0 will only have enough room if your program is fairly short. You can reduce the length of the BASIC workspace and place your data in bank 1, but there's no ROM image of the standard character set in bank 1, so in addition to your high-res data you will have to copy the character set into this bank of memory. All this will take time if you do it using BASIC. If you load 8000 bytes of high-res screen memory from a disk, plus 2048 bytes to define a character set, that will take about three minutes. From tape, it will take two or three times as long. Most people won't want to wait that long, no matter *how* wonderful your program is!

These are some of the problems of high-res graphics. Now here are some of the solutions.

First, instead of thinking in terms of loading a whole screen picture that you have previously prepared, you can begin by zeroing your high-res screen by POKEing each control address with a 0. (Remember, pattern number 0 consists of 8 empty dots.) Then you can have your program draw shapes, curves, whatever, by doing math calculations to control POKE routines such as are described in the *Commodore 64 Programmer's Reference Guide* on page 126. This will allow you to make some use of high-res, although it will still be very slow.

As for the problem of finding room for high-res memory, you can deal with this by *moving your BASIC program.* Yes, this is possible; you can locate the program at the beginning of bank 1, for instance, and use Bank 0 entirely for video data of various kinds.

Moving the BASIC program is not a very simple operation, but let's assume you do it. How do you then actually control high-res graphics?

Suppose your 8000 bytes of memory for graphics data begin at address A. The number in that address will determine the dot pattern on the top row of the top-left pixel of the screen. (I'm still talking in pixels, even though we're not using the old video memory any more, because Commodore high-res is organized as if pixels still exist as the basic building blocks of the video picture.)

The number in memory address A+1 will determine the dot pattern in the second row of the top-left pixel on the screen. And so on down to the eighth row, controlled by address A+7—as Figure 12.1 shows.

Now we move one pixel to the right. The top row of that pixel has its

A	A+8	A+16
A+1	A+9	A+17
A+2	A+10	A+18
A+3	A+11	A+19
A+4	A+12	A+20
A+5	A+13	A+21
A+6	A+14	
A+7	A+15	
A+320	A+328	
A+321	A+329	
A+322	A+330	
A+323	A+331	
A+324		
A+325		

Figure 12.1: Dot-rows in video pixels, and the memory addresses that control them in high-res mode, assuming A is the starting address of high-res data.

dot pattern controlled by memory address A+8, and so on. You see how this is almost exactly like filling the screen with programmable characters.

Unfortunately, this makes programming a real chore. The whole point of high-res graphics is to be able to draw thin lines and delicate shapes. But suppose you want a thin diagonal line running across the screen. First you have to find the memory address that controls each row of each pixel that the line crosses. Then each of those addresses will have to be POKEd with a code number, which you'll have to calculate or get from the pattern-matching chart in Appendix N. Since the screen is 200 dots high, you'll need at least 200 POKEs just to draw a single line.

The procedure can be systematized. You can work out a formula to find the address of each dot-row, and another formula to give you the right dot pattern. Commodore supplies such a formula on page 126 of the *Programmer's Reference Guide*. But it works slooooowly. It is of some interest, as a way of drawing a couple of demonstration lines or curves, provided the viewer isn't in an impatient mood. It is of no use at all for video games.

Coping with Color

There's another high-res snag that I haven't even mentioned yet, and that is color. As far as color is concerned, the screen is still divided into 1000 pixels. In each pixel, you can specify one color for each dot that's "filled in," and a second color (not necessarily screen background color) for each "empty" dot. You do this by POKEing numbers into what used to be video memory. You take each of the 1000 addresses from 1024 through 2023, decide the number of the color for filled-in dots in that pixel, and multiply that number by 16. You then add the color number you want for "empty dots" in that pixel, and POKE the sum of these numbers into the video address controlling that pixel.

Frankly, I don't think any of this is practical in BASIC. I won't even try to supply a demonstration program; it's a big hassle, and the results are not impressive.

Multicolor bit-mapping is even harder to deal with. In this mode, dots are considered in pairs, as they are with multicolor sprites. 0–0 dot pairs are assigned plain old screen background color. 1–1 dot pairs are assigned a color determined by POKEing plain old ordinary color memory. 1–0 and 0–1 dot pairs are colored according to the system just described, POKEing numbers into what used to be video memory.

BASIC Limitations

Why does it all have to be so complicated? For two reasons. First, Commodore kept the price of their computer low by economizing on their version of BASIC. They *could* have added new BASIC words such as PLOT, that activate extra built-in routines to do all your calculations for you. On more expensive computers, PLOT lets you specify the beginning of a high-res line, using a pair of numbers, like the distance numbers defining the position of a sprite. You then specify the end of the line in the same way, tell the computer to DRAWTO, and—instantly, the line appears, joining those two points. Another command specifies the color of the line.

Assembly Language

The other reason why high-res graphics seem to be so much trouble on this computer is that we're trying to cope with them in BASIC, when we should really be using assembly language. BASIC happens to be the easiest computer language to learn, which is why many computers have it built in. But it isn't the only computer language; there are dozens of others.

Assembly language is a way of writing coded commands for moving individual bytes inside computer memory, in and out of the CPU (Central Processing Unit). There are no short-cut words like PRINT; you have to spell out each tiny step in a code which the computer can understand one byte at a time. This is tedious, but the great advantage is speed: the computer doesn't have to interpret statements any more. *You're* talking *its* language, so it carries out your commands literally thousands of times faster than in BASIC. Many arcade games are written in assembly language. So are the games you buy on cartridges for home computers.

The POKE statement we have used so often in this book produces an effect that, in assembly language, is fairly simply controlled and very quickly executed. It's merely a matter of moving a byte of data from one place to another. Since so many of the graphics routines on the Commodore 64 require POKE statements, it almost looks as though this computer was designed by, and for, people who use assembly language.

For instance, to clear the screen in high-res mode, using BASIC you would have to write a loop to POKE a 0 into every one of the 8000 addresses that supply high-res video data. This routine would take perhaps thirty seconds to run. If you wrote it in assembly language, the programming would not be much more complicated, because this is the kind of task that assembly language does especially easily. And the operation would be carried out by the computer in a fraction of a second.

Should you try to learn assembly language yourself? It depends how interested you really are in computers, and how much free time you have. Also, you need a true aptitude for programming, since this language is much harder to understand than BASIC.

If you really want to write elaborate videogames, there's certainly no substitute for the speed of assembly language. You can write the opening of a game in BASIC, and then, when speed becomes important, switch the computer to machine-language routines which you wrote separately and loaded along with the BASIC part of your program.

There are some good introductory books that will help you understand assembly code. *Programming the 6502,* by Rodnay Zaks, is my favorite. Like this book, it's published by SYBEX.

But once you begin getting into machine code, computers are likely to become more than a hobby. The amount of time you will invest, and the quality of the results you will get, will make you want to start marketing your own programs. There are already thousands of people out there trying to do exactly that. Will your software really be better than theirs?

First, I think, you should practice more with BASIC. Even if the games run slowly, they'll help you estimate your own abilities to come up with new ideas and good-looking graphics.

Next, you should try some of the programming aids that are now being marketed for the Commodore 64. These are cartridges or programs on tape or disk that install extra machine-language routines to enhance Commodore BASIC, especially its graphics capabilities.

I haven't been able to try all these aids myself, so I can't give you a buyer's guide. But you should visit your local dealer and ask about the following:

>Basic Tools, by Comm∗Data
>
>SpriteByter, by FoxSoft
>
>Color Craft, by Sim Computer Products
>
>64 Panorama, by Midwest Micro
>
>Video/Music Support, by Commodore
>
>Spritemaster 64, by Access Software
>
>Screen-Graphics 64, and Sprite Aid, by Abacus
>
>GrafDOS, by Interesting Software
>
>Doodle!, by OMNI Unlimited

Some of these are sprite-building programs, similar to the Sprite Generator I have listed in this book. Others, including Basic Tools, Video/Music Support, and Screen-Graphics 64, help you to control high-res graphics and other advanced features which are theoretically available on the Commodore 64. And they greatly increase the speed of these features.

All "add-on" programming aids tend to suffer from some limitations, however. For instance, in order to make use of the code that you create while using one of the graphics aids, you may have to have in memory a kind of interpreter, which has to be loaded at the same time you load your graphics data. This takes up time and memory.

If you're seriously interested in graphics, you might try other brands of computer to see whether their enhanced versions of BASIC will be sufficient for your game-programming needs. Some have graphics that are much easier to program in BASIC than the Commodore 64, and respond more quickly.

Finally, after you've practiced a bit, joined user groups, exchanged programs with friends, and discovered the limits of your skills and your equipment—then, you may find that you can't settle for anything less than assembly language. At this point, you'll probably feel that computers have become an obsession you can't shake off. In which case, you won't need to make any decision about whether to go into programming professionally, because you simply won't be able to stop.

Either way, I hope you had fun with the game ideas in this book, and I hope you have more fun inventing your own.

Summary

This chapter has explained the following:

- How to turn high-res graphics on and off.
- How high-res mode resembles a screen full of programmable characters.
- How to accommodate high-res graphics in memory.
- How to control the contents of each high-res "pixel."
- How to add two more colors with multicolor bit-mapping.
- How other brands of BASIC work.

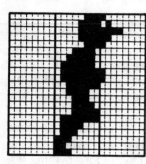

Appendix A
Color Code Numbers

To produce the color you want, POKE the appropriate memory address with the number of the color. POKE 53281 to determine screen background color. POKE 53280 to determine screen border color. POKE color memory (see Appendix F) to determine the color of an individual character on the screen. Video locations 1024 through 2023 (see video memory map in Appendix E) are colored by memory addresses 55296 through 56295.

 0 : Black
 1 : White
 2 : Red
 3 : Cyan (greenish blue)
 4 : Magenta (purplish red)
 5 : Green
 6 : Blue
 7 : Yellow

 8 : Orange
 9 : Brown
10 : Bright Red
11 : Dark Gray
12 : Medium Gray
13 : Bright Green
14 : Bright Blue
15 : Light Gray

Appendix B
Special CHR$ Codes

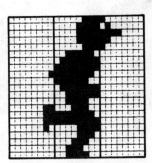

In the following tables, the code number, inserted in a PRINT CHR$( ) command, produces the special result.

Text Color

5 : White	151 : Dark Gray
28 : Red	152 : Medium Gray
30 : Green	153 : Bright Green
31 : Blue	154 : Bright Blue
129 : Orange	155 : Light Gray
144 : Black	156 : Magenta
149 : Brown	158 : Yellow
150 : Bright Red	159 : Cyan

Cursor Movement

17 : Down	145 : Up
29 : Right	157 : Left

Miscellaneous Keyboard Emulation

8 : Disable C= key and SHIFT key combination
9 : Enable C= key and SHIFT key combination
13 : Carriage Return + Line Feed
14 : Switch to Character Set Two
18 : Reverse video on
19 : Home Cursor (does not clear screen)
20 : Delete Previous Character
133 : Function key f1

134 : Function key f3
135 : Function key f5
136 : Function key f7
137 : Function key f2
138 : Function key f4
139 : Function key f6
140 : Function key f8
142 : Switch to Character Set One
146 : Reverse video off
147 : Home Cursor AND Clear Screen
148 : Insert Space (emulates SHIFTed INST/DEL)

Appendix C
Displayable Characters Using POKE Statements

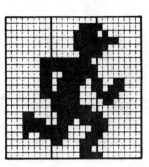

These are the characters you will see in response to the statement:

POKE V,N

where V is a video address, and N is the code number of the character.

Remember that on some models of the Commodore 64, color memory is automatically set to match the color of the screen background. This means that characters POKEd into video memory will be colored the same as their background, and will therefore be invisible until you POKE a contrasting color into color memory (see Appendix F). Remember that color memory resets itself to match screen background color every time you clear the screen on some models of the Commodore 64.

You can switch between the two character sets shown in the following pages by pressing the C= key while holding down a SHIFT key, or by using the statement:

PRINT CHR$(142)

to select Character Set One, or:

PRINT CHR$(14)

to select Character Set Two.

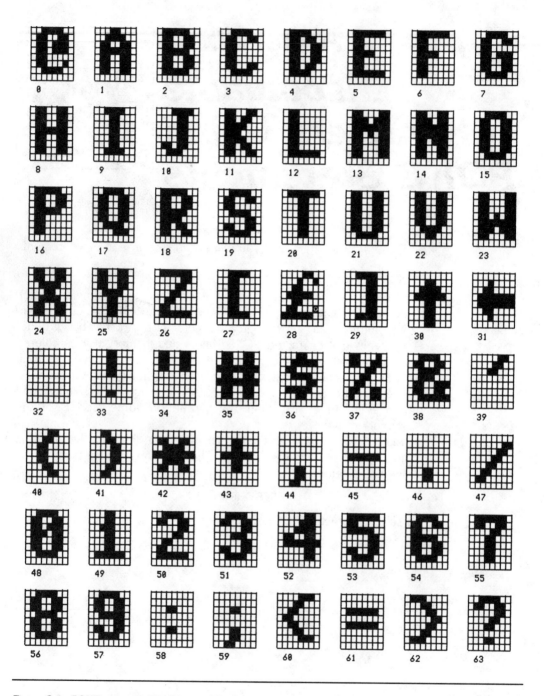

Figure C.1 : POKE codes 0–63 : Character Set 1.

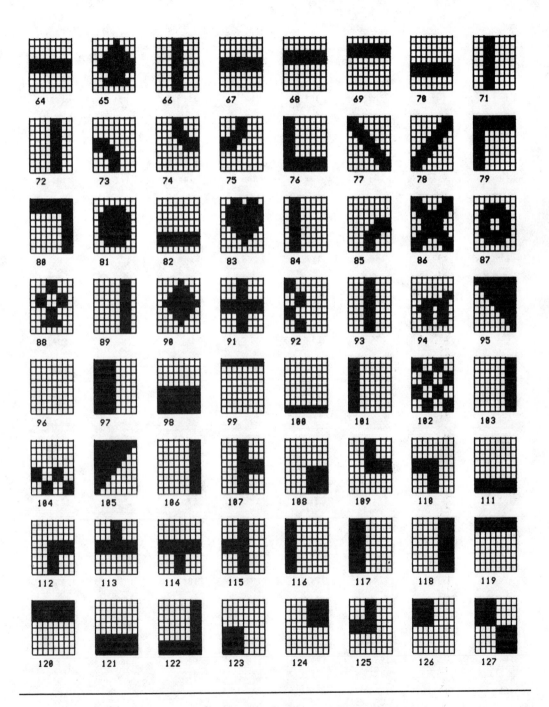

Figure C.2 : POKE codes 64–127 : Character Set 1 graphics symbols.

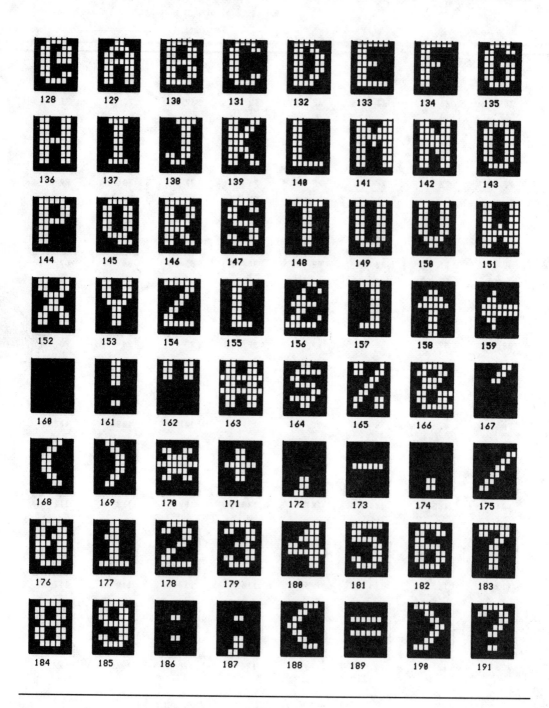

Figure C.3 : POKE codes 128–191 : Character Set 1 reverse video.

Figure C.4 : POKE codes 192–255 : Character Set 1 reverse video graphics symbols.

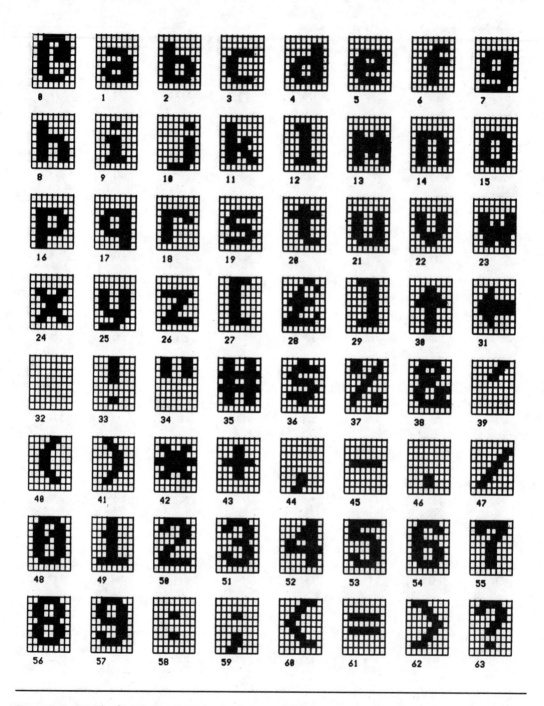

Figure C.5 : POKE codes 0–63 : Character Set 2 lowercase.

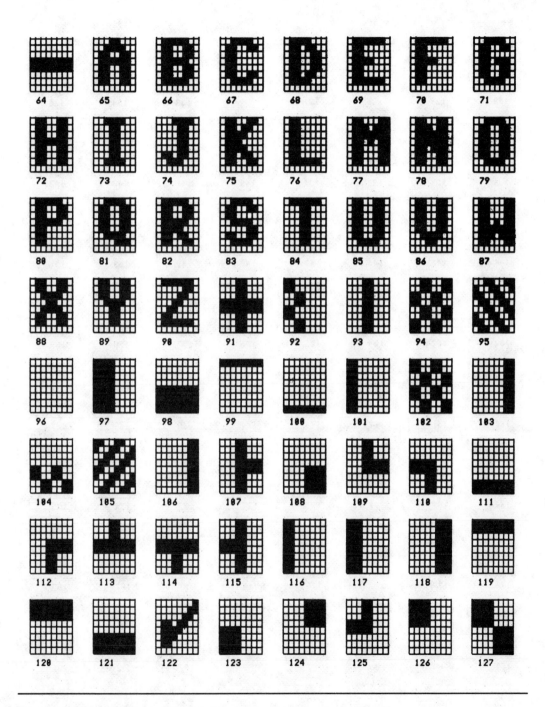

Figure C.6 : POKE codes 64–127 : Character Set 2 uppercase.

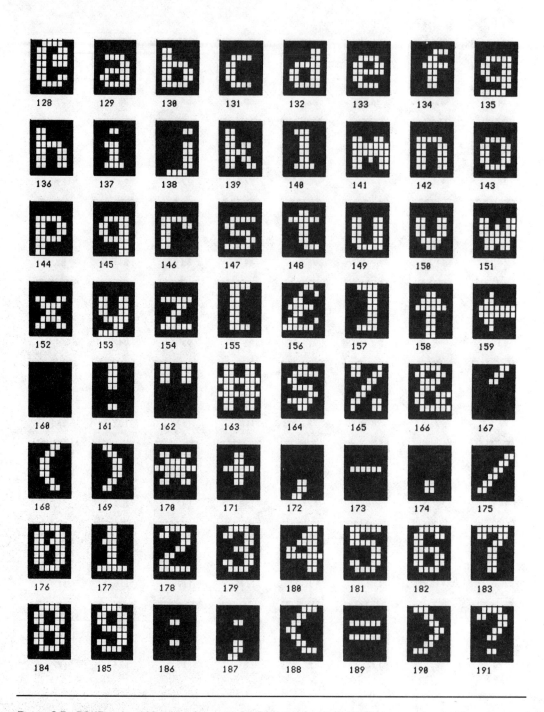

Figure C.7: POKE codes 128–191: Character Set 2 lowercase reverse video.

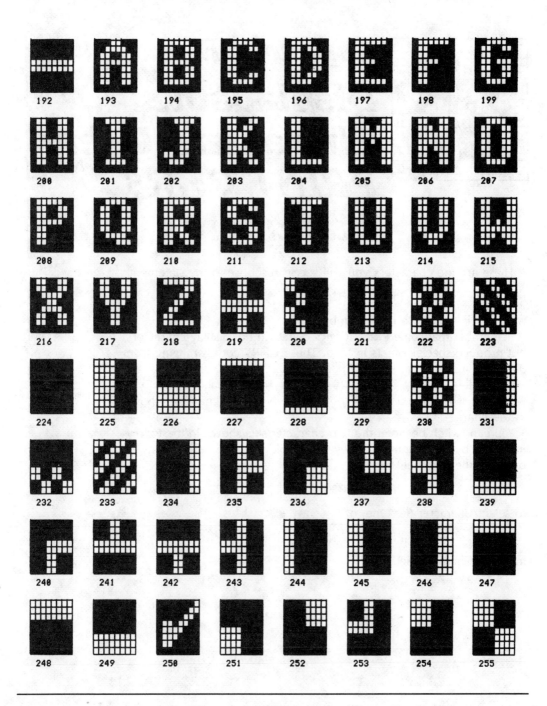

Figure C.8 : POKE codes 192–255 : Character Set 2 uppercase reverse video.

Appendix D
Displayable Characters Using PRINT CHR$ Statements

These are the characters you will see in response to the statement:

PRINT CHR$(N)

where N is the CHR$ code number.

Remember that some PRINT CHR$ codes do not display characters, but produce special effects instead. These CHR$ codes, ranging from 0–32 and 128–159, are listed in Appendix B.

Generally speaking, the CHR$ number is the same number you would get if you asked for ASC("?") where "?" is the character shown in the chart.

You can switch between the two character sets shown in the following pages by pressing the C= key while holding down a SHIFT key, or by using the statement:

PRINT CHR$(142)

to select Character Set One, or:

PRINT CHR$(14)

to select Character Set Two.

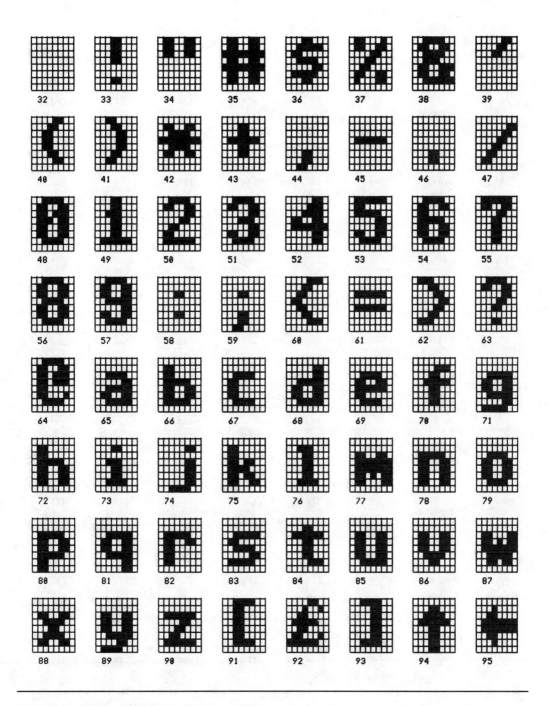

Figure D.1 : CHR$ codes 32–95 : Character Set One.

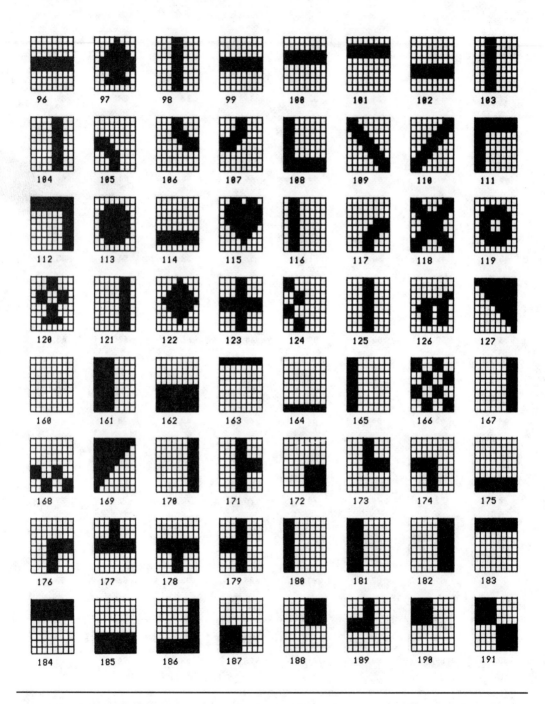

Figure D.2 : CHR$ codes 96–127 and 160–191 : Character Set One.

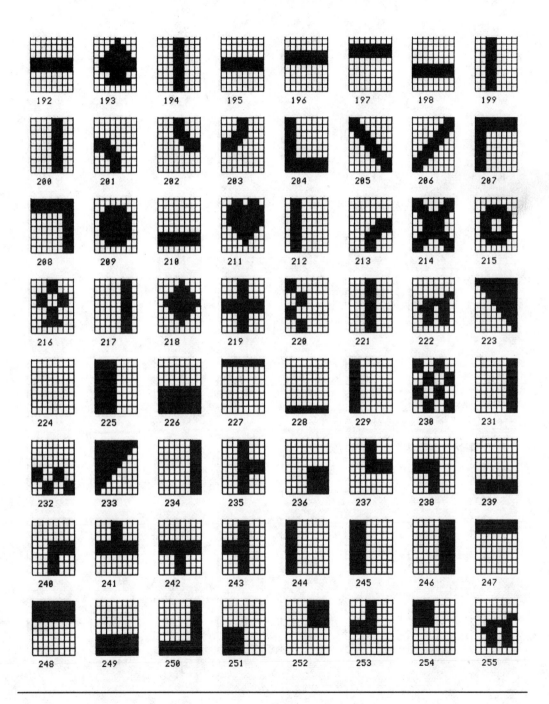

Figure D.3 : CHR$ codes 192–255 : Character Set One.

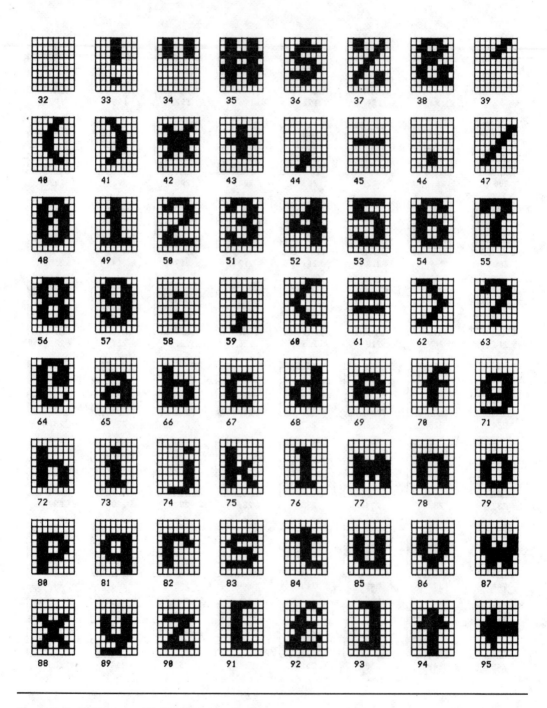

Figure D.4 : CHR$ codes 32–95 : Character Set Two.

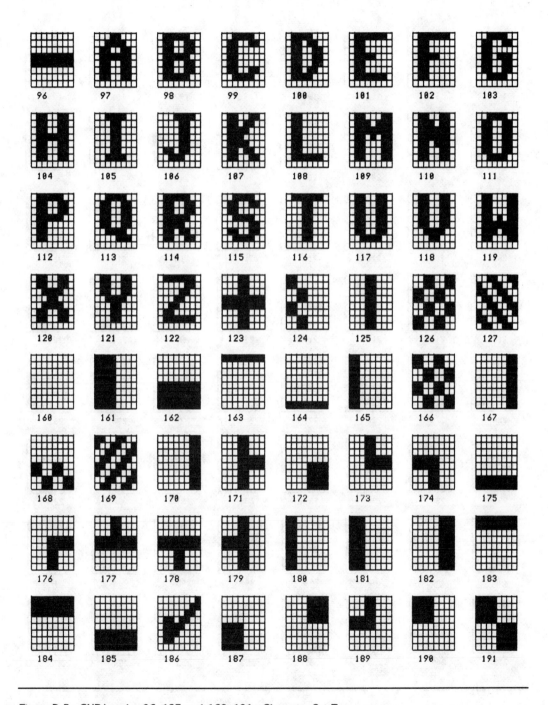

Figure D.5 : CHR$ codes 96–127 and 160–191 : Character Set Two.

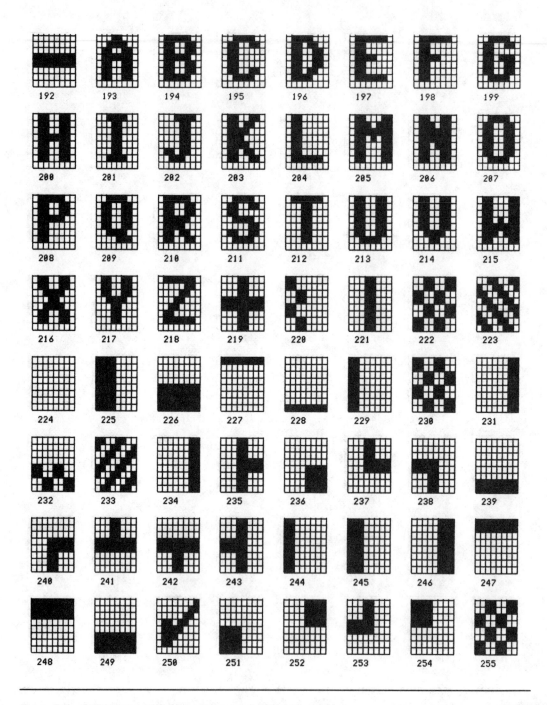

Figure D.6 : CHR$ codes 192–255 : Character Set Two.

Appendix E
Video Memory Map

To find the address of a pixel in the map, add the number opposite its line, at the left, to the column number, at the top, and then add the result to the first video address, which is 1024 (assuming you have not relocated video memory). Thus the address of the top-left pixel is 0 + 0 + 1024 = 1024. The address of the bottom-right pixel is 960 + 39 + 1024 = 2023.

Remember that on some models of the Commodore 64, a character that you POKE into video memory will not be visible until you also POKE a contrasting color into color memory.

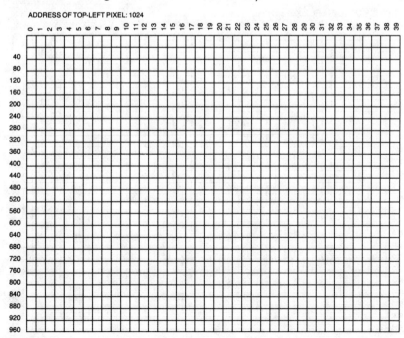

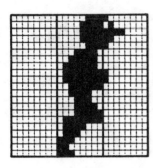

Appendix F
Color Memory Map

To find the address of a pixel in the map, add the number opposite its line, at the left, to the column number, at the top, and add the result to 55296. Thus the address of the top-left pixel is 0 + 0 + 55296 = 55296. The address of the bottom-left pixel is 960 + 39 + 55296 = 56295.

Each color address controls the color of the character in the corresponding position on the video memory map. Assuming you have not relocated video memory, subtract 54272 (the "color constant") from an address in the color memory map to find the address it controls in the video memory map.

ADDRESS OF TOP-LEFT PIXEL 55296

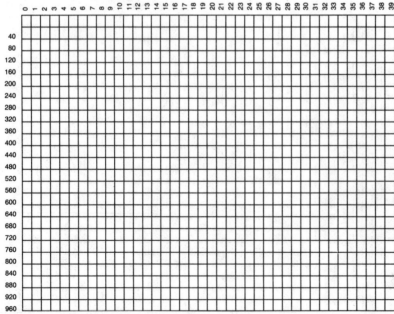

Appendix G
Tab and Line Number Map

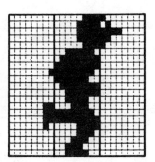

Use this map to keep track of cursor position. The numbers of the columns, along the top of the chart, should be used in PRINT TAB statements, to TAB the cursor across and place the first printed character in the column of that number.

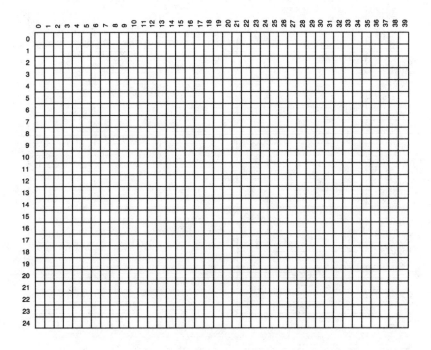

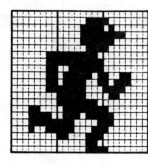

Appendix H
Computer Memory Map

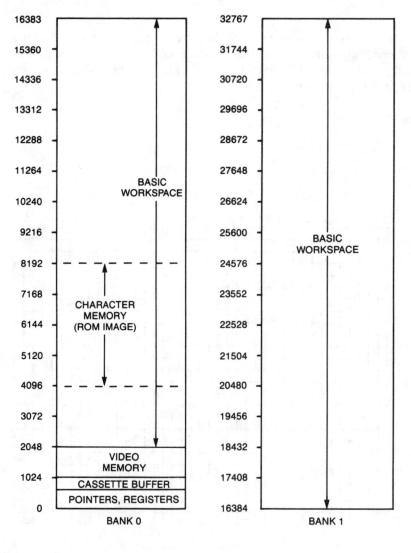

16383	
15360	
14336	
13312	
12288	
11264	**BASIC WORKSPACE**
10240	
9216	
8192	- - - - - -
7168	
6144	**CHARACTER MEMORY (ROM IMAGE)**
5120	
4096	- - - - - -
3072	
2048	
	VIDEO MEMORY
1024	**CASSETTE BUFFER**
0	**POINTERS, REGISTERS**

BANK 0

32767	
31744	
30720	
29696	
28672	
27648	
26624	
25600	**BASIC WORKSPACE**
24576	
23552	
22528	
21504	
20480	
19456	
18432	
17408	
16384	

BANK 1

This map has been marked out at intervals of one kilobyte (1024 bytes). All numbers are in decimal notation. Some indications are approximate. For instance, video memory actually runs from 1024 through 2023, rather than through 2047; addresses 2040 through 2047 are used for sprite data pointers. See Appendix J for precise information.

If you have a cassette system, the C-64 Wedge, which is shown installed from 52224 through 53247, will not be present. It will only be present on a disk system if you choose to load it from your Commodore system disk.

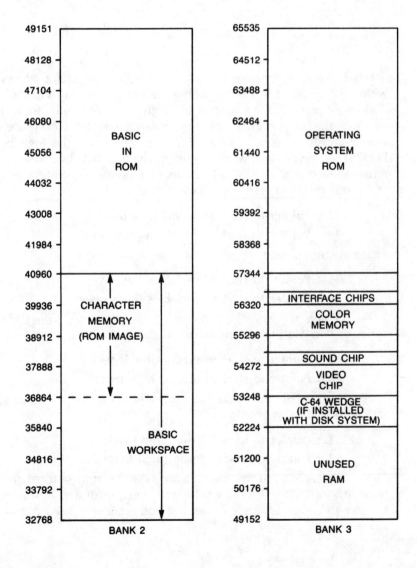

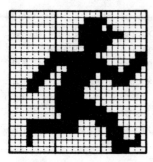

Appendix J
Useful Memory Addresses

This listing is not complete, but does include all useful addresses within the scope of this book. Addresses are in decimal notation.

Memory pointers are encoded in "high byte, low byte" form. For example, the pointers establishing the end of the BASIC workspace are stored in addresses 55 and 56. PEEK(56) gives you the high byte. PEEK(55) gives you the low byte. Multiply the high byte by 256 and add it to the low byte to find the address that the pointer is pointing to. Use POKE statements to reset the pointers as desired.

43 : Pointer to start of BASIC (low byte)

44 : Pointer to start of BASIC (high byte)

These pointers determine where your program begins.

45 : Pointer to start of variables (low byte)

46 : Pointer to start of variables (high byte)

These pointers tell you where the computer stores the values of the variables you use in your program.

47 : Pointer to start of arrays (low byte)

48 : Pointer to start of arrays (high byte)

These pointers tell you where the computer stores the values of subscripted variables in your program.

51 : Pointer to lowest string (low byte)

52 : Pointer to lowest string (high byte)

These pointers tell you the lowest address of the strings stored so far, from the top of the BASIC workspace, moving down. Reset these pointers to avoid garbage collection, if you no longer need old string values.

55 : Pointer to end of BASIC workspace (low byte)

56 : Pointer to end of BASIC workspace (high byte)

These pointers can be reset to reduce workspace size and make spare memory above the workspace available for your use. This POKE should be followed by CLR to zero all variables and reset the lowest-string pointers in addresses 51 and 52.

63 : Current DATA line number (low byte)

64 : Current DATA line number (high byte)

65 : Current DATA address (low byte)

66 : Current DATA address (high byte)

Current DATA line number tells you the line number of the DATA statement in your program that the computer is going to read next. You might imagine all you have to do is POKE these pointers to make the computer read a DATA line number of your choice, but it isn't that simple, because the DATA line number pointers are controlled by the current DATA address pointers. So, first you need to find the address of the DATA line that you want. Do this by READing and PRINTing DATA statements till you reach the one just before the one you want (you can do this in BASIC Immediate Mode). Then PEEK(65) and PEEK(66) for the DATA line address, and later have your program POKE those pointers with the address, to specify the DATA statement you want the program to read. Remember, if you edit your program, that its listing may grow or shrink, and the addresses of the DATA lines may change accordingly.

139 : RND seed

140 : RND seed

141 : RND seed

142 : RND seed

143 : RND seed

These are the numbers the computer uses to create random numbers.

160 : Clock (advances approximately every 18 minutes)

161 : Clock (advances approximately every 4 seconds)

162 : Clock (advances every 1/60th second)

The clock runs all the time the computer is turned on, regardless of other operations. The number in address 162 increases every 1/60th of a second. Each time it counts from 0 through 255, the number in address 161 increases by one. Each time that reaches 255, the number in 160 increases by one. Reset the clock by POKEing these addresses, or use the statement TI$ = "000000".

198 : Number of characters in keyboard buffer

The number of characters in the keyboard buffer can be POKEd with a 0 if you want the computer to ignore any keys that have been pressed. This "empties" the buffer.

203 : Which key pressed

PEEKing this address yields a code number according to which key is being pressed. It yields a 64 if no key is currently being pressed. This is a similar operation to the BASIC statement, GET, but the code numbers are not related or convertible to ASCII or CHR$ numbers. One advantage of PEEKing 203 for a key is that it avoids accumulating strings, as in a GET A$ statement, and thus avoids garbage collection. Also, PEEK(203) avoids the keyboard buffer. It checks the keyboard only at that specific instant. Keys pressed previously will be ignored. To discover the code numbers, try running this one-line program:

```
10 PRINT PEEK(203):GOTO 10
```

It will display on the screen the code number of any letter you press.

214 : Screen line number of cursor

This address can be POKEd to shift the cursor to the line of your choice (0–24). The POKE must be followed by a carriage return (i.e. a single, unadorned PRINT statement) to reorient other associated pointers, so the cursor moves where you want it. If the screen is filled with graphics characters, however, the results may be unpredictable, as two lines of graphics characters may be interpreted as a single program line, causing the cursor to skip a line.

631 : Stores first character in keyboard buffer
640 : Stores 10th (last) character in buffer

The keyboard buffer consists of ten memory addresses, 631–640, in which typed characters are stored if the computer is not currently processing keyboard entries. If you POKE 198,0 the computer assumes the buffer is empty, regardless of the contents of its memory addresses. If you POKE 198,1 the computer processes only the first character, in address 631. If you POKE 198,2 the computer processes the character in 631, then moves the character in 632 to 631 and processes it, and so on.

You can use this feature to make the computer do things after the end of a program. Have your program PRINT a BASIC instruction onto the screen, and reposition the cursor on that line. Then have the program POKE 631,13 and POKE 198,1 (13 being the code for a carriage return). Then END the program. The computer switches into immediate mode, finds one character in its keyboard buffer, and processes it. The 13 code is the equivalent of the operator pressing RETURN. Thus the instruction on the screen is executed. It could be an instruction to load another program. The Sprite Demonstration program in Chapter Six uses this feature to display a sprite control instruction on the screen, which is then executed in immediate mode while the user watches.

648 : Pointer to start of video memory (high byte)

This tells you the first address of video memory. There is only a high-byte pointer, since video memory always begins at an address that is a multiple of 256.

650 : Key repeat: Some, none, or all

This address normally contains 0, which means that only spacebar, CRSR, and INST/DEL keys repeat when held down for more than half a second. You can POKE 650,64 to make no keys repeat, or POKE 650,128 to make all keys repeat.

657 : Enable or disable SHIFT keys

This is useful if you want to prohibit the user from inputting shifted key-combinations. Disable the SHIFT keys by POKEing this address with a 0. Restore to normal with 128.

With the exception of the sprite pointers in 2040–2047 the rest of the memory addresses do not contain pointers, but are, rather, locations that pointers point to.

The various routines that reside in addresses 53248 upward cannot be shifted to other memory locations, and are included for your information only.

1024 : Usual start of video memory
2023 : Usual end of video memory
2040 : Start of sprite data pointers
2047 : End of sprite data pointers
2048 : Start of BASIC workspace
40959 : Usual end of BASIC workspace
40960 : Start of BASIC in ROM
49151 : End of BASIC in ROM
49152 : Start of spare 4K RAM block
52224 : Start of C-64 Wedge, when installed
53247 : End of spare RAM block or C-64 Wedge
53248 : Start of video chip
54271 : End of video chip

54272 : Start of sound chip
55295 : End of sound chip
55296 : Start of color memory
56295 : End of color memory
56320 : Start of I/O interface chips
57343 : End of I/O
57344 : Start of ROM operating system
65535 : End of ROM operating system

Appendix K
Sprite Control Addresses

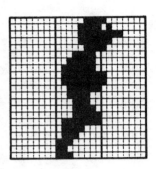

Pointers to Sprite Data

2040 : Pointer to data for sprite 0

2041 : Pointer to data for sprite 1

2042 : Pointer to data for sprite 2

2043 : Pointer to data for sprite 3

2044 : Pointer to data for sprite 4

2045 : Pointer to data for sprite 5

2046 : Pointer to data for sprite 6

2047 : Pointer to data for sprite 7

These pointers do not use the high byte/low byte system. If P is the Pointer value, and B is the number of the Bank that the video chip is using, and A is the Address of the data that the pointer is pointing to, then:

$$A = 64 \times (P + (B \times 256))$$
$$P = (A/64) - (B \times 256)$$

Sprite Bit Values

Sprite 0 : Bit value 1

Sprite 1 : Bit value 2

Sprite 2 : Bit value 4

Sprite 3 : Bit value 8

Sprite 4 : Bit value 16

Sprite 5 : Bit value 32

Sprite 6 : Bit value 64

Sprite 7 : Bit value 128

These bit values are used in some of the sprite registers (see next section). POKE registers VC+16, VC+21, VC+23, VC+27, VC+28, VC+29, VC+30, or VC+31 with the sum of the bit values of the sprites that you wish to control. For example, to turn on sprites 0, 1, and 2: POKE VC+21,7. To turn on sprite 4 in addition to any other sprites that may already be on: POKE VC+21,PEEK(VC+21)+16.

Sprite Registers

In the following list, 53248 (the starting address of the Video Chip) is represented by the constant VC. Thus VC+1 is 53249, VC+2 is 53250, and so on.

> **VC + 0 : X distance of sprite 0**
> **VC + 1 : Y distance of sprite 0**
> **VC + 2 : X distance of sprite 1**
> **VC + 3 : Y distance of sprite 1**
> **VC + 4 : X distance of sprite 2**
> **VC + 5 : Y distance of sprite 2**
> **VC + 6 : X distance of sprite 3**
> **VC + 7 : Y distance of sprite 3**
> **VC + 8 : X distance of sprite 4**
> **VC + 9 : Y distance of sprite 4**
> **VC + 10 : X distance of sprite 5**
> **VC + 11 : Y distance of sprite 5**
> **VC + 12 : X distance of sprite 6**
> **VC + 13 : Y distance of sprite 6**
> **VC + 14 : X distance of sprite 7**
> **VC + 15 : Y distance of sprite 7**

Each X distance register determines the horizontal distance, in dots, of the left edge of each sprite from the left edge of the sprite video map, lying beyond the left edge of the screen (see Appendix L). Each Y Distance register determines the vertical distance of the top edge of each sprite from the top edge of the sprite video map, lying beyond the top edge of the screen. Distances are measured in dots. Eight dots = one pixel.

VC + 16 : X distance exceeds 255 register

This register should be POKEd with the total bit value(s) of any sprite(s) that must move horizontally past the point where the X distance = 255. Their X distance registers should then be POKEd with 0, and future X distances will be measured from the 255 line.

VC + 21 : Sprite on/off register

POKE this register with the sum of the bit values of the sprites to be displayed. POKE VC+21,0 to turn all sprites off—the PRINT CHR$(147) screen-clearing statement will not have this effect.

VC + 23 : Double-height register

POKE this register with the sum of the bit values of sprites to be expanded vertically.

VC + 27 : Sprite-to-pixel priority register

POKE this register with the sum of the bit values of sprites that you want to move behind images in video memory pixels.

VC + 28 : Multicolor sprite on/off register

POKE this register with the sum of the bit values of sprites to be displayed in multicolor mode.

VC + 29 : Double-width register

POKE this register with the sum of the bit values of sprites to be expanded horizontally.

VC + 30 : Sprite-to-sprite collision register

When PEEKed, this register will give the sum of the bit values of sprites whose colored image areas are touching. PEEKing this register resets it to zero if the sprites are no longer touching. If there has been a collision involving a sprite of bit value BV, PEEK(VC+30) AND BV = BV.

VC + 31 : Sprite-to-pixel collision register

When PEEKed, this register will give the sum of the bit values of sprites touching visible characters in video memory pixels. If a sprite of bit value BV is touching a video character, PEEK (VC+31) AND BV = BV.

VC + 37 : Color #1 of multicolor sprites
VC + 38 : Color #2 of multicolor sprites
VC + 39 : Main color of sprite 0
VC + 40 : Main color of sprite 1
VC + 41 : Main color of sprite 2
VC + 42 : Main color of sprite 3
VC + 43 : Main color of sprite 4
VC + 44 : Main color of sprite 5
VC + 45 : Main color of sprite 6
VC + 46 : Main color of sprite 7

The main-color registers should be POKEd with 0 through 15 to determine the main sprite colors. Multicolor #1 and multicolor #2 will be shared by all multicolored sprites. The main color of each sprite can be specified individually.

Pairs of dots in multicolor sprites will show colors as follows:

    0-1 dot pairs : multicolor #1
    1-1 dot pairs : multicolor #2
    1-0 dot pairs : main sprite color
    0-0 dot pairs : transparent to background color

Appendix L
Sprite Video Map

Sprite distances are measured from beyond the normal screen area. Gray rectangles on the map indicate possible positions of normal-size (unexpanded) sprites, including off-screen positions, from which the sprites can move into the visible area. The location of a sprite is given as the X distance (horizontal) and Y distance (vertical) of its top-left dot, even if that dot is blank (contains no color). Expanded sprites will be twice as wide and/or high as the gray areas shown.

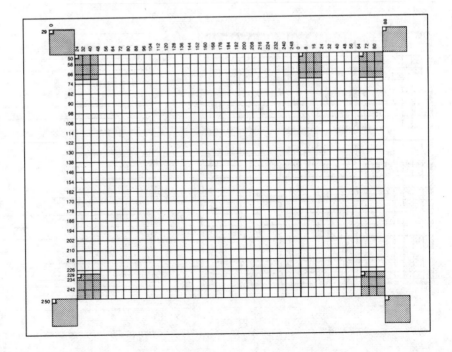

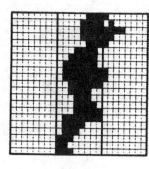

Appendix M
Sprite Grid and Code-Number Chart

To construct a sprite, make a few photocopies of this grid and chart. Draw your sprite by filling in grid squares. Then take each group of eight squares and find a match for its pattern in the patterns in Appendix N. Write the number of the matching pattern in the appropriate space in the chart. Then transcribe the sequence of 63 numbers, from left to right, top to bottom, into the sprite DATA statements in your program. See Chapter Six.

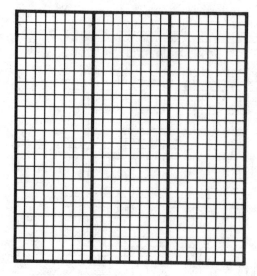

Figure M.1: Sprite grid

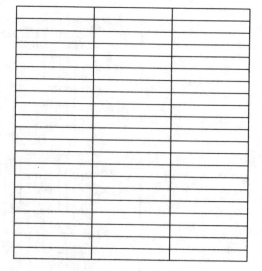

Figure M.2: Sprite code-number chart.

Appendix N
Pattern Matching Aid for Sprites and Alternate Character Sets

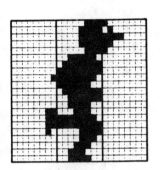

Use this chart to find the code number that defines each set of eight dots in your sprite or video character. All possible permutations of eight dots and spaces are illustrated in the chart.

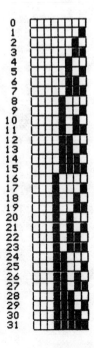

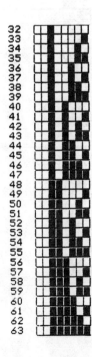

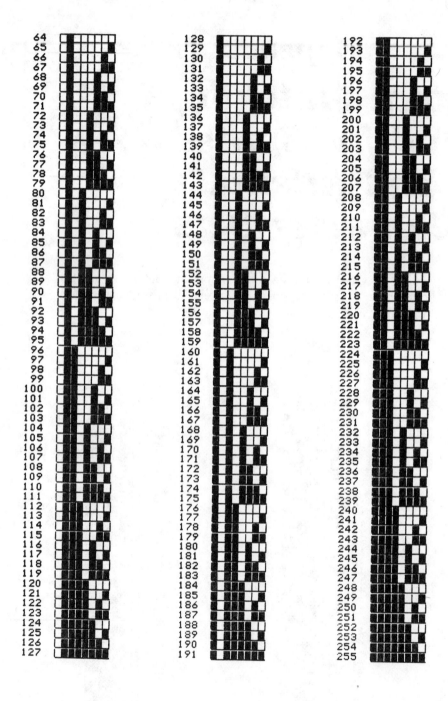

Appendix P
Display Alphabet Built from Commodore Graphics Characters

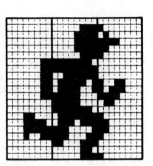

The code numbers are the ASCII (POKE) codes of the characters used to assemble the display letter.

233	160	223
160	32	160
160	160	160
160	32	160

160	160	223
160	98	105
160	226	223
160	160	105

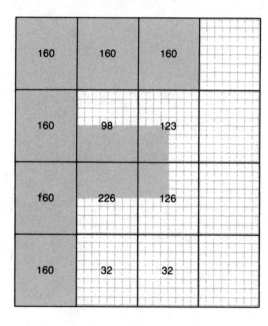

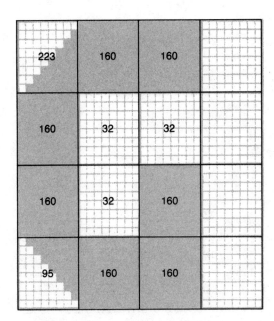

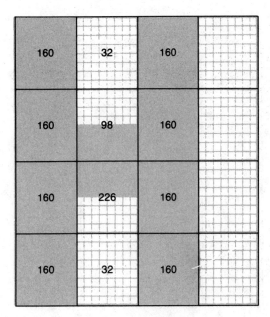

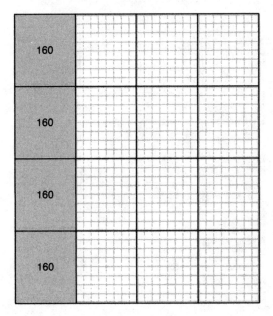

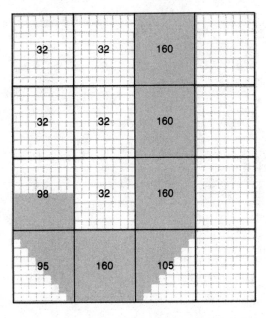

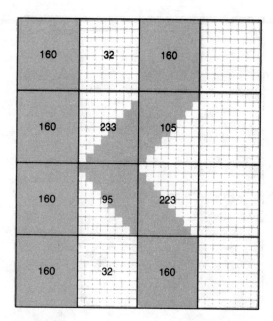

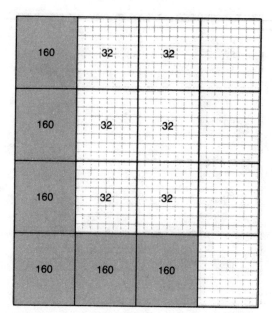

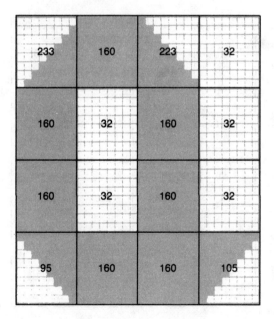

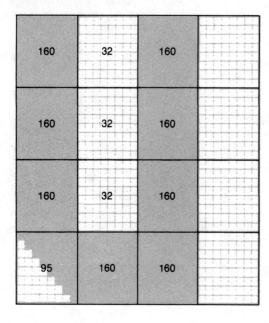

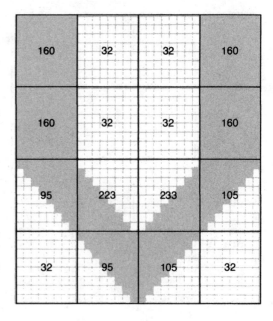

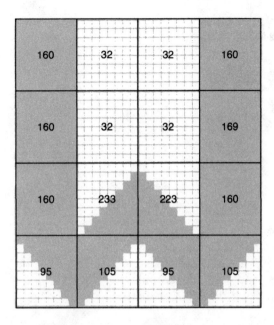

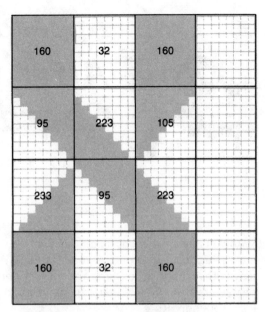

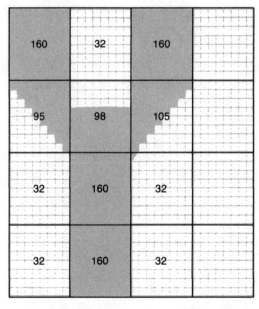

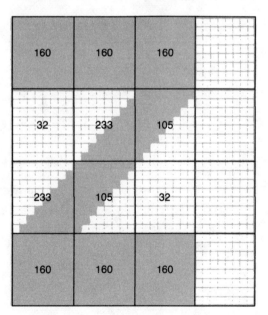

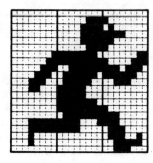

Appendix Q
Alternate
Character Set

Advantages of this character set over the standard Commodore set include uppercase letters assigned standard ASCII codes, lowercase letters with proper ascenders and descenders, and versatile graphics characters from which you can build good-looking display alphabets (see Appendix R).

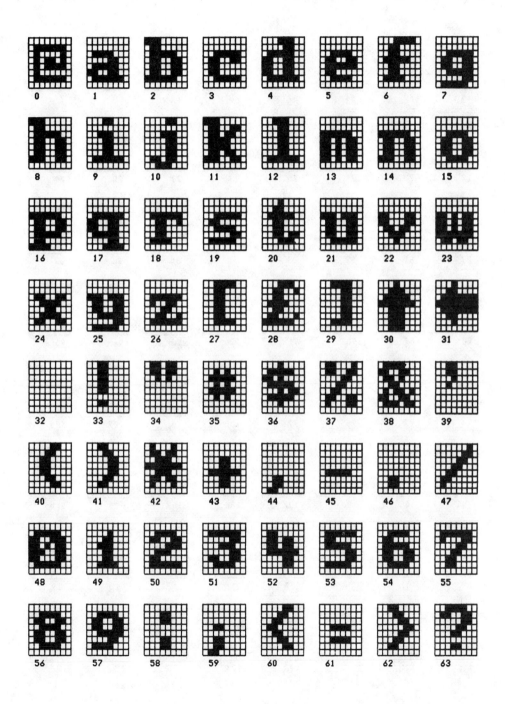

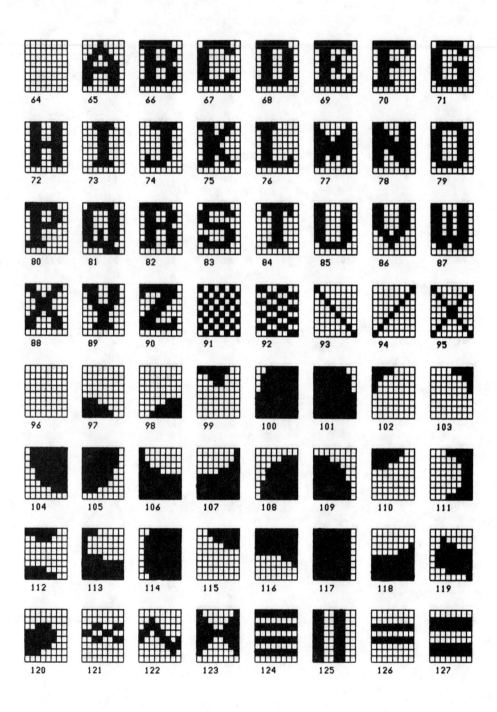

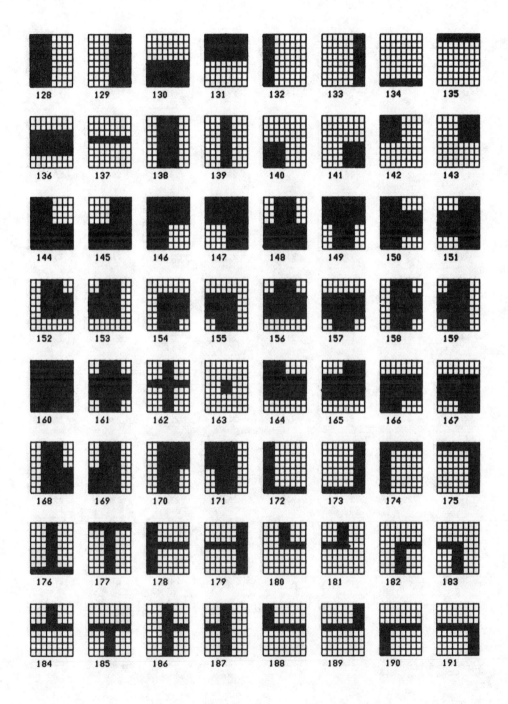

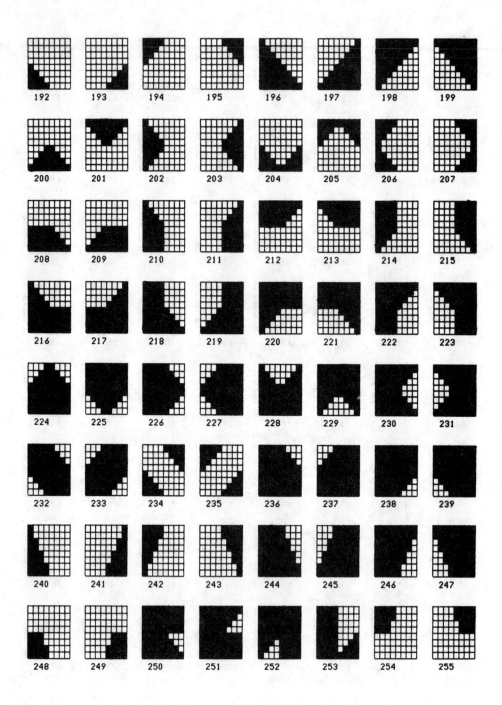

Appendix R
Display Alphabet Built from Alternate Character Set

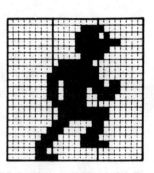

This alphabet can only be built from the graphics characters in the alternate character set depicted in Appendix Q, which must first be installed in memory.

32	32	249	248	32	32
32	32	245	244	32	32
32	241	246	247	240	32
32	245	146	147	244	32

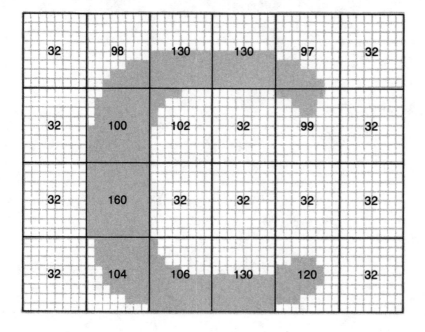

141	130	130	130	97	32
32	160	32	111	105	32
32	160	131	116	109	32
141	160	130	118	105	32

32	98	130	130	97	32
32	100	102	32	99	32
32	160	32	32	32	32
32	104	106	130	120	32

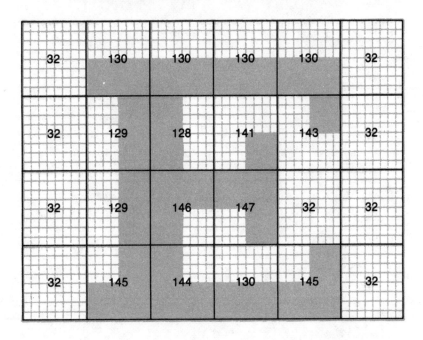

32	130	130	130	97	32
32	129	128	103	101	32
32	129	128	32	160	32
32	145	144	107	105	32

32	130	130	130	130	32
32	129	128	141	143	32
32	129	146	147	32	32
32	145	144	130	145	32

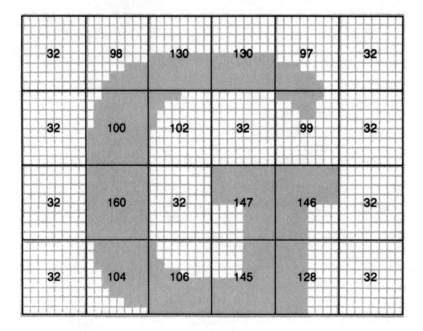

32	130	130	130	130	32
32	129	128	141	143	32
32	129	146	147	32	32
32	145	144	32	32	32

32	98	130	130	97	32
32	100	102	32	99	32
32	160	32	147	146	32
32	104	106	145	128	32

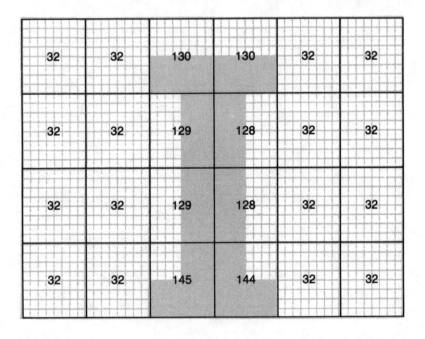

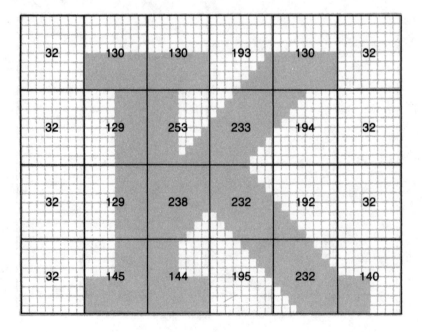

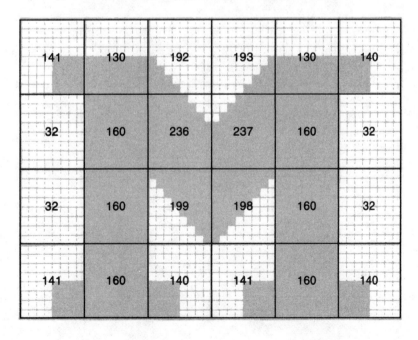

32	130	130	32	32	32
32	129	128	32	32	32
32	129	128	32	32	32
32	145	144	130	145	32

141	130	192	193	130	140
32	160	236	237	160	32
32	160	199	198	160	32
141	160	140	141	160	140

141	130	192	141	130	140
32	160	236	192	160	32
32	160	199	236	160	32
141	160	140	199	160	32

32	98	130	130	97	32
32	100	102	103	101	32
32	160	32	32	160	32
32	104	106	107	105	32

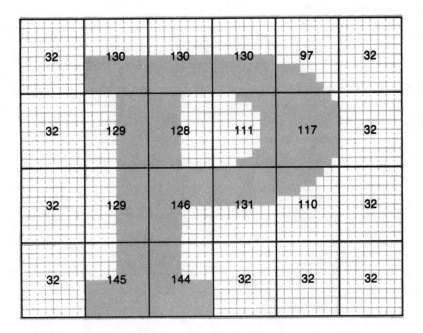

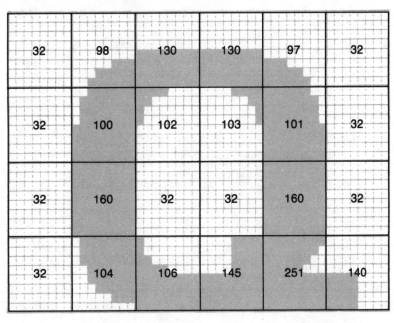

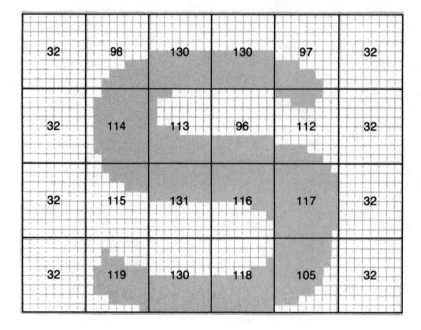

141	130	130	130	97	32
32	160	32	111	117	32
32	160	221	250	110	32
141	160	140	199	216	32

32	98	130	130	97	32
32	114	113	96	112	32
32	115	131	116	117	32
32	119	130	118	105	32

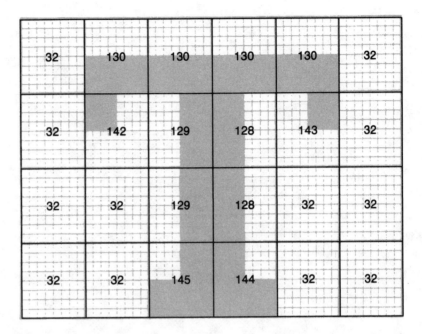

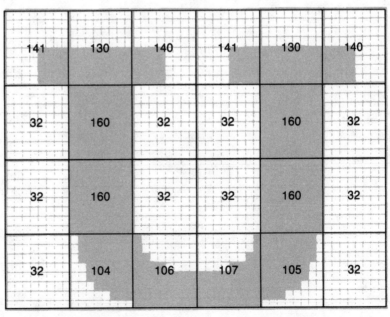

141	130	140	141	130	140
32	247	240	241	246	32
32	243	244	245	242	32
32	32	247	246	32	32

141	130	140	141	130	140
32	160	249	248	160	32
32	160	245	244	160	32
32	247	246	247	246	32

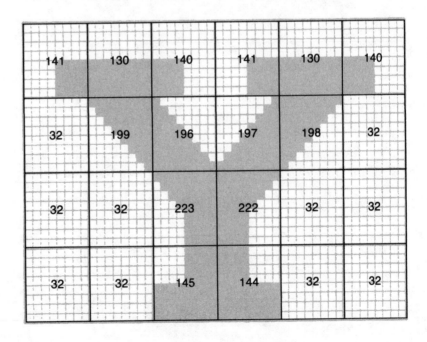

32	130	130	130	130	32
32	142	197	160	198	32
32	197	160	198	32	32
32	160	251	130	145	32

Appendix S
Hints on Using the 1541 Disk Drive

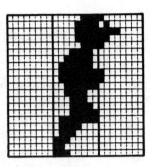

When the 1541 disk drive was first introduced for the Commodore 64, there were a few problems. To judge from readers' query letters in computer magazines, it has taken Commodore some time to correct these problems. In particular, the drive can seem very "fussy" about saving programs on disks. It sometimes refuses repeatedly to save onto certain disks, and keeps stopping and flashing its red error light.

As far as I can tell, the problem begins when you format a new disk using the "N0:" command (listed in your disk drive instruction manual). When I have followed this procedure, and then tried immediately to save a program on the new disk, I have run into difficulties. However, the following procedure seems to solve the problem.

1. When you want to prepare a brand-new disk using the "N0:" command, first load a program from your Commodore system disk (the disk supplied with your computer) titled "C-64 WEDGE." RUN this program, which installs several useful features, including the ability to read disk error messages, when they occur, simply by pressing the @ key and then RETURN.

2. Having "installed" the wedge program, substitute your brand-new disk in the disk drive. Make sure the disk does not have a write-protect sticker wrapped around its edge notch. Make sure also that this is a new, blank disk, or a disk with no data that you want to preserve. The next operation will totally erase it.

3. Type:

        @15,"N0:DISK NAME,00"

and press RETURN. Instead of DISK NAME you can substitute any words totalling 16 letters and spaces or less. Instead of the two zeroes after the comma, you can use any two digits for identification. In response to this command, your disk drive will "home" itself (a nasty rattling noise), then format the disk, which takes about a minute. During this operation, the red light should be steadily lit. If it flickers or flashes, open the drive, turn *everything* off and then back on again, and start over from Step 1.

4. After the disk has been formatted, the disk drive's red light goes out. At this point, *turn off the computer and the disk drive.* Then re-start your system, (always turn on the disk drive before you turn on the computer), load a test program from another disk, and try saving it on your new disk. In my experience, if you totally reset the system this way by shutting it down before you start using your new disk, you'll get no errors.

5. But if you do still have trouble saving onto your new disk, it's fair to say that the disk will always give you trouble. Don't keep trying—start all over again, and NEW it afresh, from Step 1 onward. Once you end up with a disk which will accept data, it should always accept data. (Well, nearly always....)

Appendix T
Headline Generator
Program Listing

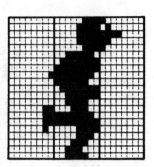

```
10 GOTO 5000
97 REM
98 REM------- Select a Character ------
99 REM
100 GOSUB 9100
110 PRINT TAB(22)"CHOOSE A LETTER"
130 PRINT TAB(22)"OR SYMBOL: ":PRINT
140 GOSUB 9000:IF A<32 OR A>95 THEN 140
150 IF A>63 THEN A=A-64
160 POKE VA+153,A
170 CM=GM+(A*64)
180 IF PEEK(CM)<T THEN GOSUB 4200
200 GOSUB 300
210 PRINT TAB(22)"CHOOSE ANOTHER?"
220 GOSUB 9000
230 GOSUB 7500
240 IF A=89 THEN 100
250 GOTO 900
297 REM
298 REM------- Edit a Character -------
299 REM
300 GOSUB 4000
310 X=1:Y=1
320 P=PEEK(VM(X,Y)):M=0
330 POKE VM(X,Y),86:GOSUB 550
340 IF M=1 THEN 400
350 POKE VM(X,Y),P:GOSUB 550
360 IF M=0 THEN 330
400 A=ASC(A$):IF A>57 OR A<F THEN 420
410 L=0:IF A=F THEN L=15
412 POKE VM(X,Y)+CC,L
414 POKE VM(X,Y),G(A-F)
416 X=X+1:GOTO 490
420 POKE VM(X,Y),P:IF A=88 THEN 600
430 IF A<F1 OR A>F7 THEN M=0:GOTO 330
440 IF A=F1 THEN IF Y>1 THEN Y=Y-1
450 IF A=F7 THEN IF Y<H THEN Y=Y+1
460 IF A=F3 THEN X=X-1
470 IF A=F5 THEN X=X+1
480 IF X=0THEN X=9:Y=Y-1:IF Y=0THEN Y=H
490 IF X=T THENX=1:Y=Y+1:IFY>H THEN Y=1
500 GOTO 320
540 REM------------------------
550 FOR N=1 TO 50
560 GET A$:IF A$<>""THEN N=50:M=1
570 NEXT N
```

```
580 RETURN
590 REM-------------------------
600 GOSUB 9100
610 PRINT TAB(22)"DO YOU WANT TO"
620 PRINT TAB(22)"MEMORIZE THIS?"
630 PRINT
640 GOSUB 9000
650 IF A=78 THEN RETURN
660 IF A<>89 THEN 640
670 PRINT TAB(22)"SCANNING"
680 PRINT TAB(22)".";
690 REM---------- First Find Width
700 W=10
710 FOR M=9 TO 1 STEP -1
720 FOR N=1 TO H
730 P=PEEK(VM(M,N))
740 IF P<>G(T) AND P>TH THEN W=M
750 NEXT N
760 PRINT".";:IF W=M THEN M=1
770 NEXT M
780 POKE CM,W
790 IF W=10 THEN 890
795 REM-------- Now Scan Letter
800 L=CM
810 FOR M=1 TO W
820 FOR N=1 TO H
830 P=PEEK(VM(M,N))
840 IF P=G(T) THEN P=TH
850 L=L+1:POKE L,P
860 NEXT N
870 PRINT".";
880 NEXT M
890 PRINT:PRINT:RETURN
897 REM
898 REM---------- Main Menu -----------
899 REM
900 GOSUB 9100
910 PRINT TAB(22)"1. REVIEW":PRINT
920 PRINT TAB(22)"2. EDIT":PRINT
930 PRINT TAB(22)"3. SAVE":PRINT:PRINT
940 PRINT TAB(22)"...YOUR CHOICE?"
950 GOSUB 9000
960 IF A<49 OR A>51 THEN 950
970 ON A-48 GOTO 1000,100,980
980 RESTORE:GOSUB 2000:GOSUB 2500
990 POKE 52,120:PRINT C$:GOTO 6080
997 REM
998 REM------------ Review ------------
999 REM
1000 GOSUB 4100
1100 CN=0:S=1:V=1
1110 POKE VA+473,CN
1120 CM=GM+(64*CN)
1130 IF PEEK(CM)=T THEN 1300
1140 GOSUB 4200:IF W=>V THEN 1190
1150 FOR M=W+1 TO V
1155 FOR N=1 TO H-1
1160 POKE VM(M,N)+CC,FT
1165 POKE VM(M,N),G(T)
1170 NEXT N
```

```
1175 POKE VM(M,N),TH
1180 NEXT M
1190 V=W:POKE 198,0:GOSUB 9000
1200 IF A<49 OR A>52 THEN 1140
1210 IF A=49 THEN S=1
1220 IF A=50 THEN S=-1
1230 IF A=51 THEN GOSUB 1500
1240 IF A=52 THEN 1330
1250 PRINT H$
1260 PRINT D$D$D$D$D$D$D$D$D$TAB(33);
1300 CN=CN+S
1310 IF CN<0 THEN S=1:CN=0
1320 IF CN<64 THEN 1110
1330 GOSUB 7500:GOTO 900
1499 REM----------------
1500 GOSUB 9100:GOSUB 300:GOSUB 7500
1510 GOSUB 4100:RETURN
1997 REM
1998 REM----- Get Disk Directory ------
1999 REM
2000 M=0:POKE 53280,15:PRINT C$
2005 PRINT" SEE THE DIRECTORY?"
2010 GOSUB 9000:IF A$="N" THEN 2200
2015 PRINT:PRINT" ";
2020 OPEN 2,8,2,"$"
2030 FOR N=1 TO 254:GET#2,A$:NEXT N
2040 K=13:M=M+1:IF M=8 THEN K=11:M=0
2050 GET#2,A$
2060 IF ST>0 THEN CLOSE 2:GOTO 2200
2070 IF A$<>"" THEN A=ASC(A$):GOTO 2100
2080 FOR N=1 TO 18+K:GET#2,A$
2090 NEXT N:GOTO 2040
2100 GET#2,A$,A$
2110 FOR N=1 TO 16:GET#2,A$
2120 PRINT A$;:NEXT N
2130 PRINT" "CHR$(83-(A-129)*3)"   ";
2140 FOR N=1 TO K:GET#2,A$:NEXT N
2150 GOTO 2040
2199 REM----------------
2200 PRINT:PRINT:PRINT" ";
2210 INPUT"WHICH FILE";F$
2220 RETURN
2297 REM
2298 REM--------- Load File -----------
2299 REM
2300 OPEN 2,8,2,"0:"+F$+",S,R"
2310 INPUT#2,H
2320 FOR M=GM TO GM+4032 STEP 64
2330 GET#2,A$:W=ASC(A$)
2340 POKE M,W:IF W=T THEN 2400
2350 FOR N=M+1 TO M+W*H
2370 GET#2,A$
2380 POKE N,ASC(A$)
2390 NEXT N
2400 NEXT M
2410 CLOSE 2:RETURN
2497 REM
2498 REM--------- Save File -----------
2499 REM
2500 OPEN 2,8,2,"@0:"+F$+",S,W"
```

```
2510 PRINT#2,H
2520 FOR M=GM TO GM+4032 STEP 64
2530 W=PEEK(M):PRINT#2,CHR$(W);
2540 IF W=T THEN 2600
2550 FOR N=M+1 TO M+W*H
2560 A=PEEK(N)
2570 PRINT#2,CHR$(A);
2580 NEXT N
2600 NEXT M
2610 CLOSE 2:RETURN
3997 REM
3998 REM------ Menu for Editing -------
3999 REM
4000 PRINT TAB(22)"USE NUMBERS 0-9"
4010 PRINT TAB(22)"TO DRAW PATTERNS."
4020 PRINT
4030 PRINT TAB(22)"F1 = UP"
4040 PRINT TAB(22)"F3 = LEFT"
4050 PRINT TAB(22)"F5 = RIGHT"
4060 PRINT TAB(22)"F7 = DOWN"
4070 PRINT
4080 PRINT TAB(22)"PRESS X TO EXIT"
4090 RETURN
4097 REM
4098 REM------ Menu for Reviewing -----
4099 REM
4100 GOSUB 9100
4110 PRINT TAB(22)"1. CONTINUE":PRINT
4120 PRINT TAB(22)"2. GO BACK":PRINT
4130 PRINT TAB(22)"3. EDIT":PRINT
4140 PRINT TAB(22)"4. ABORT"
4150 PRINT:PRINT
4160 PRINT TAB(22)"CHARACTER:  "
4170 RETURN
4197 REM
4198 REM----- Display a Character -----
4199 REM
4200 K=1:W=PEEK(CM)
4210 FOR M=1 TO W
4220 FOR N=1 TO H
4230 POKE VM(M,N)+CC,0
4240 POKE VM(M,N),PEEK(CM+K)
4250 K=K+1
4260 NEXT N
4270 NEXT M
4280 RETURN
4997 REM
4998 REM-------- Set Variables --------
4999 REM
5000 POKE 650,128:POKE 56,128:CLR
5100 VA=1024:CC=55296-VA:GM=36864
5110 F=48:TH=32:T=10:FT=15
5120 F1=133:F3=134:F5=135:F7=136
5200 B$=CHR$(144)
5201 C$=CHR$(147)
5202 D$=CHR$(17)
5203 G$=CHR$(155)
5204 H$=CHR$(19)
5206 R$=CHR$(18)
5207 U$=CHR$(145)
```

```
5210 W$=CHR$(5)
5500 DIM G(10),VM(9,7),L$(26)
5510 L=VA+204
5520 FOR M=1 TO 7
5530 FOR N=1 TO 9
5540 VM(N,M)=L+N
5550 NEXT N
5560 L=L+40
5570 NEXT M
5750 G(0)=32:G(1)=160:G(2)=98:G(3)=226
5751 G(4)=223:G(5)=105:G(6)=95:G(7)=233
5752 G(8)=97:G(9)=225:G(10)=100
5800 L$(1)="37111110104111"
5801 L$(4)="3111110014115"
5802 L$(5)="3111112311001"
5803 L$(7)="37116610011011"
5804 L$(8)="3111103301111"
5805 L$(9)="11111"
5806 L$(12)="31111100010001"
5807 L$(14)="41111416004161111"
5808 L$(15)="3711610014115"
5809 L$(18)="3111110164154"
5810 L$(20)="3100011111000"
5997 REM
5998 REM----- Title & Instructions ----
5999 REM
6000 POKE 53280,3:POKE 53281,1
6010 PRINTC$CHR$(28)
6020 FOR N=1 TO 15
6030 PRINT "(24 spaces)"
6040 NEXT N:PRINTB$D$D$D$D$
6050 H=4
6060 A$="HEADLINE":X=VA+45:GOSUB 6900
6070 A$="GENERATOR":X=VA+242:GOSUB 6900
6080 PRINT"     1. RETRIEVE AN OLD ";
6085 PRINT"ALPHABET?":PRINT
6090 PRINT"     2. START A NEW ";
6095 PRINT"ALPHABET?"D$D$D$
6100 GOSUB 9000
6110 IF A<49 OR A>50 THEN 6100
6120 IF A=50 THEN 6300
6200 GOSUB 2000:GOSUB 2300
6210 GOSUB 7000:GOSUB 7500:GOTO 900
6300 PRINT"   HEIGHT OF ";
6305 PRINT"LETTERS (2-7 PIXELS):";
6310 GOSUB 9000
6320 IF A<50 OR A>55 THEN 6310
6330 H=A-48:PRINT H:GOSUB 9200
6340 GOSUB 7000:GOSUB 7500
6350 FOR N=GM TO GM+4032 STEP 64
6360 POKE N,T
6370 NEXT N
6380 GOTO 100
6897 REM
6898 REM------ Display Subroutine -----
6899 REM
6900 FOR J=1 TO LEN(A$)
6910 K=ASC(MID$(A$,J,1))-64:L=2
6920 FOR M=X TO X+VAL(LEFT$(L$(K),1))-1
6930 FOR N=M TO M+(H-1)*40 STEP 40
```

```
6940 POKE N,G(VAL(MID$(L$(K),L,1)))
6950 L=L+1
6960 NEXT N
6970 NEXT M
6980 X=M+1:NEXT J
6990 RETURN
6997 REM
6998 REM--------- Main Layout ---------
6999 REM
7000 POKE 53280,15
7010 POKE 53281,1
7020 PRINT C$G$
7030 FOR N=1 TO 15:PRINT:NEXT N
7040 FOR N=1 TO 17
7050 PRINT R$"(21 spaces)"
7060 NEXT N
7070 PRINT R$"  "U$U$U$
7080 POKE VA+999,160:POKE VA+CC+999,15
7090 L=48:FOR N=2 TO 38 STEP 4
7100 PRINT TAB(N)R$CHR$(L);
7110 L=L+1:NEXT N
7120 FOR M=VA+721 TO VA+801 STEP 40
7130 READ A$
7140 A$="000111"+A$:L=1
7150 FOR N=M TO M+38
7160 IF N/4=INT(N/4) THEN N=N+1
7170 POKE N+CC,0
7180 POKE N,G(VAL(MID$(A$,L,1)))
7190 L=L+1
7200 NEXT N:NEXT M
7210 PRINTH$B$;
7220 RETURN
7300 DATA "000111400115611007180091"
7310 DATA "222333140150061071180091"
7320 DATA "111000114500006711180091"
7497 REM
7498 REM------ Letter Grid Layout -----
7499 REM
7500 PRINT:PRINTH$G$;
7510 FOR N=1 TO 16
7520 PRINT R$"(21 spaces)"
7530 NEXT N
7540 FOR M=1 TO 9
7550 FOR N=1 TO H-1
7560 POKE VM(M,N),G(T)
7570 NEXT N
7580 POKE VM(M,H),G(O)
7590 NEXT M
7600 PRINT B$;:RETURN
8997 REM
8998 REM--------- Subroutines ---------
8999 REM
9000 GET A$:IF A$="" THEN 9000
9010 A=ASC(A$):RETURN
9100 PRINTH$:FOR N=1 TO 14
9110 PRINT TAB (22)"(17 spaces)"
9120 NEXT N
9130 PRINT H$:PRINT
9140 RETURN
9200 FOR DY=1 TO 200:NEXT DY:RETURN
```

Appendix U
Character
Generator Program
Listing

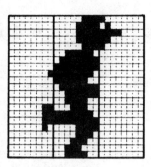

```
10 GOTO 5000
97 REM
98 REM------- Select a Character ------
99 REM
100 GOSUB 3200
120 GOSUB 4200:GOSUB 300
130 PRINT TAB(16)"ANOTHER? ";
140 PRINT"(RETURN=NEXT)
150 GOSUB 9000:GOSUB 7500
160 IF A=78 THEN 900
170 IF A=13 THEN 200
180 IF A=89 THEN 100
190 GOTO 150
200 CN=CN+1:IF CN=TH OR CN=OS THEN 200
210 CM=C+(CN*8):GOSUB 9100
220 IF CN>CR+63 THEN GOSUB 3300
230 PRINT TAB(19)"CHARACTER #"CN
240 PRINT:GOTO 120
297 REM
298 REM------- Edit a Character -------
299 REM
300 GOSUB 4000
310 X=1:Y=1:P=PEEK(VM(X,Y))
320 M=0
330 POKE VM(X,Y),CU:GOSUB 550
340 IF M=1 THEN 400
350 POKE VM(X,Y),P:GOSUB 550
360 IF M=0 THEN 330
400 IF A<>FS AND A<>TF THEN 420
412 IF A=TF THEN POKE VM(X,Y),TH
414 IF A=FS THEN POKE VM(X,Y),OS
416 X=X+1:GOTO 490
420 POKE VM(X,Y),P:IF A=1 THEN 600
430 IF A<3 OR A>6 THEN M=0:GOTO 330
440 IF A=4 THEN IF Y>1 THEN Y=Y-1
450 IF A=3 THEN IF Y<8 THEN Y=Y+1
460 IF A=5 THEN X=X-1
470 IF A=6 THEN X=X+1
480 IF X=0THEN X=8:Y=Y-1:IF Y=0THEN Y=8
490 IF X=9 THENX=1:Y=Y+1:IFY>8 THEN Y=1
500 P=PEEK(VM(X,Y))
505 IF A<7 THEN 320
```

```
510 POKE VM(X,Y),CU
515 FOR K=1 TO 10
520 NEXT K
530 GOTO 320
540 REM-------------------------
550 FOR N=1 TO 40
560 A=PEEK(KB):IF A<>SF THEN N=40:M=1
570 NEXT N
580 RETURN
590 REM-------------------------
600 POKE 198,0:GOSUB 9100
610 PRINT TAB(16)"WANT TO MEMORIZE ";
620 PRINT"THIS?":PRINT
630 GOSUB 9000
640 IF A=78 THEN RETURN
670 PRINT TAB(16)"SCANNING";
795 REM-------- Scan Letter
800 FOR N=1 TO 8
810 K=1:A=0
820 FOR M=8 TO 1 STEP -1
830 IF PEEK(VM(M,N))=OS THEN A=A+K
840 K=2*K
850 NEXT M
860 POKE CM+N-1,A
870 PRINT".";
880 NEXT N
890 PRINT:PRINT:RETURN
897 REM
898 REM---------- Main Menu -----------
899 REM
900 GOSUB 9100
910 PRINT TAB(20)"1. REVIEW"
920 PRINT TAB(20)"2. EDIT"
925 PRINT TAB(20)"3. SEE WHOLE SET"
930 PRINT TAB(20)"4. SAVE":PRINT
940 PRINT TAB(20)"...YOUR CHOICE?"
950 GOSUB 9000
960 IF A<49 OR A>52 THEN 950
970 ON A-48 GOTO 1000,100,3500,980
980 RESTORE:GOSUB 2000:GOSUB 2500
990 POKE 52,120:PRINT C$:GOTO 6080
997 REM
998 REM------------ Review ------------
999 REM
1000 GOSUB 3200:GOSUB 4100
1100 PRINT CN:PRINT U$TAB(33);
1140 GOSUB 4200
1150 S=1
1190 POKE 198,0:GOSUB 9000
1220 IF A=50 AND CN>0 THEN S=-1
1230 IF A=51 THEN GOSUB 1500
1240 IF A=52 THEN GOSUB 7500:GOTO 900
1300 CN=CN+S:CM=CM+(S*8)
1310 IF CN=>CR AND CN<=CR+63 THEN 1100
1320 IF CN=256 THEN GOSUB 7500:GOTO 900
1330 GOSUB 3300:GOTO 1100
1499 REM----------------
1500 GOSUB 9100:GOSUB 300
1510 GOSUB 4100:RETURN
1997 REM
1998 REM----- Get Disk Directory ------
```

```
1999 REM
2000 M=0:POKE 53280,15:PRINT C$
2005 PRINT" SEE THE DIRECTORY?"
2010 GOSUB 9000:IF A$="N" THEN 2200
2015 PRINT:PRINT" ";
2020 OPEN 2,8,2,"$"
2030 FOR N=1 TO 254:GET#2,A$:NEXT N
2040 K=13:M=M+1:IF M=8 THEN K=11:M=0
2050 GET#2,A$
2060 IF ST>0 THEN CLOSE 2:GOTO 2200
2070 IF A$<>"" THEN A=ASC(A$):GOTO 2100
2080 FOR N=1 TO 18+K:GET#2,A$
2090 NEXT N:GOTO 2040
2100 GET#2,A$,A$
2110 FOR N=1 TO 16:GET#2,A$
2120 PRINT A$;:NEXT N
2130 PRINT" "CHR$(83-(A-129)*3)"   ";
2140 FOR N=1 TO K:GET#2,A$:NEXT N
2150 GOTO 2040
2199 REM----------------
2200 PRINT:PRINT:PRINT" ";
2210 INPUT"WHICH FILE";F$
2220 RETURN
2297 REM
2298 REM--------- Load File ----------
2299 REM
2300 OPEN 2,8,2,"0:"+F$+",S,R"
2310 FOR N=C TO C+2047
2320 GET#2,A$
2330 POKE N,ASC(A$+CHR$(0))
2340 NEXT N
2350 CLOSE 2:RETURN
2497 REM
2498 REM--------- Save File ----------
2499 REM
2500 OPEN 2,8,2,"@0:"+F$+",S,W"
2510 FOR N=C TO C+2047
2520 PRINT#2,CHR$(PEEK(N));
2530 NEXT N
2540 CLOSE 2:RETURN
2997 REM
2998 REM----- Get Character Number ----
2999 REM
3200 GOSUB 9100
3210 PRINT TAB(19)"CHARACTER #      ";
3220 PRINT L$L$L$L$L$;:INPUT CN
3230 IF CN=TH THEN PRINT U$;:GOTO 3210
3240 IF CN=OS THEN PRINT U$;:GOTO 3210
3250 IF CN<0 THEN PRINT U$;:GOTO 3210
3260 IF CN>255 THEN PRINT U$;:GOTO 3210
3270 IF CN<CR THEN GOSUB 3300
3280 IF CN>CR+63 THEN GOSUB 3300
3290 CM=C+(8*CN):PRINT:RETURN
3299 REM--------------------
3300 IF CN>255 OR CR<0 THEN CN=0:CM=C
3310 CR=INT(CN/64)*64
3320 GOSUB 7150:GOSUB 7400:RETURN
3497 REM
3498 REM-------- See Whole Set --------
3499 REM
3500 GOSUB 9100
```

```
3510 PRINTTAB(17)"THE WHOLE SET WILL"
3520 PRINTTAB(17)"BE SHOWN IN 4 PARTS."
3530 PRINT
3540 PRINTTAB(17)"PRESS THE SPACEBAR"
3550 PRINTTAB(17)"TO PROCEED THROUGH."
3560 PRINT
3570 PRINTTAB(17)"READY?"
3580 GOSUB 9000:GOSUB 9100
3590 PRINT H$G$:GOSUB 7030
3600 CR=0:P=PEEK(53272)
3610 POKE 53272,18
3620 GOSUB 7400
3630 GOSUB 9000
3640 IF CR<192 THEN CR=CR+64:GOTO 3620
3650 POKE 53272,P
3660 CR=0
3670 GOSUB 7150:GOSUB 7400
3680 GOTO 900
3997 REM
3998 REM------ Menu for Editing -------
3999 REM
4000 PRINT TAB(19)"PRESS 1 TO INSERT"
4010 PRINT TAB(19)"PRESS 0 TO ERASE"
4020 PRINT TAB(16)"F1,F3,F5,F7 MOVE ";
4030 PRINT"CURSOR":PRINT
4040 PRINT TAB(19)"RETURN KEY: EXIT"
4050 RETURN
4097 REM
4098 REM------ Menu for Reviewing -----
4099 REM
4100 GOSUB 9100
4110 PRINT TAB(22)"1. CONTINUE"
4120 PRINT TAB(22)"2. GO BACK"
4130 PRINT TAB(22)"3. EDIT"
4140 PRINT TAB(22)"4. ABORT"
4150 PRINT:PRINT
4160 PRINT TAB(22)"CHARACTER #";
4170 RETURN
4197 REM
4198 REM----- Display a Character -----
4199 REM
4200 FOR N=1 TO 8
4210 A=PEEK(CM+N-1):K=128
4220 FOR M=1 TO 8
4230 IF A<K THEN POKE VM(M,N),TH
4240 IF A=>K THEN POKE VM(M,N),OS:A=A-K
4250 K=K/2
4260 NEXT M
4270 NEXT N
4280 RETURN
4997 REM
4998 REM-------- Switch Banks ---------
4999 REM
5000 POKE 56,128:CLR
5010 C=34816:VA=33792:D=53248
5020 POKE 56576,21
5030 POKE 648,132
5040 POKE 53272,20
5050 PRINT CHR$(147)CHR$(8)
5097 REM
5098 REM-------- Set Variables --------
```

```
5099 REM
5100 CA=55296:CC=CA-VA:CR=0
5110 F=48:TH=32:G=100:HF=185:OS=160
5120 TF=35:FS=56:SF=64:CU=91:KB=203
5200 B$=CHR$(144)
5201 C$=CHR$(147)
5202 D$=CHR$(17)
5203 G$=CHR$(155)
5204 H$=CHR$(19)
5205 L$=CHR$(157)
5206 R$=CHR$(18)
5207 U$=CHR$(145)
5208 RR$=CHR$(146)
5210 W$=CHR$(5)
5220 SP$="      (22 spaces)          "
5500 DIM G(7),VM(8,8),L$(26),NR(2)
5510 L=VA+43
5520 FOR M=1 TO 8
5530 FOR N=1 TO 8
5540 VM(N,M)=L+N
5550 NEXT N
5560 L=L+40
5570 NEXT M
5750 G(0)=32:G(1)=160:G(2)=98:G(3)=226
5751 G(4)=223:G(5)=105:G(6)=95:G(7)=233
5800 L$(1)="3711110104111"
5801 L$(3)="3711610011001"
5802 L$(5)="3111112311001"
5803 L$(7)="3711610011011"
5804 L$(8)="41111023002301111"
5807 L$(14)="41111416004161111"
5808 L$(15)="3711610014115"
5809 L$(18)="3111110164154"
5810 L$(20)="3100011111000"
5997 REM
5998 REM----- Title & Instructions ----
5999 REM
6000 POKE 53280,3:POKE 53281,1
6010 PRINTC$CHR$(28)
6020 FOR N=1 TO 17
6030 PRINT SP$;
6040 NEXT N:PRINTB$D$D$
6050 H=4
6060 A$="CHARACTER":X=VA+42:GOSUB 6900
6070 A$="GENERATOR":X=VA+242:GOSUB 6900
6080 PRINT"     1. RETRIEVE AN OLD ";
6085 PRINT"ALPHABET?"D$
6090 PRINT"     2. START A NEW ";
6095 PRINT"ALPHABET?"D$D$
6100 GOSUB 9000
6110 IF A<49 OR A>50 THEN 6100
6120 IF A=50 THEN 6300
6200 GOSUB 2000:GOSUB 2300
6210 GOSUB 7000:GOSUB 7500
6220 GOSUB 7150:GOSUB 7400:GOTO 900
6300 PRINT"     COPY COMMODORE SET ";
6305 PRINT"1 OR 2?"D$
6310 GOSUB 9000
6315 IF A<49 OR A>50 THEN 6310
6320 IF A=50 THEN D=D+2048
6340 PRINT"          COPYING ";
```

```
6350 PRINT"CHARACTER SET..."
6359 REM----- Copy Commodore Characters
6360 POKE 56334,0
6370 POKE 1,PEEK(1) AND 251
6380 FOR N=0 TO 2047
6390 POKE C+N,PEEK(D+N)
6400 NEXT N
6410 POKE 1,PEEK(1) OR 4
6420 POKE 56334,1
6430 GOSUB 7000:GOSUB 7500
6440 GOSUB 7150:GOSUB 7400
6450 GOTO 100
6897 REM
6898 REM------ Display Subroutine -----
6899 REM
6900 FOR J=1 TO LEN(A$)
6910 K=ASC(MID$(A$,J,1))-64:L=2
6920 FOR M=X TO X+VAL(LEFT$(L$(K),1))-1
6930 FOR N=M TO M+(H-1)*40 STEP 40
6940 POKE N,G(VAL(MID$(L$(K),L,1)))
6950 L=L+1
6960 NEXT N
6970 NEXT M
6980 X=M+1:NEXT J
6990 RETURN
6997 REM
6998 REM--------- Main Layout ---------
6999 REM
7000 POKE 53280,15
7010 POKE 53281,1
7020 PRINT C$G$
7030 FOR N=1 TO 8:PRINT:NEXT N
7040 FOR N=1 TO 29
7050 PRINT R$;SP$;
7060 NEXT N
7070 PRINT R$" "U$U$B$H$
7080 POKE VA+999,160:POKE VA+CC+999,15
7100 FOR L=CA+404 TO CA+964 STEP 80
7110 FOR M=L TO L+35 STEP 5
7120 POKE M,0
7130 NEXT M
7140 NEXT L:RETURN
7149 REM----------
7150 A$=STR$(CR)
7160 IF LEN(A$)>3 THEN 7180
7170 A$=" "+A$:GOTO 7160
7180 FOR N=0 TO 2
7190 NR(N)=ASC(MID$(A$,N+2,1))+128
7195 NEXT N
7199 REM---------------
7200 FOR L=VA+401 TO VA+961 STEP 80
7210 FOR M=L TO L+35 STEP 5
7220 FOR N=0 TO 2
7230 POKE M+N,NR(N)
7240 NEXT N
7250 NR(2)=NR(2)+1
7260 IF NR(2)>HF THEN GOSUB 7300
7270 NEXT M
7280 NEXT L
7290 RETURN
7299 REM---------------
```

```
7300 K=1
7310 NR(K+1)=176
7320 IF NR(K)=OS THEN NR(K)=177:RETURN
7330 NR(K)=NR(K)+1
7340 IF NR(K)>HF THEN K=0:GOTO 7310
7350 RETURN
7399 REM--------------
7400 K=CR
7410 FOR L=VA+404 TO VA+964 STEP 80
7420 FOR M=L TO L+35 STEP 5
7430 POKE M,K
7440 K=K+1
7450 NEXT M
7460 NEXT L
7470 RETURN
7497 REM
7498 REM------ Letter Grid Layout -----
7499 REM
7500 PRINT:PRINTH$G$;
7510 PRINTR$"  (15 spaces)    "
7520 FOR N=1 TO 8
7530 PRINTR$"     "RR$B$" (8 spc) "R$G$;
7540 PRINT"    "
7550 NEXT N
7560 PRINT B$:RETURN
8997 REM
8998 REM--------- Subroutines ---------
8999 REM
9000 GET A$:IF A$="" THEN 9000
9010 A=ASC(A$):RETURN
9100 PRINTH$:FOR N=1 TO 7
9110 PRINT TAB(16)" "SP$
9120 NEXT N
9130 PRINT H$
9140 RETURN
```

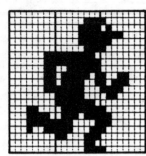

Appendix V
Sprite Generator
Program Listing

```
10 GOTO 50000
85 REM
90 REM ------------ DRAW SPRITE
95 REM
100 IF NS=47 THEN RETURN
102 NS=NS+1:MS=NS:GOSUB 20300
105 GOSUB 10500:GOSUB1900:POKE VC+21,15
110 IF MC=2 THEN POKE VC+28,15
120 GOSUB 20200:UD=0:LR=0:H=HT:X=V+94
125 Y=XS+SF*SP(MS):Z=X+CC:ED=1:GOTO 130
126 POKE Z,C(P):IF MC=2THENPOKEZ+1,C(P)
127 POKE X,S:X=X+D:Z=Z+D
130 POKE X,CU
140 GET A$:IF A$="" THEN 140
150 P=ASC(A$)
160 IF P=RT THEN GOSUB 400:GOTO 127
170 IF P=LF THEN GOSUB 500:GOTO 127
180 IF P=UP THEN IF UD>0 THEN UD=UD-1:Y=Y-3:D=-FY:GOTO 127
190 IF P=DN THEN IF UD<20 THEN UD=UD+1:Y=Y+3:D=FY:GOTO 127
200 IF P<FI THEN IF P>FE THEN P=P-FE:CL=2-P:GOSUB 300:GOTO 126
210 IF P=FI OR P=52 THEN IF MC=2 THEN P=P-FE:GOSUB 300:GOTO 126
215 POKE X,S
220 IF P=ESTHENGOSUB51400:POKEVC+21,0:POKEVC+28,0:MC=1:ED=0:RETURN
230 IF P=67 THEN GOSUB 10600:GOTO 120
240 GOTO 140
285 REM
290 REM --------------- UPDATE SPRITE
295 REM
300 IF MC=2 THEN POKE Y,(PEEK(Y)AND(TF-H-H/2))+H*CV(P):GOTO 400
320 POKE Y,(PEEK(Y)AND(TF-H))+H*(P-1)
385 REM
390 REM -------------- MOVE CURSOR RT
395 REM
400 H=H/(2*MC):D=MC:IF H=>1THENRETURN
410 H=HT:Y=Y+1:LR=LR+1:IF LR<3 THEN RETURN
420 LR=0:UD=UD+1:D=16+MC:IF UD<21 THEN RETURN
430 UD=0:D=-(824-MC):Y=Y-63:RETURN
485 REM
490 REM --------------- MOVE CURSOR LFT
495 REM
500 H=H*2*MC:D=-MC:IF H<=HT THENRETURN
510 H=MC:Y=Y-1:LR=LR-1:IF LR=>0THEN RETURN
```

```
520 LR=2:UD=UD-1:D=-(16+MC):IF UD=>0 THEN RETURN
530 UD=20:D=824-MC:Y=Y+63:RETURN
985 REM
990 REM --------------- REVIEW
995 REM
1000 IF NS<0 THEN RETURN
1010 MS=0
1020 GOSUB 1850
1030 GOSUB 20100
1040 GET A$:IF A$="" THEN 1040
1050 P=ASC(A$)
1060 IFP=RT THEN D=1:GOSUB1800:GOTO1040
1070 IFP=LF THEND=-1:GOSUB1800:GOTO1040
1080 IFP=68 THEN 2000
1090 IFP=69 THENGOSUB3000:ED=1:GOSUB120:ED=0:GOTO 1020
1100 IFP=67 THEN GOSUB 10600:GOTO 1030
1130 IF P=ES THEN POKE VC+21,0:POKE VC+28,0:MC=1:RETURN
1140 GOTO 1040
1800 MS=MS+D
1810 IF MS>NS THEN MS=0
1820 IF MS<0 THEN MS=NS
1850 P=PEEK(XS+SF*SP(MS)+63):IFP=MCTHEN1900
1860 POKE VC+21,0
1870 MC=P:IF MC=2 THEN POKE VC+28,15
1880 IF MC=1 THEN POKE VC+28,0
1900 FOR N=PS TO PS+3:POKE N,SP(MS)+BA
1910 NEXT N:POKE VC+21,15
1920 IF MS<10 THEN POKE NL,MS+FE:POKE NL-1,TH:RETURN
1930 M=INT(MS/10):POKE NL-1,M+FE:POKE NL,MS-10*M+FE:RETURN
1985 REM
1990 REM -------------------- DELETE SUBROUTINE
1995 REM
2000 GOSUB 10300:PRINT
2010 PRINT"   DELETE":PRINT:PRINT"   THIS?"
2020 GOSUB 10020:IF P<>89THENGOSUB10300:GOSUB 20100:GOTO 1
2030 M=SP(MS):NS=NS-1
2040 IF MS=NS+1 THEN MS=0:GOTO 2100
2050 FOR N=MS TO NS:SP(N)=SP(N+1)
2060 NEXT N:SP(NS+1)=M
2100 GOSUB 1900:GOTO 1020
2985 REM
2990 REM --------------- DISPLAY BIG SPRITE
2995 REM
3000 X=V+94:Y=XS+SP(MS)*SF:Z=X+CC
3010 IF MC=2 THEN 4000
3020 FOR L=Y TO Y+60 STEP 3
3030 FOR M=L TO L+2
3040 P=PEEK(M):H=HT:FOR N=1 TO 8
3050 A=C(1):IF P=>H THEN A=C(2):P=P-H
3060 POKE Z,A:Z=Z+1
3070 H=H/2:NEXT N:NEXT M
3080 Z=Z+16:NEXT L:RETURN
4000 FOR L=Y TO Y+60 STEP 3
4010 FOR M=L TO L+2
4020 P=PEEK(M):H=HT:FOR N=1TO4:A=1
4030 IF P=>H THEN A=2:P=P-H
4040 H=H/2:IF P=>H THEN A=A+2:P=P-H
4050 H=H/2:POKE Z,C(A)
4060 POKE Z+1,C(A):Z=Z+2
4070 NEXT N:NEXT M:Z=Z+16:NEXT L:RETURN
8985 REM
```

```
8990 REM ----------------- LOAD
8995 REM
9000 PRINT C$:GOSUB 9800
9100 OPEN 2,8,2,"0:"+F$+",S,R"
9110 INPUT#2,MS:IF MS+NS>46 THEN 9200
9120 FOR M=1+NS TO 1+NS+MS
9130 L=XS+SP(M)*SF
9140 FOR N=L TO L+63
9150 GET#2,A$:POKE N,ASC(A$+CHR$(0))
9160 NEXT N:NEXT M:CLOSE 2
9170 NS=NS+MS+1:GOSUB 51000:RETURN
9200 CLOSE 2:PRINT" EXCESS DATA"
9210 GOSUB 10000:RETURN
9485 REM
9490 REM ---------------- SAVE
9495 REM
9500 IF NS=-1 THEN RETURN
9510 PRINT C$:GOSUB 9800
9600 OPEN 2,8,2,"@0:"+F$+",S,W"
9610 PRINT#2,NS
9620 FOR M=0 TO NS
9630 L=XS+SP(M)*SF
9640 FOR N=L TO L+63
9650 PRINT#2,CHR$(PEEK(N));
9660 NEXT N:NEXT M:CLOSE 2
9670 PRINT" BACKUP DISK?"
9680 GOSUB 10000:IF P=89 THEN 9510
9690 GOSUB 51000:RETURN
9795 REM------------------
9800 PRINT:PRINT" FILE NAME":PRINT
9810 PRINT" ";:INPUT F$
9820 PRINT:PRINT" DISK READY?"
9830 GOSUB 10000:PRINT:RETURN
9985 REM
9990 REM ---------- INPUT SUBROUTINES
9995 REM
10000 GET A$:IF A$="" THEN 10000
10010 P=ASC(A$):RETURN
10020 GOSUB 10000
10030 IF P<>78 AND P<>89 THEN 10020
10040 RETURN
10050 GOSUB 10000
10060 IF P<MN OR P>MX THEN 10050
10070 RETURN
10285 REM
10290 REM -------------- CLEAR PROMPTS
10295 REM
10300 PRINT H$:PRINT
10310 FOR N=1 TO 8
10320 PRINT" (13 spaces) ":NEXT N
10330 PRINT H$:PRINT B$:RETURN
10385 REM
10390 REM ---------- CHANGE COLORS
10395 REM
10400 L=V+441+CC
10410 FOR M=L TO L+440 STEP 40
10420 FOR N=M TO M+11
10430 POKE N,C(1):NEXT N:NEXT M
10440 FOR N=VC+39 TO VC+42
10450 POKE N,C(2):NEXT N
10460 POKE VC+37,C(3):POKE VC+(38),C(4)
```

```
10480 RETURN
10500 M=XS+SP(MS)*SF:FOR N=M TO M+62
10510 POKE N,0:NEXT N
10520 POKE N,MC:RETURN
10585 REM
10590 REM -------------- SELECT NEW COLORS
10595 REM
10600 PRINT H$:PRINT
10610 FOR N=0 TO 7
10620 PRINT" "CN$(N)"  "CN$(N+8)
10630 NEXT N
10650 FOR M=1 TO MC*2
10660 PRINT H$TAB(10*M-7)CHR$(214)BK$;
10670 X$="":FOR N=1 TO 5
10675 GOSUB 10000
10680 IF N=1 AND P=13 THEN N=5:NEXT N:PRINTCN$(C(M)):GOTO 10750
10685 IF A$<"A" OR A$>"Z" THEN IF P<>32 THEN 10675
10686 PRINT A$CHR$(214)BK$;:X$=X$+A$
10690 NEXT N:PRINT" ";
10700 K=0:FOR N=0 TO 15
10710 IF X$=CN$(N)THEN C(M)=N:N=15:K=1
10720 NEXT N:IF K=0 THEN 10660
10750 NEXT M:GOSUB 10300:GOSUB 10400
10760 IF ED=0 THEN RETURN
10800 PRINT" COP Y THE
10810 PRINT" NEW COLORS
10820 PRINT" INTO THE
10830 PRINT" DISPLA Y
10840 PRINT" GRID?
10850 GOSUB 10020:IF P=89THENGOSUB3000
10860 RETURN
19985 REM
19990 REM ----------- MENUS
19995 REM
20000 GOSUB10300:POKENL,TH:POKENL-1,TH
20010 PRINT
20015 PRINT" 1:LOAD
20020 PRINT" 2:SAVE
20030 PRINT" 3:REVIEW
20040 PRINT" 4:NEW SPRITE
20050 PRINT" 5:COLOR TEST
20060 PRINT" 6:CLEAR MEM.
20070 MN=49:MX=54:GOSUB10050:ON P-48 GOSUB9000,9500,1000,100,52000
20080 GOTO 20000
20090 GOSUB 10300:PRINT:PRINT
20091 PRINT"    ERASE":PRINT"    ALL":PRINT"    DATA?"
20092 GOSUB 10020:IF P=78 THEN RETURN
20093 RUN
20100 GOSUB 10300:PRINT
20110 PRINT" F5:NEXT
20120 PRINT" F3:PREVIOUS
20130 PRINT"  D:DELETE
20140 PRINT"  E:EDIT
20150 PRINT"  C:NEW COLRS
20180 PRINT"  X:EXIT
20190 RETURN
20200 GOSUB 10300:PRINT
20210 PRINT"  F1:UP
20211 PRINT"  F3:LEFT
20212 PRINT"  F5:RIGHT
20213 PRINT"  F7:DOWN
```

```
20214 PRINT" 1-4:COLOR
20215 PRINT"   C:NEW COLS
20218 PRINT"   X:EXIT
20220 RETURN
20300 GOSUB 10300:PRINT
20310 PRINT"   1:SINGLE
20320 PRINT"     COLOR
20330 PRINT
20340 PRINT"   2:MULTI-
20350 PRINT"     COLOR
20360 MN=49:MX=50:GOSUB10050
20370 MC=P-48:RETURN
49985 REM
49990 REM ------------- SWITCH BANKS
49995 REM
50000 POKE 56576,21:POKE 53272,4
50010 POKE 648,128:POKE 650,128
50020 PRINT CHR$(142)CHR$(147)
50030 POKE 52,128:POKE 56,128:CLR
50035 REM
50040 REM ------------ CONSTANTS
50045 REM
50050 V=32768:CC=22528:VC=53248
50060 VB=53281:XS=33792:PS=V+1016:TH=32
50070 BA=16:CU=86:RT=135:ES=88:NL=V+970
50075 BA=16:FE=48:FI=51:UP=133:DN=136
50080 FY=40:SF=64:HT=128:TF=255:S=160
50085 REM
50090 REM --------------- VARIABLES
50095 REM
50100 A=0:B=0:D=0:H=0:J=0:K=0:L=0:M=0
50110 N=0:P=0:X=0:Z=0
50120 MC=1:NS=-1:MS=0
50130 UD=0:LR=0:MX=0:MN=0:ED=0
50135 REM
50140 REM ------------- DIMD VARS
50145 REM
50150 DIM C(4):DIM SP(47)
50155 FOR N=1 TO 47
50156 SP(N)=N:NEXT N
50160 C(1)=1:C(2)=0:C(3)=3:C(4)=7
50165 DIM CV(4):CV(1)=0:CV(2)=1
50166 CV(3)=.5:CV(4)=1.5
50185 REM
50190 REM ------------- STRINGS
50195 REM
50200 H$=CHR$(19):C$=CHR$(147)
50210 B$=CHR$(144):W$=CHR$(5)
50220 R$=CHR$(18):S$=CHR$(146)
50250 BK$=CHR$(157):A$="":F$=""
50260 DIM CN$(15)
50270 FOR N=0 TO 15:READ CN$(N):NEXT N
50280 DATA "BLACK","WHITE","RED  "
50290 DATA "CYAN ","MAGEN","GREEN"
50300 DATA "BLUE ","YELLO","ORANG"
50310 DATA "BROWN","LRED ","DGRAY"
50320 DATA "MGRAY","LGREE","LBLUE"
50330 DATA "LGRAY"
50385 REM
50390 REM --------------- SPRITE SETUP
50395 REM
```

```
50400 FOR N=0 TO 7:READ M
50410 POKE VC+N,M:NEXT
50420 DATA 36,143,76,143,36,185,76,185
50430 POKE VC+23,12:POKE VC+29,10
50500 GOSUB 51000:GOTO 20010
50985 REM
50990 REM --------------- SCREEN LAYOUT
50995 REM
51000 POKE VB,12:POKE VB-1,12:PRINT C$;
51005 FOR N=1 TO 4
51006 PRINTW$STR$(N)":"B$CN$(C(N));
51007 IF N<4 THEN PRINT"  ";
51008 NEXT N:PRINTW$
51010 M=48:FOR N=V+119 TO V+919 STEP FY
51020 POKE N+CC,0:POKE N,M
51030 M=M+1:IF M=58 THEN M=48
51040 NEXT N
51100 M=48:FOR N=V+997 TO V+974 STEP -1
51110 POKE N,M:POKE N+CC,0
51120 M=M+1:IF M=56 THEN M=48
51130 NEXT N
51200 PRINT H$W$
51210 FOR N=1 TO 10:PRINT:NEXT
51220 FOR N=1 TO 4:GOSUB 51500:NEXT
51230 PRINT
51240 FOR N=1 TO 7:GOSUB 51500:NEXT
51250 PRINT:PRINT" SPRITE #";
51260 GOSUB 10400:POKE VC+28,0
51400 PRINT H$W$:PRINT
51410 FOR N=1 TO 21
51420 PRINTTAB(14)R$" (24 spaces) ":NEXT
51430 PRINTB$H$:PRINT:RETURN
51500 PRINT" "R$"     "S$" "R$"         ":RETURN
51510 GOSUB 10400:RETURN
51985 REM
51990 REM --------------- COLOR TEST
51995 REM
52000 PRINT C$:K=V+10+CC
52010 FOR M=0 TO 15
52020 PRINT CN$(M)"     "R$" (20 spaces) "S$
52030 K=K+FY:FOR N=K TO K+19
52040 POKE N,M:NEXT N:NEXT M
52050 GOSUB 10000:GOSUB 51000:RETURN
```

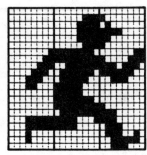

Appendix W
Graphics Generator
Program Listing

```
10 REM-------GRAPHICS GENERATOR-------
20 REM
30 GOSUB 1000
40 P=PEEK(X):Q=PEEK(X+CC)
50 POKE X+CC,O:POKE X,CU
60 GET A$:IF A$="" THEN 60
70 IF A$="U" THEN D=-40:GOTO 180
80 IF A$="D" THEN D=40:GOTO 180
90 IF A$="L" THEN D=-1:GOTO 180
100 IF A$="R" THEN D=1:GOTO 180
110 IF A$="I" THEN P=A:Q=C:D=1:GOTO 180
120 IF A$="E" THEN P=S:Q=1:D=1:GOTO 180
130 IF A$="A" THEN 300
140 IF A$="C" THEN 500
150 IF A$="S" THEN 800
160 IF A$="H" THEN 600
170 GOTO 60
180 POKE X+CC,Q
190 POKE X,P
200 IF X+D>VA+NN THEN X=X-1000
210 IF X+D<VA THEN X=X+1000
220 X=X+D:GOTO 40
297 REM
298 REM--------NEW ASCII CODE---------
299 REM
300 B$="ASCII OF NEW GRAPHICS:      "
310 GOSUB 900:M=Y+24:A=0
320 GOSUB 2000
330 IF A$<"0" OR A$>"2" THEN 320
340 POKEM,ASC(A$):A=A+100*VAL(A$):M=M+1
350 GOSUB 2000
360 IF A$<"0" OR A$>"9" THEN 350
370 POKE M,ASC(A$):A=A+10*VAL(A$):M=M+1
380 GOSUB 2000
390 IF A$<"0" OR A$>"9" THEN 380
400 POKE M,ASC(A$):A=A+VAL(A$)
410 GOSUB 950:IF A>255 THEN 300
420 GOTO 60
497 REM
498 REM--------NEW COLOR CODE---------
499 REM
500 B$="CODE OF NEW COLOR:    "
```

```
510 GOSUB 900:M=Y+20:C=0
520 GOSUB 2000
530 IF A$<"0" OR A$>"1" THEN 520
540 POKE M,ASC(A$):C=C+10*VAL(A$):M=M+1
550 GOSUB 2000
560 IF A$<"0" OR A$>"9" THEN 550
570 POKE M,ASC(A$):C=C+VAL(A$)
580 GOSUB 950:IF C>15 THEN 500
590 GOTO 60
597 REM
598 REM---------HELP MESSAGE----------
599 REM
600 B$="U=UP:D=DOWN:L=LEFT:R=RIGHT"
610 GOSUB 900:GOSUB 2000:GOSUB 950
620 B$="I=INSERT:E=ERASE:H=HELP"
630 GOSUB 900:GOSUB 2000:GOSUB 950
640 B$="A=ASCII:C=COLOR:S=SAVE"
650 GOSUB 900:GOSUB 2000:GOSUB 950
660 GOTO 60
797 REM
798 REM----------SAVE PICTURE----------
799 REM
800 B$="READY TO SAVE?":GOSUB 900
810 GOSUB 2000
820 IF A$<>"Y" AND A$<>"N" THEN 810
830 GOSUB 950:IF A$="N" THEN 60
835 POKE X,P:POKE X+CC,Q
840 OPEN 2,8,2,"@0:"+F$+",S,W"
850 FOR N=VA TO VA+999
860 PRINT#2,CHR$(PEEK(N+CC));
870 PRINT#2,CHR$(PEEK(N));
880 NEXT N
890 CLOSE 2:GOTO 40
897 REM
898 REM--------DISPLAY A MESSAGE-------
899 REM
900 FOR N=1 TO LEN(B$)
910 A(N)=PEEK(N+Y):B(N)=PEEK(N+Y+CC)
920 POKE N+Y+CC,0
925 M=ASC(MID$(B$,N,1))
930 IF M>SF THEN M=M-SF
935 POKE N+Y,M
940 NEXT N:RETURN
950 FOR N=1 TO LEN(B$)
960 POKE N+Y,A(N)
970 POKE N+Y+CC,B(N)
980 NEXT N:RETURN
997 REM
998 REM------------START-UP------------
999 REM
1000 POKE 53281,1:POKE 53280,1
1010 PRINT CHR$(147)CHR$(144)
1020 PRINT"GRAPHICS GENERATOR":PRINT
1030 PRINT"COMMAND CODES:":PRINT
1040 PRINT"U = UP"
1050 PRINT"D = DOWN"
1060 PRINT"L = LEFT"
1070 PRINT"R = RIGHT"
1080 PRINT"I = INSERT"
1090 PRINT"E = ERASE"
1110 PRINT"C = NEW COLOR"
```

```
1120 PRINT"A = NEW ASCII CODE"
1130 PRINT"S = SAVE"
1140 PRINT"H = HELP":PRINT
1200 P=0:Q=0:D=0:M=0:N=0
1300 VA=1024:CC=54272:X=1524:Y=VA+959
1310 A=160:C=0:CU=86:S=32:SF=64:NN=999
1350 DIM A(40),B(40)
1400 A$="":B$="":F$=""
1500 POKE 650,128
1600 INPUT"SCREEN BACKGROUND COLOR";M
1610 POKE 53281,M:PRINT
1620 INPUT"SCREEN BORDER COLOR";M
1630 POKE 53280,M:PRINT
1650 PRINT"WANT TO LOAD & EDIT?":PRINT
1660 GOSUB 2000:IF A$="Y" THEN 1800
1700 PRINT"WHICH FILE WILL YOU"
1710 INPUT"SAVE THE PICTURE IN";F$
1720 PRINT CHR$(147)
1730 RETURN
1797 REM
1798 REM---------LOAD PICTURE----------
1799 REM
1800 INPUT"FILE NAME";F$
1810 OPEN 2,8,2,"0:"+F$+",S,R"
1820 FOR N=VA TO VA+999
1830 GET#2,A$
1840 POKE N+CC,ASC(A$+CHR$(0))
1850 GET#2,A$
1860 POKE N,ASC(A$+CHR$(0))
1870 NEXT N
1880 CLOSE 2:GOTO 40
1999 REM
2000 GET A$:IF A$="" THEN 2000
2010 RETURN
```

Appendix X
Complete Listing for Air Attack— Final Version

```
10 GOSUB 1000
50 IF TI$>"000200" THEN 900
60 PRINT MID$(TI$,4,1)":"RIGHT$(TI$,2);
70 PRINT TAB(FT)SC:PRINT U$;
97 REM
98 REM--------- MOVE AIRPLANE ---------
99 REM
100 L=L+1
120 IF YA+IY<VU THEN L=0:N=3-N
130 IF YA+IY>VD THEN L=0:N=3-N
140 IF XA+IX<VL ORXA+IX>VRTHENL=0:N=N+4
150 IF N>7 THEN N=N-8
160 IF L>T THEN L=0:N=INT(RND(1)*8)
170 IX=SGN(D(N))*8:IY=ABS(D(N))-SX
175 XA=XA+IX:YA=YA+IY
180 POKE SP,A(N)
190 POKE VC,XA:POKE VC+1,YA
197 REM
198 REM---------- MOVE GUN ----------
199 REM
200 GET A$
210 IG=0
220 IF A$="1" AND XG-SX=>VL THEN IG=-SX
230 IF A$="2" AND XG+SX<=VR THEN IG=SX
240 XG=XG+IG
250 POKE VC+2,XG
297 REM
298 REM---------- MOVE BULLET ---------
299 REM
300 IF A$=CHR$(BS) THEN 370
310 IF YB=0 THEN 50
320 YB=YB-T
330 IF YB<VU THEN YB=0
340 POKE VC+5,YB
350 IF PEEK(VC+TH)>0 THEN 800
360 GOTO 50
365 REM---------- FIRE GUN ---------
370 XB=XG
380 YB=208
390 POKE VC+4,XB:POKE VC+5,YB:GOTO 50
797 REM
```

```
798 REM------ BULLET HITS TARGET ------
799 REM
800 POKE VC+TH,0:POKE VC+21,3
810 A=7:B=253:GOSUB 860
820 A=8:B=254:GOSUB 860
830 A=9:B=255:GOSUB 860
840 POKE VC+21,2:SC=SC+1
845 GOSUB 880
850 GOSUB 2800:GOTO 50
855 REM---------- DELAY LOOP
860 POKE VC+39,A
870 POKE SP,B
880 FOR C=1 TO 100:NEXT C
890 RETURN
897 REM
898 REM--------- TIME RUNS OUT --------
899 REM
900 POKE 53280,1:POKE 53281,1
910 PRINT C$:POKE VC+21,0
920 PRINT"YOUR SCORE:";SC
930 PRINT:PRINT
940 PRINT"PLAY AGAIN?"
950 GET A$:IF A$="" THEN 950
960 IF A$="Y" THEN GOSUB 2700:GOTO 50
970 END
997 REM
998 REM----- ESTABLISH CONSTANTS ------
999 REM
1000 VA=1024:CA=55296:CC=CA-VA:VC=53248
1005 SX=16:TH=30:SP=2040
1006 T=10:FT=15:BS=32
1010 VU=58:VD=150:VL=24:VR=255
1015 A(0)=246:A(1)=247:A(2)=249
1016 A(3)=250:A(4)=248:A(5)=245
1017 A(6)=245:A(7)=248
1020 D(0)=24:D(1)=-24:D(2)=-8:D(3)=8
1021 D(4)=-16:D(5)=16:D(6)=16:D(7)=-16
1025 G(0)=32:G(1)=160:G(2)=98:G(3)=226
1026 G(4)=223:G(5)=105:G(6)=95:G(7)=233
1040 POKE 650,128
1047 REM
1048 REM----- ESTABLISH VARIABLES -----
1049 REM
1050 A=0:B=0:C=0:D=0:E=0
1060 H=0:L=0:N=0:X=0:SC=0
1070 AA=0:AB=0:AG=0
1080 XA=0:YA=0:XG=0:XB=0:YB=0
1097 REM
1098 REM------ ESTABLISH STRINGS ------
1099 REM
1100 DIM L$(26)
1101 L$(1)="6071117111111523016230411111"
1102 L$(1)=L$(1)+"04111"
1103 L$(3)="5711161111111000113021430025"
1109 L$(9)="21111111111"
1111 L$(11)="611111111111071507116015411"
1112 L$(11)=L$(11)+"150041"
1118 L$(18)="5111111111101601111141541"
1120 L$(20)="4100001111111111110000"
1140 A$="":U$=CHR$(145):C$=CHR$(147)
1797 REM
```

```
1798 REM-------- SHOW HEADLINE --------
1799 REM
1800 H=5:POKE 53280,3:POKE 53281,3
1810 PRINT C$
1820 A$="AIR":X=VA+172:GOSUB 2500
1830 A$="ATTACK":X=VA+442:GOSUB 2500
1840 FOR A=1 TO 19
1850 PRINT
1860 NEXT A
1870 PRINT TAB(9)"PRESS ANY KEY ";
1880 PRINT"TO BEGIN"
1890 GET A$:IF A$="" THEN 1890
1997 REM
1998 REM-------- INSTRUCTIONS ---------
1999 REM
2000 POKE 53280,1:POKE 53281,1
2010 PRINT C$;CHR$(144)
2020 PRINT"THE OBJECT OF THIS GAME"
2030 PRINT"IS TO SHOOT DOWN AN ENEMY"
2040 PRINT"AIRPLANE.":PRINT:PRINT
2050 PRINT"USE KEYS 1 AND 2 TO MOVE"
2060 PRINT"YOUR GUN LEFT AND RIGHT."
2070 PRINT"PRESS THE SPACEBAR"
2080 PRINT"TO FIRE.":PRINT:PRINT
2090 PRINT"YOU HAVE TWO MINUTES"
2100 PRINT"TO SCORE AS MANY HITS"
2110 PRINT"AS YOU CAN.":PRINT:PRINT
2120 PRINT"PRESS ANY KEY TO BEGIN."
2130 GET A$:IF A$="" THEN 2130
2140 PRINT:PRINT
2150 PRINT"LOADING SPRITE DATA..."
2160 GOSUB 2600
2170 RETURN
2497 REM
2498 REM----- HEADLINE SUBROUTINE -----
2499 REM
2500 FOR A=1 TO LEN(A$)
2510 B=ASC(MID$(A$,A,1))-64
2520 C=2
2530 FOR D=X TO X+VAL(LEFT$(L$(B),1))-1
2540 FOR E=D TO D+(H-1)*40 STEP 40
2550 POKE E+CC,2
2560 POKE E,G(VAL(MID$(L$(B),C,1)))
2570 C=C+1
2575 NEXT E
2580 NEXT D
2585 X=D+1
2590 NEXT A
2595 RETURN
2597 REM
2598 REM------ READ & POKE DATA -------
2599 REM
2600 FOR A=15680 TO 16320 STEP 64
2610 FOR B=A TO A+62
2620 READ C:POKE B,C
2630 NEXT B
2640 NEXT A
2697 REM
2698 REM-------- SET UP SCREEN --------
2699 REM
2700 POKE 53280,3:POKE 53281,3
```

```
2710 PRINT C$;
2750 PRINT SPC(5)"TIME"SPC(10)"HITS"
2760 PRINT U$;
2770 TI$="000000":SC=0:L=10:K=3
2800 POKE SP,245
2810 POKE SP+1,251:POKE SP+2,252
2820 XA=160:YA=100:XG=160:YB=0
2830 POKE VC,XA:POKE VC+1,YA
2840 POKE VC+2,XG:POKE VC+3,229
2850 POKE VC+5,YB:POKE VC+16,0
2860 POKE VC+39,2:POKE VC+40,5
2870 POKE VC+41,0:POKE VC+30,0
2880 POKE VC+21,7
2890 RETURN
2997 REM
2998 REM-------- AIRPLANE DATA --------
2999 REM
3000 DATA 3,128,0,3,192,0,1,224,0,1,240
3010 DATA 0,0,248,0,0,252,0,192,126,0
3020 DATA 224,127,0,240,127,128,255,255
3030 DATA 254,255,255,255,255,255,254
3040 DATA 240,127,128,224,127,0,192,126
3050 DATA 0,0,252,0,0,248,0,1,240,0,1
3060 DATA 224,0,3,192,0,3,128,0
3099 REM
3100 DATA 12,3,0,28,3,0,60,7,0,124,7,0
3110 DATA 254,15,0,255,15,0,15,159,0,7
3120 DATA 223,0,3,255,0,1,255,0,0,255,0
3130 DATA 3,255,0,15,255,0,63,255,0,255
3140 DATA 255,128,255,255,192,0,3,224,0
3150 DATA 1,240,0,0,248,0,0,120,0,0,56
3199 REM
3200 DATA 0,192,48,0,192,56,0,224,60
3210 DATA 0,224,62,0,240,127,0,240,255
3220 DATA 0,249,240,0,251,224,0,255,192
3230 DATA 0,255,128,0,255,0,0,255,192,0
3240 DATA 255,240,0,255,252,1,255,255,3
3250 DATA 255,255,7,192,0,15,128,0,31,0
3260 DATA 0,30,0,0,28,0,0
3299 REM
3300 DATA 0,1,192,0,3,192,0,7,128,0,15
3310 DATA 128,0,31,0,0,63,0,0,126,3,0
3320 DATA 254,7,1,254,15,127,255,255
3330 DATA 255,255,255,127,255,255,1,254
3340 DATA 15,0,254,7,0,126,3,0,63,0,0
3350 DATA 31,0,0,15,128,0,7,128,0,3,192
3360 DATA 0,1,192
3399 REM
3400 DATA 28,0,0,30,0,0,31,0,0,15,128,0
3410 DATA 7,192,0,3,255,255,1,255,255,0
3420 DATA 255,252,0,255,240,0,255,192,0
3430 DATA 255,0,0,255,128,0,255,192,0
3440 DATA 251,224,0,249,240,0,240,255,0
3450 DATA 240,127,0,224,62,0,224,60,0
3460 DATA 192,56,0,192,48
3499 REM
3500 DATA 0,0,56,0,0,120,0,0,248,0,1
3510 DATA 240,0,3,224,255,255,192,255
3520 DATA 255,128,63,255,0,15,255,0,3
3530 DATA 255,0,0,255,0,1,255,0,3,255,0
3540 DATA 7,223,0,15,159,0,255,15,0,254
```

```
3550 DATA 15,0,124,7,0,60,7,0,28,3,0,12
3560 DATA 3,0
3597 REM
3598 REM---------- GUN DATA -----------
3599 REM
3600 DATA 0,60,0,0,126,0,0,126,0,0,60,0
3610 DATA 0,60,0,0,60,0,0,60,0,0,60,0
3620 DATA 0,60,0,0,60,0,0,126,0,0,255,0
3630 DATA 1,255,128,3,255,192,7,255,224
3640 DATA 15,255,240,31,255,248,63,255
3650 DATA 252,63,255,252,63,255,252,63
3660 DATA 255,252
3697 REM
3698 REM--------- BULLET DATA ---------
3699 REM
3700 DATA 0,0,0,0,0,0,0,0,0,0,0,0,0,0,0,0
3710 DATA 0,0,0,0,0,0,0,0,0,0,0,0,0,0,0,0
3720 DATA 0,0,0,0,0,0,0,0,0,0,0,0,0,0,0,0
3730 DATA 0,24,0,0,60,0,0,126,0,0,126,0
3740 DATA 0,60,0,0,24,0
3797 REM
3798 REM------- EXPLOSION DATA --------
3799 REM
3800 DATA 0,0,0,0,0,0,0,16,0,0,16,0,2
3810 DATA 24,64,3,25,192,1,223,128,0
3820 DATA 255,128,0,255,0,0,127,240,0
3830 DATA 255,192,3,254,0,15,255,0,0
3840 DATA 255,128,1,237,192,1,204,96,3
3850 DATA 12,0,2,4,0,0,4,0,0,0,0,0,0,0
3899 REM
3900 DATA 0,120,0,0,120,12,48,124,24,28
3910 DATA 126,120,31,127,240,15,255,240
3920 DATA 15,255,224,7,255,224,7,255
3930 DATA 248,31,255,254,127,255,255
3940 DATA 255,255,248,255,255,224,63
3950 DATA 255,240,7,255,248,3,255,252,7
3960 DATA 255,254,7,255,63,15,255,15,15
3970 DATA 222,3,31,30,0
3999 REM
4000 DATA 0,0,0,0,112,0,0,56,0,0,56,64
4010 DATA 14,0,96,15,0,224,6,28,0,0,14
4020 DATA 0,0,128,0,97,195,12,112,193
4030 DATA 142,224,1,199,0,24,0,0,56,0,1
4040 DATA 24,96,7,0,112,7,128,48,0,28
4050 DATA 16,0,28,0,0,24,0,0,0,0
```

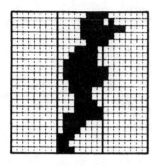

Appendix Y
Pre-Recorded Program Disks and Tapes

Some of the program listings in this book are quite long. It will take you several hours to type each one into your own computer; and, as always, one mistake can stop a program from working properly.

If you want to avoid this hassle, you can obtain the programs on disk or tape from the author. For $15, including postage, you will receive your choice of a disk or a cassette tape containing:

> The Air Attack game—final version
> The Sprite Demonstration program
> The Graphics Generator
> The Headline Generator
> The Character Generator
> The Sprite Generator
> Data files with the alternate character set
> Data files with three alphabets of headline letters
> Data files for the running sprite

Two versions of each program will be supplied. One version will be in BASIC, exactly as listed in this book. The other will be a compiled version, which runs several times faster, and is easier to use.

Make checks or money orders payable (in U.S. dollars) to:

> Charles Platt
> P.O. Box 556
> New York, NY 10113

INDEX

Selections from The SYBEX Library

Buyer's Guides

THE BEST OF TI 99/4A™ CARTRIDGES
by Thomas Blackadar
150 pp., illustr., Ref. 0-137
Save yourself time and frustration when buying TI 99/4A software. This buyer's guide gives an overview of the best available programs, with information on how to set up the computer to run them.

FAMILY COMPUTERS UNDER $200
by Doug Mosher
160 pp., illustr., Ref. 0-149
Find out what these inexpensive machines can do for you and your family. "If you're just getting started . . . this is the book to read before you buy."—Richard O'Reilly, Los Angeles newspaper columnist

PORTABLE COMPUTERS
by Sheldon Crop and Doug Mosher
128 pp., illustr., Ref. 0-144
"This book provides a clear and concise introduction to the expanding new world of personal computers."—Mark Powelson, Editor, *San Francisco Focus Magazine*

THE BEST OF VIC-20™ SOFTWARE
by Thomas Blackadar
150 pp., illustr., Ref. 0-139
Save yourself time and frustration with this buyer's guide to VIC-20 software. Find the best game, music, education, and home management programs on the market today.

SELECTING THE RIGHT DATA BASE SOFTWARE

SELECTING THE RIGHT WORD PROCESSING SOFTWARE

SELECTING THE RIGHT SPREADSHEET SOFTWARE
by Kathy McHugh and Veronica Corchado
80 pp., illustr., Ref. 0-174, 0-177, 0-178
This series on selecting the right business software offers the busy professional concise, informative reviews of the best available software packages.

Introduction to Computers

OVERCOMING COMPUTER FEAR
by Jeff Berner
112 pp., illustr., Ref. 0-145
This easy-going introduction to computers helps you separate the facts from the myths.

COMPUTER ABC'S
by Daniel Le Noury and Rodnay Zaks
64 pp., illustr., Ref. 0-167
This beautifully illustrated, colorful book for parents and children takes you alphabetically through the world of computers, explaining each concept in simple language.

PARENTS, KIDS, AND COMPUTERS
by Lynn Alpers and Meg Holmberg
208 pp., illustr., Ref. 0-151
This book answers your questions about the educational possibilities of home computers.

THE COLLEGE STUDENT'S COMPUTER HANDBOOK
by Bryan Pfaffenberger
350 pp., illustr., Ref. 0-170
This friendly guide will aid students in selecting a computer system for college study, managing information in a college course, and writing research papers.

COMPUTER CRAZY
by Daniel Le Noury
100 pp., illustr., Ref. 0-173
No matter how you feel about computers, these cartoons will have you laughing about them.

DON'T!
(or How to Care for Your Computer)
by Rodnay Zaks
214pp., 100 illustr., Ref. 0-065
The correct way to handle and care for all elements of a computer system, including what to do when something doesn't work.

YOUR FIRST COMPUTER
by Rodnay Zaks
258 pp., 150 illustr., Ref. 0-045
The most popular introduction to small computers and their peripherals: what they do and how to buy one.

INTERNATIONAL MICROCOMPUTER DICTIONARY
120 pp., Ref. 0-067
All the definitions and acronyms of micro-computer jargon defined in a handy pocket-sized edition. Includes translations of the most popular terms into ten languages.

FROM CHIPS TO SYSTEMS: AN INTRODUCTION TO MICROPROCESSORS
by Rodnay Zaks
552 pp., 400 illustr., Ref. 0-063
A simple and comprehensive introduction to microprocessors from both a hardware and software standpoint: what they are, how they operate, how to assemble them into a complete system.

Personal Computers

ATARI

YOUR FIRST ATARI® PROGRAM
by Rodnay Zaks
150 pp., illustr., Ref. 0-130
A fully illustrated, easy-to-use introduction to ATARI BASIC programming. Will have the reader programming in a matter of hours.

BASIC EXERCISES FOR THE ATARI®
by J.P. Lamoitier
251 pp., illustr., Ref. 0-101
Teaches ATARI BASIC through actual practice using graduated exercises drawn from everyday applications.

THE EASY GUIDE TO YOUR ATARI® 600XL/800XL
by Thomas Blackadar
175 pp., illustr., Ref. 0-125
This jargon-free companion will help you get started on the right foot with your new 600XL or 800XL ATARI computer.

ATARI® BASIC PROGRAMS IN MINUTES
by Stanley R. Trost
170 pp., illustr., Ref. 0-143
You can use this practical set of programs without any prior knowledge of BASIC! Application examples are taken from a wide variety of fields, including business, home management, and real estate.

Commodore 64/VIC-20

THE COMMODORE 64™/VIC-20™ BASIC HANDBOOK
by Douglas Hergert

144 pp., illustr., Ref. 0-116

A complete listing with descriptions and instructive examples of each of the Commodore 64 BASIC keywords and functions. A handy reference guide, organized like a dictionary.

THE EASY GUIDE TO YOUR COMMODORE 64™
by Joseph Kascmer

160 pp., illustr., Ref. 0-129

A friendly introduction to using the Commodore 64.

YOUR FIRST VIC-20™ PROGRAM
by Rodnay Zaks

150 pp., illustr., Ref. 0-129

A fully illustrated, easy-to-use introduction to VIC-20 BASIC programming. Will have the reader programming in a matter of hours.

THE VIC-20™ CONNECTION
by James W. Coffron

260 pp., 120 illustr., Ref. 0-128

Teaches elementary interfacing and BASIC programming of the VIC-20 for connection to external devices and household appliances.

YOUR FIRST COMMODORE 64™ PROGRAM
by Rodnay Zaks

182 pp., illustr., Ref. 0-172

You can learn to write simple programs without any prior knowledge of mathematics or computers! Guided by colorful illustrations and step-by-step instructions, you'll be constructing programs within an hour or two.

COMMODORE 64™ BASIC PROGRAMS IN MINUTES
by Stanley R. Trost

170 pp., illustr., Ref. 0-154

Here is a practical set of programs for business, finance, real estate, data analysis, record keeping and educational applications.

IBM

THE ABC'S OF THE IBM® PC
by Joan Lasselle and Carol Ramsay

100 pp., illustr., Ref. 0-102

This is the book that will take you through the first crucial steps in learning to use the IBM PC.

THE BEST OF IBM® PC SOFTWARE
by Stanley R. Trost

144 pp., illustr., Ref. 0-104

Separates the wheat from the chaff in the world of IBM PC software. Tells you what to expect from the best available IBM PC programs.

THE IBM® PC-DOS HANDBOOK
by Richard Allen King

144 pp., illustr., Ref. 0-103

Explains the PC disk operating system, giving the user better control over the system. Get the most out of your PC by adapting its capabilities to your specific needs.

BUSINESS GRAPHICS FOR THE IBM® PC
by Nelson Ford

200 pp., illustr., Ref. 0-124

Ready-to-run programs for creating line graphs, complex illustrative multiple bar graphs, picture graphs, and more. An ideal way to use your PC's business capabilities!

THE IBM® PC CONNECTION
by James W. Coffron

200 pp., illustr., Ref. 0-127

Teaches elementary interfacing and BASIC programming of the IBM PC for connection to external devices and household appliances.

BASIC EXERCISES FOR THE IBM® PERSONAL COMPUTER
by J.P. Lamoitier
252 pp., 90 illustr., Ref. 0-088
Teaches IBM BASIC through actual practice, using graduated exercises drawn from everyday applications.

USEFUL BASIC PROGRAMS FOR THE IBM® PC
by Stanley R. Trost
144 pp., Ref. 0-111
This collection of programs takes full advantage of the interactive capabilities of your IBM Personal Computer. Financial calculations, investment analysis, record keeping, and math practice—made easier on your IBM PC.

YOUR FIRST IBM® PC PROGRAM
by Rodnay Zaks
182 pp., illustr., Ref. 0-171
This well-illustrated book makes programming easy for children and adults.

YOUR IBM® PC JUNIOR
by Douglas Hergert
250 pp., illustr., Ref. 0-179
This comprehensive reference guide to IBM's most economical microcomputer offers many practical applications and all the helpful information you'll need to get started with your IBM PC Junior.

DATA FILE PROGRAMMING ON YOUR IBM® PC
by Alan Simpson
275 pp., illustr., Ref. 0-146
This book provides instructions and examples of managing data files in BASIC. Programming designs and developments are extensively discussed.

Apple

THE EASY GUIDE TO YOUR APPLE II®
by Joseph Kascmer
160 pp., illustr., Ref. 0-122
A friendly introduction to using the Apple II, II plus and the new IIe.

BASIC EXERCISES FOR THE APPLE®
by J.P. Lamoitier
250 pp., 90 illustr., Ref. 0-084
Teaches Apple BASIC through actual practice, using graduated exercises drawn from everyday applications.

APPLE II® BASIC HANDBOOK
by Douglas Hergert
144 pp., illustr., Ref. 0-155
A complete listing with descriptions and instructive examples of each of the Apple II BASIC keywords and functions. A handy reference guide, organized like a dictionary.

APPLE II® BASIC PROGRAMS IN MINUTES
by Stanley R. Trost
150 pp., illustr., Ref. 0-121
A collection of ready-to-run programs for financial calculations, investment analysis, record keeping, and many more home and office applications. These programs can be entered on your Apple II plus or IIe in minutes!

YOUR FIRST APPLE II® PROGRAM
by Rodnay Zaks
150 pp., illustr., Ref. 0-136
A fully illustrated, easy-to-use introduction to APPLE BASIC programming. Will have the reader programming in a matter of hours.

THE APPLE® CONNECTION
by James W. Coffron
264 pp., 120 illustr., Ref. 0-085
Teaches elementary interfacing and BASIC programming of the Apple for connection to external devices and household appliances.

TRS-80

YOUR COLOR COMPUTER
by Doug Mosher
350 pp., illustr., Ref. 0-097
Patience and humor guide the reader through purchasing, setting up, programming, and using the Radio Shack TRS-80/TDP Series 100 Color Computer. A complete introduction.

THE FOOLPROOF GUIDE TO SCRIPSIT™ WORD PROCESSING
by Jeff Berner
225 pp., illustr., Ref. 0-098
Everything you need to know about SCRIPSIT—from starting out, to mastering document editing. This user-friendly guide is written in plain English, with a touch of wit.

Timex/Sinclair 1000/ZX81

YOUR TIMEX/SINCLAIR 1000 AND ZX81™
by Douglas Hergert
159 pp., illustr., Ref. 0-099
This book explains the set-up, operation, and capabilities of the Timex/Sinclair 1000 and ZX81. Includes how to interface peripheral devices, and introduces BASIC programming.

THE TIMEX/SINCLAIR 1000™ BASIC HANDBOOK
by Douglas Hergert
170 pp., illustr., Ref. 0-113
A complete alphabetical listing with explanations and examples of each word in the T/S 1000 BASIC vocabulary; will allow you quick, error-free programming of your T/S 1000.

TIMEX/SINCLAIR 1000™ BASIC PROGRAMS IN MINUTES
by Stanley R. Trost
150 pp., illustr., Ref. 0-119
A collection of ready-to-run programs for financial calculations, investment analysis, record keeping, and many more home and office applications. These programs can be entered on your T/S 1000 in minutes!

MORE USES FOR YOUR TIMEX/SINCLAIR 1000™
Astronomy on Your Computer
by Eric Burgess
176 pp., illustr., Ref. 0-112
Ready-to-run programs that turn your TV into a planetarium.

Other Popular Computers

YOUR FIRST TI 99/4A™ PROGRAM
by Rodnay Zaks
182 pp., illustr., Ref. 0-157
Colorfully illustrated, this book concentrates on the essentials of programming in a clear, entertaining fashion.

THE RADIO SHACK® NOTEBOOK COMPUTER
by Orson Kellogg
128 pp., illustr., Ref. 0-150
Whether you already have the Radio Shack Model 100 notebook computer, or are interested in buying one, this book will clearly explain what it can do for you.

THE EASY GUIDE TO YOUR COLECO ADAM™
by Thomas Blackadar
175 pp., illustr., Ref. 0-181
This quick reference guide shows you how to get started on your Coleco Adam with a minimum of technical jargon.

YOUR KAYPRO II/4/10™
by Andrea Reid and Gary Deidrichs
250 pp., illustr., Ref. 0-166
This book is a non-technical introduction to the KAYPRO family of computers. You will find all you need to know about operating your KAYPRO within this one complete guide.

Software and Applications

Operating Systems

THE CP/M® HANDBOOK
by Rodnay Zaks
320 pp., 100 illustr., Ref 0-048
An indispensable reference and guide to CP/M—the most widely-used operating system for small computers.

MASTERING CP/M®

by Alan R. Miller

398 pp., illustr., Ref. 0-068

For advanced CP/M users or systems programmers who want maximum use of the CP/M operating system . . . takes up where our *CP/M Handbook* leaves off.

THE BEST OF CP/M® SOFTWARE

by John D. Halamka

250 pp., illustr., Ref. 0-100

This book reviews tried-and-tested, commercially available software for your CP/M system.

REAL WORLD UNIX™

by John D. Halamka

250 pp., illustr., Ref. 0-093

This book is written for the beginning and intermediate UNIX user in a practical, straightforward manner, with specific instructions given for many special applications.

THE CP/M PLUS™ HANDBOOK

by Alan R. Miller

250 pp., illustr., Ref. 0-158

This guide is easy for the beginner to understand, yet contains valuable information for advanced users of CP/M Plus (Version 3).

Business Software

INTRODUCTION TO WORDSTAR™

by Arthur Naiman

202 pp., 30 illustr., Ref. 0-077

Makes it easy to learn how to use WordStar, a powerful word processing program for personal computers.

PRACTICAL WORDSTAR™ USES

by Julie Anne Arca

200 pp., illustr., Ref. 0-107

Pick your most time-consuming office tasks and this book will show you how to streamline them with WordStar.

MASTERING VISICALC®

by Douglas Hergert

217 pp., 140 illustr., Ref. 0-090

Explains how to use the VisiCalc "electronic spreadsheet" functions and provides examples of each. Makes using this powerful program simple.

DOING BUSINESS WITH VISICALC®

by Stanley R. Trost

260 pp., Ref. 0-086

Presents accounting and management planning applications—from financial statements to master budgets; from pricing models to investment strategies.

DOING BUSINESS WITH SUPERCALC™

by Stanley R. Trost

248 pp., illustr., Ref. 0-095

Presents accounting and management planning applications—from financial statements to master budgets; from pricing models to investment strategies.

VISICALC® FOR SCIENCE AND ENGINEERING

by Stanley R. Trost and Charles Pomernacki

225 pp., illustr., Ref. 0-096

More than 50 programs for solving technical problems in the science and engineering fields. Applications range from math and statistics to electrical and electronic engineering.

DOING BUSINESS WITH 1-2-3™

by Stanley R. Trost

250 pp., illustr., Ref. 0-159

If you are a business professional using the 1-2-3 software package, you will find the spreadsheet and graphics models provided in this book easy to use "as is" in everyday business situations.

THE ABC'S OF 1-2-3™

by Chris Gilbert

225 pp., illustr., Ref. 0-168

For those new to the LOTUS 1-2-3 program, this book offers step-by-step instructions in mastering its spreadsheet, data base, and graphing capabilities.

UNDERSTANDING dBASE II™
by Alan Simpson
220 pp., illustr., Ref. 0-147
Learn programming techniques for mailing label systems, bookkeeping and data base management, as well as ways to interface dBASE II with other software systems.

DOING BUSINESS WITH dBASE II™
by Stanley R. Trost
250 pp., illustr., Ref. 0-160
Learn to use dBASE II for accounts receivable, recording business income and expenses, keeping personal records and mailing lists, and much more.

DOING BUSINESS WITH MULTIPLAN™
by Richard Allen King and Stanley R. Trost
250 pp., illustr., Ref. 0-148
This book will show you how using Multiplan can be nearly as easy as learning to use a pocket calculator. It presents a collection of templates that can be applied "as is" to business situations.

DOING BUSINESS WITH PFS®
by Stanley R. Trost
250 pp., illustr., Ref. 0-161
This practical guide describes specific business and personal applications in detail. Learn to use PFS for accounting, data analysis, mailing lists and more.

INFOPOWER: PRACTICAL INFOSTAR™ USES
by Jule Anne Arca and Charles F. Pirro
275 pp., illustr., Ref. 0-108
This book gives you an overview of Info-Star, including DataStar and ReportStar, WordStar, MailMerge, and SuperSort. Hands on exercises take you step-by-step through real life business applications.

WRITING WITH EASYWRITER II™
by Douglas W. Topham
250 pp., illustr., Ref. 0-141
Friendly style, handy illustrations, and numerous sample exercises make it easy to learn the EasyWriter II word processing system.

Business Applications

INTRODUCTION TO WORD PROCESSING
by Hal Glatzer
205 pp., 140 illustr., Ref. 0-076
Explains in plain language what a word processor can do, how it improves productivity, how to use a word processor and how to buy one wisely.

COMPUTER POWER FOR YOUR LAW OFFICE
by Daniel Remer
225 pp., Ref. 0-109
How to use computers to reach peak productivity in your law office, simply and inexpensively.

OFFICE EFFICIENCY WITH PERSONAL COMPUTERS
by Sheldon Crop
175 pp., illustr., Ref. 0-165
Planning for computerization of your office? This book provides a simplified discussion of the challenges involved for everyone from business owner to clerical worker.

COMPUTER POWER FOR YOUR ACCOUNTING OFFICE
by James Morgan
250 pp., illustr., Ref. 0-164
This book is a convenient source of information about computerizing you accounting office, with an emphasis on hardware and software options.

Languages

C

UNDERSTANDING C
by Bruce Hunter
200 pp., Ref 0-123
Explains how to use the powerful C language for a variety of applications. Some programming experience assumed.

FIFTY C PROGRAMS
by Bruce Hunter
200 pp., illustr., Ref. 0-155
Beginning as well as intermediate C programmers will find this a useful guide to programming techniques and specific applications.

BUSINESS PROGRAMS IN C
by Leon Wortman and Thomas O. Sidebottom
200 pp., illustr., Ref. 0-153
This book provides source code listings of C programs for the business person or experienced programmer. Each easy-to-follow tutorial applies directly to a business situation.

BASIC

YOUR FIRST BASIC PROGRAM
by Rodnay Zaks
150pp. illustr. in color, Ref. 0-129
A "how-to-program" book for the first time computer user, aged 8 to 88.

FIFTY BASIC EXERCISES
by J. P. Lamoitier
232 pp., 90 illustr., Ref. 0-056
Teaches BASIC by actual practice, using graduated exercises drawn from everyday applications. All programs written in Microsoft BASIC.

INSIDE BASIC GAMES
by Richard Mateosian
348 pp., 120 illustr., Ref. 0-055
Teaches interactive BASIC programming through games. Games are written in Microsoft BASIC and can run on the TRS-80, Apple II and PET/CBM.

BASIC FOR BUSINESS
by Douglas Hergert
224 pp., 15 illustr., Ref. 0-080
A logically organized, no-nonsense introduction to BASIC programming for business applications. Includes many fully-explained accounting programs, and shows you how to write them.

EXECUTIVE PLANNING WITH BASIC
by X. T. Bui
196 pp., 19 illustr., Ref. 0-083
An important collection of business management decision models in BASIC, including Inventory Management (EOQ), Critical Path Analysis and PERT, Financial Ratio Analysis, Portfolio Management, and much more.

BASIC PROGRAMS FOR SCIENTISTS AND ENGINEERS
by Alan R. Miller
318 pp., 120 illustr., Ref. 0-073
This book from the "Programs for Scientists and Engineers" series provides a library of problem-solving programs while developing proficiency in BASIC.

CELESTIAL BASIC
by Eric Burgess
300 pp., 65 illustr., Ref. 0-087
A collection of BASIC programs that rapidly complete the chores of typical astronomical computations. It's like having a planetarium in your own home! Displays apparent movement of stars, planets and meteor showers.

YOUR SECOND BASIC PROGRAM
by Gary Lippman
250 pp., illustr., Ref. 0-152
A sequel to *Your First BASIC Program*, this book follows the same patient, detailed approach and brings you to the next level of programming skill.

Pascal

INTRODUCTION TO PASCAL (Including UCSD Pascal™)
by Rodnay Zaks
420 pp., 130 illustr., Ref. 0-066
A step-by-step introduction for anyone wanting to learn the Pascal language. Describes UCSD and Standard Pascals. No technical background is assumed.

THE PASCAL HANDBOOK
by Jacques Tiberghien
486 pp., 270 illustr., Ref. 0-053
A dictionary of the Pascal language, defining every reserved word, operator, procedure and function found in all major versions of Pascal.

APPLE® PASCAL GAMES
by Douglas Hergert and Joseph T. Kalash
372 pp., 40 illustr., Ref. 0-074
A collection of the most popular computer games in Pascal, challenging the reader not only to play but to investigate how games are implemented on the computer.

INTRODUCTION TO THE UCSD p-SYSTEM™
by Charles W. Grant and Jon Butah
300 pp., 10 illustr., Ref. 0-061
A simple, clear introduction to the UCSD Pascal Operating System; for beginners through experienced programmers.

PASCAL PROGRAMS FOR SCIENTISTS AND ENGINEERS
by Alan R. Miller
374 pp., 120 illustr., Ref. 0-058
A comprehensive collection of frequently used algorithms for scientific and technical applications, programmed in Pascal. Includes such programs as curve-fitting, integrals and statistical techniques.

DOING BUSINESS WITH PASCAL
by Richard Hergert and Douglas Hergert
371 pp., illustr., Ref. 0-091
Practical tips for using Pascal in business programming. Includes design considerations, language extensions, and applications examples.

Assembly Language Programming

PROGRAMMING THE 6502
by Rodnay Zaks
386 pp., 160 illustr., Ref. 0-046
Assembly language programming for the 6502, from basic concepts to advanced data structures.

6502 APPLICATIONS
by Rodnay Zaks
278 pp., 200 illustr., Ref. 0-015
Real-life application techniques: the input/output book for the 6502.

ADVANCED 6502 PROGRAMMING
by Rodnay Zaks
292 pp., 140 illustr., Ref. 0-089
Third in the 6502 series. Teaches more advanced programming techniques, using games as a framework for learning.

PROGRAMMING THE Z80
by Rodnay Zaks
624 pp., 200 illustr., Ref. 0-069
A complete course in programming the Z80 microprocessor and a thorough introduction to assembly language.

Z80 APPLICATIONS
by James W. Coffron
288 pp., illustr., Ref. 0-094
Covers techniques and applications for using peripheral devices with a Z80 based system.

PROGRAMMING THE 6809
by Rodnay Zaks and William Labiak
362 pp., 150 illustr., Ref. 0-078
This book explains how to program the 6809 in assembly language. No prior programming knowledge required.

PROGRAMMING THE Z8000
by Richard Mateosian
298 pp., 124 illustr., Ref. 0-032
How to program the Z8000 16-bit microprocessor. Includes a description of the architecture and function of the Z8000 and its family of support chips.

PROGRAMMING THE 8086/8088
by James W. Coffron
300 pp., illustr., Ref. 0-120
This book explains how to program the 8086 and 8088 in assembly language. No prior programming knowledge required.

Other Languages

FORTRAN PROGRAMS FOR SCIENTISTS AND ENGINEERS
by Alan R. Miller
280 pp., 120 illustr., Ref. 0-082
In the "Programs for Scientists and Engineers" series, this book provides specific scientific and engineering application programs written in FORTRAN.

A MICROPROGRAMMED APL IMPLEMENTATION
by Rodnay Zaks
350 pp., Ref. 0-005
An expert-level text presenting the complete conceptual analysis and design of an APL interpreter, and actual listing of the microcode.

Hardware and Peripherals

MICROPROCESSOR INTERFACING TECHNIQUES
by Rodnay Zaks and Austin Lesea
456 pp., 400 illustr., Ref. 0-029
Complete hardware and software interconnect techniques, including D to A conversion, peripherals, standard buses and troubleshooting.

THE RS-232 SOLUTION
by Joe Campbell
225 pp., illustr., Ref. 0-140
Finally, a book that will show you how to correctly interface your computer to any RS-232-C peripheral.

SYBEX Computer Books
are different.

Here is why . . .

At SYBEX, each book is designed with you in mind. Every manuscript is carefully selected and supervised by our editors, who are themselves computer experts. We publish the best authors, whose technical expertise is matched by an ability to write clearly and to communicate effectively. Programs are thoroughly tested for accuracy by our technical staff. Our computerized production department goes to great lengths to make sure that each book is well-designed.

In the pursuit of timeliness, SYBEX has achieved many publishing firsts. SYBEX was among the first to integrate personal computers used by authors and staff into the publishing process. SYBEX was the first to publish books on the CP/M operating system, microprocessor interfacing techniques, word processing, and many more topics.

Expertise in computers and dedication to the highest quality product have made SYBEX a world leader in computer book publishing. Translated into fourteen languages, SYBEX books have helped millions of people around the world to get the most from their computers. We hope we have helped you, too.

SYBEX COMPUTER BOOKS

For a complete catalog of our publications please contact:

U.S.A.
SYBEX, Inc.
2344 Sixth Street
Berkeley,
California 94710
Tel: (800) 227-2346
　　(415) 848-8233
Telex: 336311

FRANCE
SYBEX S.A.R.L.
6–8 Impasse du Curé
75018 Paris
France
Tel: 01/203–9595
Telex: 211801

GERMANY
SYBEX-Verlag GmbH
Vogelsanger Weg 111
4000 Düsseldorf 30
West Germany
Tel: (0211) 626 411
Telex: 8588163